PRINCIPLES OF CONDUCT

Principles
of Conduct

by

JOHN MURRAY

Formerly Professor of Systematic Theology,
Westminster Theological Seminary, Philadelphia, Pa.

THE TYNDALE PRESS

39 Bedford Square, London, WC1B 3EY

First Published January 1957

Reprinted September 1971

ISBN 0 85111 704 X

PRINTED IN GREAT BRITAIN BY COMPTON PRINTING LIMITED
LONDON AND AYLESBURY

CONTENTS

CONTENTS

PREFACE

THE occasion for the preparation and publication of these studies in the field of biblical ethics is the invitation, extended to me in the Fall of 1953, by the faculty of Fuller Theological Seminary, Pasadena, California to deliver the Payton Lectures for the year 1955. In compliance with this invitation, and in terms of the Payton Lectureship, five lectures were given at Fuller Theological Seminary in March 1955. In the present volume this series of lectures has been considerably expanded.

★   ★   ★

One of the main purposes of the lectures and of this volume is to seek to show the basic unity and continuity of the biblical ethic. I have attempted to apply to the ethic of Scripture something of the biblico-theological method, understanding 'Biblical Theology' in the sense defined by Geerhardus Vos as 'that branch of Exegetical Theology which deals with the process of the self-revelation of God deposited in the Bible'.[1] I am not claiming that these studies adhere rigidly to this method of historico-genetic delineation, and I am far from pretending to have covered the whole field of biblical ethics. I have dealt only with *aspects*. My aim, however, has been to show how fruitful ethical studies conducted along this line can be and how in this field, as well as in others, we may discover the organic unity and continuity of divine revelation.

The ten commandments, it will surely be admitted, furnish the core of the biblical ethic. When we apply the biblico-theological method to the study of Scripture it will be seen that the ten commandments as promulgated at Sinai were but the concrete and practical form of enunciating principles which did not then for the first time come to have relevance but were relevant from the beginning. And it will also be seen that, as they did not *begin* to have relevance at Sinai, so they did not cease to have relevance when the Sinaitic economy had passed away. It is biblico-theo-

[1] *Biblical Theology: Old and New Testaments*, Grand Rapids, 1954, p. 13.

7

logical study that demonstrates that these commandments embody principles which belong to the order which God established for man at the beginning, as also to the order of redemption. In other words, we discover that they belong to the organism of divine revelation respecting God's will for man.

*   *   *

It must be understood that in speaking of progressive revelation, and of 'Biblical Theology' as based upon that revelation, the standpoint entertained in these studies differs from the older liberal viewpoint as well as from that of more recent proponents of Biblical Theology who are hospitable to the critical reconstructions of biblical history. Revelation is to be regarded as the disclosure to man on the part of God of his mind and will; and *progressive* revelation means that revelation has a history of increasing and accumulating disclosure until it reaches its finale in the manifestation of the Son of God and the inscripturation embodied in the completed New Testament canon. Scripture is the permanent deposit of that process of revelation. And, in distinction from the older liberal conception, 'Biblical Theology' is not to be conceived of as the presentation of the contents of the moral and religious consciousness of the leading religious spirits during the biblical period, nor as the historico-genetic delineation of the development of the religious consciousness reflected in the Bible; it is rather the historico-genetic delineation of the process of divine revelation. While we must not be indifferent to the contents of the moral and religious consciousness reflected in the Bible, yet a delineation of this would not provide us with a Biblical *Theology*. This science, as conceived of in these studies, is oriented to revelation from God and the deposit of that revelation in Scripture. It is this orientation that must always be kept in view and, although the response in human consciousness is of deep concern, yet we must not gauge the content or intent of revelation by the measure of the response given by men. In distinction from the viewpoint widely current at the present time and represented, for example, by Scandinavian scholars, the standpoint espoused in this volume is that the representation given in the Scripture is the true transcript of what the history of revelation and redemption really was. The unity which we find in the Bible reflects the organic unity of the process of divine revelation of which the Bible itself is the depository.

*   *   *

It may be objected that the standpoint reflected in this book fails to take account of the mythological character of certain parts of Scripture on which a good deal of the material in these studies is based, particularly Genesis 1-3. It is true that the argument is not conducted in terms of the mythological interpretation of Scripture. By implication such an interpretation is rejected. That Genesis 2 and 3, for example, is story, but does not represent history, the present writer does not believe. An express attempt to refute such an interpretation has not been undertaken. But if I have been successful in demonstrating the organic unity and continuity of the ethic presented in the Bible, this fact should itself constitute one of the most potent arguments against the mythological interpretation of Genesis 2 and 3, as also of other passages. This is just saying that the historical character of the revelation deposited in the Bible does not comport with a non-historical view of that which supplies the foundation and starting-point of that history. It is surely apparent how far-reaching must be the reconstruction of the Bible's representation respecting the history of revelation if we are to reject the historicity of the fall of Adam as the first man. It is the conviction of the present writer that a mythological interpretation is not compatible with the total perspective which the biblical witness furnishes. To state the case positively, the concreteness of Genesis 2 and 3, as historically interpreted, is thoroughly consonant with the concreteness which characterizes the subsequent history of Old Testament revelation. It would no doubt be helpful to some who entertain the same standpoint as is reflected in these studies to have digressed at various points to deal with the demythologization of Scripture so much in vogue at the present time. But, apart from the fact that others are more competent than the writer to deal with such questions, such digressions might have detracted from the purpose which this series of studies is intended to promote.

*   *   *

I wish to express my deep appreciation to the faculty of Fuller

Theological Seminary for the privilege extended to me of delivering the Payton Lectures in 1955 and for the hospitality and courtesies enjoyed when the lectures were being given. I wish also to thank the Board of Trustees of Westminster Theological Seminary for a leave of absence, during the first few months of which I was able to complete these studies and prepare the manuscript for the press. My thanks are extended to Mrs. Jack Peterson and Mrs. John Zinkand for their help in preparing the typescript and to Miss T. E. N. Ozinga for assistance in proof-reading and in preparing the indices.

Permission to quote from the following publications has been kindly granted.

David R. Mace: *Hebrew Marriage: A Sociological Study* (The Epworth Press, London, 1953; Philosophical Library, New York); Emil Brunner: *The Divine Imperative*, Copyright, 1947, by W. L. Jenkins (The Westminster Press, Philadelphia); Lewis Sperry Chafer: *Systematic Theology*, Vol. IV (Dallas Seminary Press, Dallas, 1948); Charles Feinberg: *Premillennialism or Amillennialism?* (Zondervan Publishing House, Grand Rapids, 1936), Copyright, Charles Feinberg.

The Wm. B. Eerdmans Publishing Co., Grand Rapids has granted permission to quote from the following:

F. W. Grosheide: *Commentary on the First Epistle to the Corinthians* (1953); E. K. Simpson: *The Pastoral Epistles* (1954); Geerhardus Vos: *Biblical Theology: Old and New Testaments* (1954); Jac. J. Müller: *The Epistles of Paul to the Philippians and to Philemon* (1955).

I wish to extend to the publishers, the Inter-Varsity Fellowship of Evangelical Unions, London, England, and the Wm. B. Eerdmans Publishing Co., Grand Rapids, Michigan, U.S.A., my heartiest thanks for their undertaking and for the numerous courtesies received from them in connection with this publication.

Philadelphia, Pa.   JOHN MURRAY
July 21, 1956

CHAPTER I

INTRODUCTORY QUESTIONS

THE word 'ethics' is derived from the Greek ἔθος or ἦθος.[1] It means custom or usage and sometimes custom or practice as prescribed by law. The one instance in the New Testament which exemplifies more closely than any other the idea to which it has been applied in Christian usage is I Corinthians 15: 33: 'evil associations corrupt good manners' (ἤθη χρηστά). 'Good manners' obviously designate the manner of life and conduct which is in agreement with the Christian faith and profession. In terms of this concept ethics would refer to the manner of life, to the pattern of conduct, or, in a word, to conduct.

The term which more frequently expresses this concept in the New Testament is not that from which our word 'ethics' is derived, but another, namely, ἀναστροφή, a word which more aptly lends itself to express the thought of 'way of life' or 'way of conduct'.   And ἀναστροφή, that is to say 'manner of life', which is in agreement with and is expressive of the Christian faith is ἀναστροφή which is καλή or ἀγνή or ἀγαθή or ἁγία (James 3: 13; I Peter 3: 2, 16; II Peter 3: 11).[2] This is to say that the manner of life which the Christian faith demands and produces is one of goodness, purity, and holiness.[3]

[1] The former occurs twelve times in the New Testament (Luke 1: 9; 2: 42; 22: 39; John 19: 40; Acts 6: 14; 15: 1; 16: 21; 21: 21; 25: 16; 26: 3; 28: 17; Hebrews 10: 25), the latter only once and then in the plural (I Corinthians 15: 33). Cf. also the verb ἔθω which occurs four times in the New Testament (Matthew 27: 15; Mark 10: 1; Luke 4: 16; Acts 17: 2), and in the LXX once in the canonical books (Numbers 24: 1). Apparently neither ἔθος nor ἦθος is used in the canonical books of the LXX.

[2] ἀναστροφή occurs thirteen times in the New Testament, on nine occasions in the good sense; cf. ἀναστρέφω in II Corinthians 1: 12; I Timothy 3: 15; Hebrews 13: 18; I Peter 1: 17. Perhaps the most significant instance is II Peter 3: 11 where we have the plural ἐν ἁγίαις ἀναστροφαῖς to indicate the variety and fulness of the manner of life which is compatible with godliness (εὐσεβείαις) and commends the Christian confession.

[3] The Latin for ἤθη is *mores*, which is the equivalent of our English word 'morals'.

When we use the word 'ethics' to designate a way of life we are not necessarily using the expression 'way of life' in an appreciative sense. It may be used depreciatively. Hence, when we wish to evaluate a way of life, we are required to qualify it in some way as good or bad, as Christian or un-Christian. The New Testament, however, has a distinctly appreciative use of the expression 'the way'. The Christian confession and manner of life are characterized as 'the way' or 'that way' (Acts 9: 2; 19: 9, 23; 22: 4; 24: 22). We can hardly dissociate this absolute use of the word 'way' from the word of our Lord, 'I am the way, the truth, and the life' (John 14: 6), even though it is difficult to define the line of connection. In any case this nomenclature does evince the total distinctiveness of the faith, worship, and life of the disciples of Christ. And this distinctiveness found its focal point in faith and devotion directed to him who declared himself to be 'the way' as well as the truth and the life. The New Testament does not have a constricted conception of what it calls 'the way'; it does not confine 'the way' to what we so frequently have in view when we speak of the way of life.[4] This specialized use of the expression 'the way' comprehends all that is distinctive of the Christian faith as 'the way of righteousness' (Matthew 21: 32; II Peter 2: 21), 'the way of salvation' (Acts 16: 17), 'the way of God' (Matthew 22: 16; Acts 18: 26), 'the way of the Lord' (Acts 18: 25), 'the right ways of the Lord' (Acts 13: 10), 'the way of truth' (II Peter 2: 2), and 'the way of peace' (Luke 1: 79; Romans 3: 17). The way of life after the mode of New Testament usage would comprise far more than falls within the sphere of ethics. Hence, if we use the expression in its more restricted sense as the synonym of ethics, it is not because we are forgetful of the richness and fulness of the New Testament concept of 'the way' as the way of all that belongs to eternal life.

If ethics is concerned with manner of life and behaviour, biblical ethics is concerned with the manner of life and behaviour which the Bible requires and which the faith of the Bible produces. When we say 'manner of life' or 'behaviour' we must also take into account the correlative considerations.

1. While we may use the word 'conduct' or 'behaviour' to

---

[4] In Acts 2: 28 (*cf.* Psalm 16: 11) the expression occurs but has undoubtedly specific reference to the resurrection of our Lord.

denote the sum-total of actions which constitute the pattern of life, yet behind all overt action is the dispositional character or complex which is the psychological determinant of action. Hence ethics must take into account the dispositional complex of which the overt act is the expression. This is to say, biblical ethics has paramount concern with the heart out of which are the issues of life.

2. The conduct that is in view in ethics, even when conduct is considered in terms of overt action, is not simply the aggregate of actions. Ethics views actions in their organic relations to one another. There is a certain unity and coherence of pattern; each action stands related to the others and cannot be understood or assessed except in that relationship.

3. The behaviour with which biblical ethics is concerned is not simply the behaviour of individuals; the principle of society bears intimately upon all ethical studies and it bears also upon biblical ethics. Hence the biblical ethic takes account, not only of individuals as individuals and of their behaviour as such, but of individuals in their corporate relationships. There is corporate responsibility and there is corporate action.

4. The behaviour in which we are interested when we seek to determine the biblical ethic is not the sum-total of the behaviour of a particular believer, not even of a peculiarly exemplary believer, nor the sum-total of the behaviour of believing society. We have to reckon with the imperfection of every saint in this world and with the imperfection that attaches to the most highly developed Christian society. There is still sin, oftentimes grievous sin; and therefore we find inconsistency and contradiction in the holiest of men and in the most sanctified society. The sum-total of behaviour cannot show the unity and coherence which the biblical ethic would require—there is no perfect pattern of behaviour exemplified in the individual believer or in the organism of believers.

The study of biblical ethics, therefore, is not that of surveying empirically the sum-total of the behaviour of those who are portrayed for us in the Bible as believers. What such a study would furnish is simply a description of the behaviour of believers. And since there is so much sin and inconsistency in the behaviour of believers at their best, whether they are viewed individually or in their corporate relations, we could not by any such empirical method delineate the biblical ethic. The biblical ethic is that manner of life which is consonant with, and demanded by, the biblical revelation. Our attention must be focused upon divine demand, not upon human achievement, upon the revelation of God's will for man, not upon human behaviour. In the biblical ethic we are concerned with the norms, or canons, or standards of behaviour which are enunciated in the Bible for the creation, direction, and regulation of thought, life, and behaviour consonant with the will of God.

It is quite obvious that this statement of the case poses several questions. And the most basic of these is the question: Is there, in the sense defined, a biblical ethic? Is there one coherent and consistent ethic set forth in the Bible? Is there not diversity in the Bible, and diversity of a kind that embraces antithetical elements? Are there not in the Bible canons of conduct that are contrary to one another? To be specific: Is there not an antithesis between the canons of conduct sanctioned and approved of God in the Old Testament and those sanctioned and approved of God in the New in respect of certain central features of human behaviour? It is a patent fact that the behaviour of the most illustrious of Old Testament believers was characterized by practices which are clearly contradictory of the elementary demands of the New Testament ethic. Monogamy is surely a principle of the Christian ethic. Old Testament saints practised polygamy. In like manner, under the Old Testament divorce was practised on grounds which could not be tolerated in terms of the explicit provisions of the New Testament revelation. And polygamy and divorce were practised without overt disapprobation in terms of the canons of behaviour which were recognized as regulative in the Old Testament period.

These are questions which must be faced, remembering that in these instances of polygamy and divorce we are not dealing with deviations from the explicitly revealed provisions of Old Testament law as, for example, the adultery and murder committed by David for which he was so sharply reproved in terms of recognized law. Such examples of wrongdoing do not perplex our inquiry in the least degree. They are in the same category as instances of wrongdoing in the New Testament itself for which there is, in like manner, condemnation and reproof. We may be reminded again that the ethic we are seeking is not that elicited from the empirical facts of history and experience—there is always inconsistency and contradiction there—but that enunciated in and approved by the Bible itself. Our study is not empirical ethics but the biblically approved ethic. The polygamy and divorce with which we are now concerned would meet with the severest reproof and condemnation in the New Testament; but in the Old Testament there appears to be no overt pronouncement of condemnation and no infliction of disciplinary judgment. Are we not compelled to recognize that the New Testament not only marks a distinct development in the progress of revelation, but also, in some of the basic particulars of human behaviour, institutes a change from one set of canons to another, and that therefore there is not only development and addition, but reversal and abrogation? Is the case such that it was perfectly consonant with the law established and revealed by God in the Old Testament for a man to have more than one wife at the same time, and for a man to put away his wife for relatively light cause, whereas in the New Testament it is unequivocally wrong and severely censurable for a man to have more than one wife and to put away one's wife except for the cause of adultery? Is there this open contrast in respect of conduct as elementary and far-reaching as the marital relations of man and wife? We are required to face squarely the question of the relation of the Old Testament to the New in respect of the criteria of upright and holy living.

It would be easy to say that, under the Old Testament, the principle of monogamy had not been established and that the necessity of multiplying and replenishing the earth constituted at least one obvious reason why this limitation should not be placed upon the man's sexual impulses and prolific propensities. It could also be argued that the law of monogamy is not one that springs from the nature and perfections of God, but is positive, and receives its sanction simply from the sovereign will of God. In terms of this line of thought it might be God's will to institute monogamy as the rule for one period of time and in one set of circumstances while the institution of polygamy had been perfectly proper at another time and in another set of circumstances. In this respect polygamy and divorce would be in very much the same category as many other regulations connected with the older economy which, obviously, because of their temporary character, have no relevance in the changed conditions of the new covenant.

However appealing and plausible such a solution might appear to be, it is faced with the difficulty that it does not fit the pertinent revelatory data in both Testaments, particularly the Old Testament data as interpreted by the New Testament. The only thesis that appears to me to be compatible with these data is that polygamy and divorce (for light cause) were permitted or tolerated under the Old Testament, tolerated in such a way that regulatory provisions were enacted to prevent some of the grosser evils and abuses attendant upon them, and tolerated in the sense that they were not openly condemned and censured with civil and ecclesiastical penalties, but that nevertheless they were not legitimated. That is to say, these practices were basically wrong; they were violations of a creation ordinance, even of an ordinance which had been revealed to man at the beginning. Therefore they were inconsistent with the standards and criteria of holy living which had been established by God at the beginning. They were really contrary to the revealed will of God and rested under his judgment.

The insistent question immediately arises: How could this be? How could God allow his people, in some cases the most eminent of Old Testament saints, to practise what was a violation of his preceptive will? It is a difficult question. Yet the position taken is the only one that satisfies the authoritative deliverance of our Lord in reference to divorce.[5] He tells us explicitly that for the

[5] With reference to divorce in the Old Testament this thesis is argued by the present writer in the volume *Divorce* (Philadelphia, 1953), pp. 3-8, 13-16, 29-33, 43-45. The same line of thought applies to polygamy. In a later chapter in the present volume monogamy as the original creation ordinance is established from Gen. 2: 23, 24 and the relevant passages in the New Testament.

J. D. Michaelis in his *Commentaries on the Laws of Moses* (translated by Alexander Smith, London, 1814) contends that the Mosaic laws permitted more than one wife. The following quotations will provide the gist of his argument. 'How much soever some may have denied it, nothing is more certain than

(*continued on p. 17*)

hardness of their hearts Moses suffered the Israelites to put away their wives, but that from the beginning it was not so (Matthew 19: 3-8; Mark 10: 2-9). If Jesus could enunciate this position in reference to divorce, there is no good reason why the same principle should not be applied to polygamy. The position would then be that because of perversity they were permitted to take more wives than one. Polygamy was not penalized by civil or ecclesiastical censures, even though in terms of the creation ordinance it was a violation of the divine institution. Men were permitted to take more wives than one, but from the beginning it was not so. Sufferance there indeed was, but no legitimation or sanction of the practice.

---

that by the civil laws of Moses, a man was allowed to have more wives than one. . . . It is certain that *before* the time of Moses, polygamy was in use among the ancestors of the Israelites, and that even Abraham and Jacob lived in it' (Vol. II, p. 1). 'As then, Moses, adhering to established usage, nowhere prohibited a man's taking a second or a third wife, along with the first, it is clear that, as a civil right, it continued allowable; for what has hitherto been customary, and permitted, remains so, in a civil sense, as long as no positive law is enacted against it' (*ibid.*, p. 4). 'The law of Deut. xxi. 15-17 . . . presupposes the case of a man having *two* wives, one of whom he peculiarly loves, while the other, whom he hates, is the mother of his first-born' (p. 5). 'The law of Exod. xxi. 9, 10 . . . expressly permits the father, who had given his son a slave for a wife, to give him, some years after, a second wife, of freer birth; and prescribes how the first was then to be treated. . . . When Moses in Lev. xviii. 18 prohibits a man from marrying the sister of his wife, to vex her while she lives, it manifestly supposes the liberty of taking another wife beside the first, and during her life-time, provided only it was *not* her sister' (p. 6).

This treatment of the relevant evidence is about as strong a case as can reasonably be made for the sufferance of polygamy under the law of Moses. It is to be noted that he has spoken of the 'civil right' of polygamy or 'the permission of polygamy by Moses, on civil grounds' (*idem*). It is significant that Michaelis, in the final analysis, takes the position that this permission, in terms of civil right, is in the same category as divorce, to wit, that it was tolerated because of hardness of heart. 'I am therefore of opinion', he says, 'that with regard to the polygamy allowed among the Israelites, we can say nothing else than what Christ has said on the subject of divorce. Moses tolerated it *on account of their hardness of heart*, and because it would have been found a difficult matter to deprive them of a custom already so firmly established' (p. 15). *Cf.* David R. Mace: *Hebrew Marriage* (New York, 1953), pp. 134ff. For the view that monogamy was superimposed upon a polygamous foundation *cf.* Louis M. Epstein: *Marriage Laws in the Bible and the Talmud* (Cambridge, Mass., 1942), pp. 5ff.

The tension which appears in this interpretation is something which must be recognized. It is not ours to resolve all difficulties in our understanding of God's ways with men. It is not ours to understand some of the patent facts of God's providence. But the fact of progressive revelation, though it does not resolve all the difficulty for our understanding, does, nevertheless, place the question in a perspective that considerably relieves the tension.

The progressiveness of divine revelation bears closely upon God's judgment upon sin because it bears upon the gravity of an offence. 'To whomsoever much is given, of the same shall much be required' (Luke 12: 48). The greater the degree of revelation, the greater the responsibility and the more severe the judgment of God upon the transgression. In the earlier periods of revelation transgression of a law would not be as aggravated as that same transgression becomes in the fuller and brighter light of the revelation of its wrong and of the sanction with which it is attended. Hence polygamy, though it was a violation of the original institution and therefore inherently wrong under the Old Testament, would not have involved the same degree of guilt or of punitive sanction which it undoubtedly entails in the clear light of the New Testament. Furthermore, it is not only the fuller revelation of truth that must be taken into account, but also the more widely diffused and efficaciously operative manifestation of the Spirit of holiness, signalized by the event of Pentecost. We must not underestimate the distinctiveness of the privilege and of the responsibility that belongs to the situation in which we of the New Testament era are placed. In these last days God has spoken to us in the Son. We have the completion of the revelatory process. Behind us lies the objective accomplishment of redemption on the basis of which the completed revelation has been given. And ours is the epochal event of Pentecost, in virtue of which the Holy Spirit works more fully and efficaciously in the hearts and lives of men to bring to more effective fruition the canons of behaviour which were established at the beginning but, by reason of human blindness and hardness of heart, were not assessed or applied in their divine obligation or sanction. Progressive revelation, progressive realization of redemption, and progressive disclosure of the grace of the Spirit have been the method by which God's redemptive purpose in the world has been fulfilled. It has pleased God to work through process because he works in history. History has significance in the unfolding of his saving designs. The tutelary nonage of the Old Testament period is a fact in this historical process. In its historical context Israel's hardness of heart was also a fact which God himself took into account in the exercise of his disciplinary judgment. Sufferance was accorded in these cases of polygamy and divorce. But it was the sufferance of forbearance, not the sufferance of approval or sanction.

If this thesis is correct, then the underlying premiss is that there is basic agreement between the Old Testament and the New on the norms or standards of behaviour in question in connection with these two practices. That is to say, the basic institutions related to matrimony in both Testaments are monogamy and the permanency of the marital bond. And if, in respect of the two practices which appear to evince a deep-seated cleavage between the Old Testament ethic and that of the New, we find this basic agreement, this will provide us with a pattern in terms of which we may seek the solution of other difficulties. It also warns us against the facile assumption that there is basic discrepancy between the ethic of the respective Testaments. To say the least, we are pointed in the direction of seeking and finding a basic identity all along the line of the biblical ethic.

We may now turn our attention to two fundamental questions relevant to the biblical ethic. Are we justified in speaking of norms, or standards, as the canons of biblically sanctioned and approved behaviour? And, assuming that there are norms or standards, whence are they derived? If we deal with the second question, we shall find that we have virtually answered the first.

It could be very plausibly argued that the norms and standards of the biblical ethic are simply the precipitate of the sanctified moral consciousness, that the renewed consciousness of man, renewed after the image of God, has an intuitive sense of what is right and good. Since the heart of a believer is renewed after the image of God in knowledge, righteousness, and holiness, it must reflect the divine perfection. Hence, as the renewed person is confronted with the various situations of life, the renewed heart and mind spontaneously respond in ways that reflect and even bespeak the divine exemplar after which the heart has been renewed. And this intuitive answer dictates the proper behaviour in each existential situation. Over a period of time this type of response, exemplified in a great number of individuals, establishes a tradition or consensus of behaviour, for the reason that the image after which men are renewed is the same and the utterances which this image dictates are similar in similar situations. It is easy to see how, in the course of time, the common consciousness and the similarity of its utterances produce a series of patterns which are gradually crystallized and become formulated as the norms or canons of Christian behaviour. Thus, it may be argued, the biblical ethic is formed, codified, and systematized.

We may not abruptly dismiss this construction of the biblical ethic. In this conception there is an important stratum of truth. We know on the authority of the apostle that, in the case of those who are without the law of special revelation, there is the work of the law written in their hearts and they do by nature the things of the law (Romans 2: 14, 15). This can mean nothing less than that the Gentiles, who were outside the pale of the special revelation of law and gospel, were constrained by an inscription in their moral constitution to do certain things which were formally in agreement with the requirements of the law of God and to refrain from certain things which the law of God forbade. By what we may call constitutional impulse or constraint they were led to certain patterns of behaviour that could be called the things of the law. And co-ordinate with this operation of the law, or consequent upon it, there was the self-excusing and self-accusing activity of conscience. We shall have to account for a good deal of the common virtues which we find among non-Christian nations and civilizations, and for the commendable restraints which these peoples exemplify, in terms of this work of the law. If this is the case where there is only the native and constitutional engraving of the work of the law on men's hearts, how much more potent and effective must be the work of the law when the person is renewed after the image of God in knowledge, righteousness, and holiness, and when, in the express terms of Scripture, 'I will put my law in their inward parts, and in their heart will I write it' (Jeremiah 31: 33) has become true. In the nature of the case it must follow that the renewed and sanctified person does by renewed nature the things of the law, and does them with the understanding and will which the renewal of nature implies. We must make full allowance, therefore, for the activity of the renewed heart and mind in a way that is consonant with, and expressive of, the renewed character. This inference is so necessary that the line of thought which it draws can be made to appear as the only proper line of thought in explaining the origin and development of the biblical ethic.

Another consideration appears to lend the strongest support to the foregoing argument. It is the great truth, embedded in the Old Testament as well as in the New, that love is the fulfilling of the law, and that on two commandments, 'Thou shalt love the Lord thy God' and 'Thou shalt love thy neighbour as thyself', hang all the law and the prophets (*cf.* Romans 13: 10; Matthew 22: 37-40). Among students of Christian ethics no datum is more universally admitted or regarded as more incontrovertibly established than this, that love is the fulfilling of the law.

It must be recognized, of course, that the love spoken of in this connection is love in the human heart, the outflow of love to God and our fellowmen. It is true, of course, that this love to God and men is constrained in the human breast because the love of God to us is shed abroad in our hearts. We love him because he first loved us. But when love is said to be the fulfilment of the law, it is the love to God that is in view. Hence, incontestably, the fulfilment of the law springs from love to God and our fellowmen. And this must mean that the practice of the biblical *ethos*, the bringing to expression and fruition of the behaviour required and approved by the biblical revelation, springs from this love. It must follow that, to the extent to which this love governs us, to that extent we fulfil the demands of the biblical ethic. Where there is the perfection of love there will be the perfection of both ethical character and behaviour. Love never fails, and perfect love casts out fear.

Is not the inference inevitable, therefore, that the norms and canons which define or exemplify the biblical ethic are simply the readings of love's dictates, the crystallizations and formulations of the necessary outflow of love to God and our fellowmen? Or, to put it in terms of the earlier analysis, is not the biblical ethic the sum-total of the ways in which the renewed consciousness of man reacts to the demands of the diversified concrete situations in which he is placed? The common principles which characterize this ethic proceed from the fact that the renewed consciousness will react in principially similar ways to situations that are essentially similar in nature and circumstance. This construction of the scriptural ethic, it could be said, makes full allowance for what is standard and normal, on the one hand, and yet allows for the variety or diversity that is necessitated by personal individuality and the particularity or singularity of each situation.

In the analysis and resolution of this question we are concerned with the cardinal issues of the biblical ethic, and at this point, therefore, we shall have to enter upon a rather extended discussion.

1. Love is without question the fulfilling of the law. It might be more accurate to say that love is the fulfilment of the law. It will surely not be challenged if we say that love is both emotive and motive; love is feeling and it impels to action. If it does not impel to the fulfilment of the law, it is not the love of which the Scripture here speaks. In a word, the action to which love impels is the action which is characterized as the fulfilment of the law. Again, since love is in the category of feeling which creates affinity with the object and constrains the outflow of affection for the object, the fulfilment which love constrains is not the fulfilment of coerced and unwilling formal compliance, but the fulfilment of cheerful and willing obedience. Without such constraining and impelling love there is really no fulfilment of the law. Law prescribes the action, but love it is that constrains or impels to the action involved. This appears to be the essence of Paul's thought in Romans 13: 8-10. The emphasis is upon the necessity of love for our neighbour as that which constrains to the absence of ill-doing and the practice of well-doing. It is impossible for the prescriptions of law to have scope in our relationships to our fellowmen unless love reigns supreme, love as both expulsive and impulsive affection, expulsive of evil and impulsive to good.

Perhaps we have not yet expressed the kernel of Paul's thought when he says that 'love is the fulfilment of the law'. The thought appears to be that it is love that carries into effect the law of God; love constitutes the fulfilment of the law. It is the motive and active principle of fulfilment. Love renders to the requirements enunciated in the law the full measure of the obedience demanded. If we may use the metaphor, love fills to the brim the cup which the law puts into our hands. Love is the first drop; it is the last drop; and it is all the drops in between. From start to finish it is love that fulfils the law. When love is all-pervasive and inclusive, then the fulfilment of the law is completed. It is obvious how embracive this concept of love is; it is not otiose emotion but love as both emotive and motive, intensely pre-occupied with him who is its supreme object, and therefore intensely active in the doing of his will. Any analysis of the biblical ethic that fails to assess the import and function of love in these characteristic features misses the witness of the Old Testament as well as of the New.

2. In the attempt to discover the origin of the norms and canons of the biblical ethic, we must not forget that love to God with all our heart and soul and strength and mind and love to our neighbour as ourselves are themselves commandments. We are *commanded* to love God and our neighbour. The antithesis which is oftentimes set up between love and commandment overlooks this elementary fact. Love itself is exercised in obedience to a commandment—'Thou shalt love'. We cannot get away from the fact that love in this case is not ultimate or original. Love is dictated by a consideration that is prior to itself. Love is obedience to a commandment which comes from a source other than itself; it does not autonomously excogitate or create itself. We must resist that perverse conception of the nature of love that we cannot be commanded to love, that love must be spontaneous and cannot be evoked by demand. It is true that the command or demand will not itself create the love. Commandment of itself has no power to generate love or elicit obedience. But it by no means follows that love is not commanded. Love is commanded, and love is exercised in response to the commandment even though it is not the commandment that creates or generates that response. In this respect the commandment to love is like every other commandment. The commandment to feed the hungry, for example, does not itself create the disposition or will to do so; but feeding the hungry is action elicited in response to the commandment.

This fact—that to love is itself a commandment—should serve to expose at the outset the fallacy and perversity of that pattern of thought which is intolerant of the notion of keeping or observing commandments. If this notion is not biblical then we shall have to eliminate the commandments on which hang all the law and the prophets.

3. When Jesus said, 'On these two commandments hang all the law and the prophets', or Paul wrote, 'Love is the fulfilment of the law', there is in both cases an obvious distinction between love and the law that hangs on it, and between love and the law that it fulfils. Jesus did not say, 'Love is the whole law', nor Paul, 'Love is the law'. In neither case do love and law have the same denotation. Hence there must be content to the law that is not defined by love itself. We may speak, if we will, of the law of love. But, if so, what we must have in view is the commandment to love or the law which love fulfils. We may not speak of the law of love if we mean that love is itself the law. Love cannot be equated with the law nor can law be defined in terms of love. A good deal of ethical theory has ignored the most elementary canon of interpretation when it seeks to develop the ethic of love in abstraction from the denotation and connotation of the law of which our Lord and the apostle spoke.

4. When we examine the witness of the Scripture itself as to the origin of the canons of behaviour which the Scripture approves, we do not find that love is allowed to discover or dictate its own standards or patterns of conduct. We do not find that the renewed heart is allowed spontaneously to excogitate the ethic of the saints of God. We do not find that love is conceived of as an autonomous, self-acting agency which of itself, apart from any extraneous prescription or regulation, defines its own norms of behaviour. We do find that, from the beginning, there are objectively revealed precepts, institutions, commandments which are the norms and channels of human behaviour. Even man in innocence was not permitted to carve for himself the path of life; it was charted for him from the outset.

5. It is easy to see the difficulties that would embarrass love if it were left to itself to devise the ways and means of its self-realization. We think very naïvely indeed if we suppose that love can spontaneously decide the mode of its expression. It is only because we have become habilitated to the biblical revelation of law and commandment, because our thinking has been in-

formed to such an extent by the revelation of God's will as deposited in the Scripture, that we could ever have entertained the thought that love dictates the law of its activity or the modes of its behaviour. If we should envisage a situation in which love would be abstracted from all special revelation respecting God's will for thought and conduct, we could discern more readily the impossibility of the hypothesis that love prescribes its own law or that love is the law. This love which is the fulfilling of the law has always existed and been operative in the context of revelation from God respecting his will. And the hypothesis amounts to an abstraction that has never been true in human experience. Experiment in terms of the hypothesis is likewise an impossibility; we can never abstract our consciousness or its operations from the influence exerted upon it by that revelation with which it is informed. And neither could we abstract love from the indelible influence exerted upon it by the context of revelation within which it has come to exist.

6. In connection with the law written upon the heart of the renewed person, we must recognize that the law referred to in those contexts where this inscription is mentioned (Jeremiah 31: 33; Hebrews 8: 10; 10: 16) is the law which, as respects its content, has been revealed and deposited for us in the Scripture. The thought of the passages is not that we come to know what the law is by reading the inscription upon the heart. The thought is rather that there is generated in the heart an affinity with and a love to the law, to the end that there may be cheerful, spontaneous, loving fulfilment of it (cf. Psalm 40: 8, 9). The writing of the law upon the heart in the renewing operations of grace is parallel and similar to that which must have been true in Adam's state of integrity. Adam was created in the image of God in knowledge, righteousness, and holiness. The analogy of Scripture teaching would indicate that this implied the inscription of the law of God upon his heart.[6] But it is abundantly clear that this

---

[6] Cf. Romans 2: 14, 15; Jeremiah 31: 33. If man as fallen has 'the work of the law' written upon his heart so that he by nature does the things of the law, how much more must this have been true in original integrity. And if the renewal of man after the image of God can be described in terms of writing the law upon the heart, surely creation in the divine image at the beginning must have carried with it the inscription of the law upon the hearts of our

(continued on p. 26)

inscription did not obviate the necessity of giving to Adam positive directions respecting the activity which was to engage interest, occupation, and life in this world. We must not focus our attention upon the specific prohibition of Eden respecting the tree of the knowledge of good and evil to such an extent that we overlook the other commandments given to Adam, commandments germane to the most basic interests of life in this world (cf. Genesis 1: 27, 28; 2: 2, 3, 15, 24). All of these commandments bear closely upon our question; but some of them are more directly pertinent. The procreative mandate, for example, had respect to the exercise of one of his fundamental instincts. Adam as created must have been endowed with the sex impulse which would have sought satisfaction and outlet in the sex act. But he was not left to the dictates of the sex impulse and of the procreative instinct; these were not a sufficient index to God's will for him. The exercise of this instinct was expressly commanded and its exercise directed to the achievement of a well-defined purpose. Furthermore, there was the marital ordinance within which alone the sex act was legitimate.

These original mandates are germane to our present inquiry precisely because they are so closely related to the powers and instincts with which man is naturally endowed, and they show unmistakeably that native endowment or instinct is not sufficient for man's direction even in the state of original integrity. The exercise of native instincts, the institutions within which they are to be exercised, and the ends to be promoted by their exercise are prescribed by specially revealed commandments. If all this is true in a state of sinless integrity, when there was no sin to blind vision or depravity to pervert desire, how much more must expressly prescribed directions be necessary in a state of sin in which intelligence is blinded, feeling depraved, conscience defiled, and will perverted!

The conclusion to which we are driven, therefore, is that the notion we are controverting, namely, that love is its own law and the renewed consciousness its own monitor, is a fantasy which has no warrant from Scripture and runs counter to the witness of the biblical teaching.

---

first parents. The image of God in which man is recreated cannot be principially different from that in which he was at first created.

CHAPTER II

CREATION ORDINANCES

WE have had occasion already to refer to the commandments
or mandates given to man in the state of integrity. These creation
ordinances, as we may call them, are the procreation of offspring,
the replenishing of the earth, subduing of the same, dominion
over the creatures, labour, the weekly Sabbath, and marriage.
When we consider them and seek to assess their significance, we
discover how relevant they are to the elementary instincts of man
and to the interests that lay closest to his heart, how inclusive they
are in respect of the occupations which would have engaged man's
thought and action, and how intimately related they are one to
another. Implied in the institution of procreation are the acts and
processes for both man and woman by which the mandate was
to be carried into effect and the family and social responsibilities
resulting from the fulfilment of the mandate. We have to envisage
also the far-reaching implications for the structure of society.
When we consider the second mandate, the replenishing of the
earth, we must appreciate that the geographical expansion
involved was not merely for the purpose of filling the earth with
people, but also for the purpose of subduing the earth and its
resources, and of exercising dominion over the fish of the sea,
the fowl of the air, and everything that moves upon the face of
the earth. There is a complementation of these mandates and they
interpenetrate one another.

We may examine in more detail a few of these ordinances in
order to discover their precise character and their bearing upon
the biblical ethic in general.

THE ORDINANCES OF PROCREATION AND MARRIAGE

It is obvious that these, which came first and last in the record of
the mandates which antedated the fall (Genesis 1: 28; 2: 23, 24),
are closely related to each other. Marriage is the institution
established by God for the fulfilment of the procreative mandate.
'And the man said, This is now bone of my bones, and flesh of

27

my flesh: she shall be called woman, because she was taken out
of man. Therefore shall a man leave his father and his mother,
and shall cleave unto his wife; and they shall be one flesh.' Our
question now is: What does this institution involve for man in
his original state of integrity, and how much of what was involved
in this institution did man know, even if there had been no further
revelation than that enunciated in these two verses? In a word,
what was the institution and how much could Adam have known?

It makes no difference to the inspired and authoritative character of verse 24 whether it is regarded as an interpretive comment
of the inspired writer or as a continuation of Adam's own utterance. This passage is appealed to as the word of God by our Lord
himself (Matthew 19: 5; cf. Mark 10: 7, 8; Ephesians 5: 31). If
Adam is the spokesman, then he was the inspired mouthpiece of
God in uttering these words. If verse 24 is an interpretation and
application of the word spoken by Adam (verse 23), and added by
the writer, then the writer was the inspired organ. The most
probable, if not necessary, view is that verse 24 is a continuation
of Adam's own word. The sequence of the thought of the two
verses is so natural and the inference of verse 24 so integrally
related to verse 23 that we should expect both to stand together
as the utterance of Adam.

The question does arise, however, whether we can be sure that,
if verse 24 is not a word of Adam himself, the truth set forth in
verse 24 and the institution that it involves were known to Adam
and constituted part of the revelatory data given to him in the
state of innocence. There are good reasons for an affirmative
answer.

(1) The word of verse 23 was spoken by Adam himself. Verse
24 is an inference drawn from verse 23, and this is just to say that
the truth enunciated in verse 24 is implicit in verse 23. The expressions 'bone of my bones, and flesh of my flesh' in verse 23
are parallel to, and the basis of, the two main elements of verse 24,
namely, 'shall cleave unto his wife: and they shall be one flesh'.
To say the least, it is difficult to believe that Adam did not draw
from his own words their implications and applications. (2) The
comments of our Lord on this text make plain that the institution
which is the subject of verse 24 was in operation from the beginning. Matthew 19: 8 says this expressly. With reference to the

Mosaic provision for divorce Jesus says, 'from the beginning it was not so'. Indisputably this alludes to Genesis 2: 24 and implies that the institution enunciated there existed from the beginning and made no allowance for the dissolution of the marital bond. And when Jesus said earlier in this same discourse that 'he who created from the beginning made them male and female' (Matthew 19: 4) and proceeded forthwith to quote Genesis 2: 24 as the word of him who created male and female, the import is plainly to the effect that Genesis 2: 24 had been revealed from the beginning as that which gave meaning and purpose to the male and female composition of the race. If the institution of Genesis 2: 24 existed from the beginning, as our Lord says (Matthew 19: 8), if it was spoken from the beginning as something complementary to and explanatory of the bisexual character of the human race, as our Lord implies (Matthew 19: 4, 5), then this institution must have been known to Adam—from the beginning he was the only one to whom it could have been revealed.

We must proceed therefore on the premiss that the institution of Genesis 2: 24 was known to Adam; and the most reasonable assumption is that, not only was he the person to whom it was first revealed, but he himself was also the organ of revelation in giving utterance to it. With such a premiss in mind we must now examine the terms of Genesis 2: 24 in order to discover its precise import. The thesis I am going to propound is that it enunciates monogamy and the permanency of the bond of marriage. The grounds for this thesis are as follows.

1. The *prima facie* sense of Genesis 2: 24 is that one man is to be joined to one woman and that the *two* become one flesh— 'a man shall leave his father and his mother, and shall cleave unto his wife: and they shall be one flesh'. If we interject the thought of digamy, not to speak of polygamy, we bring such complication into the situation and the relationship described in verse 24 that we should have the greatest difficulty in reconciling the terms of verse 24 with a digamous relationship of either the man or the woman.

2. The fullest revelation we possess on the question of marriage, that by our Lord and the apostle Paul, appeals to Genesis 2: 24 as the definitive word of institution (Matthew 19: 3-9; Mark 10: 3-9; Ephesians 5: 31). It will surely not be questioned that these

New Testament passages enunciate the principle of monogamy, and the only interpretation we can place upon this appeal to Genesis 2: 24 on the part of our Lord and of Paul is that they found in this verse authority for the highest and purest ethic of the marital relationship. And this means for us that it is in the light of the New Testament revelation respecting the standards which govern the institution of marriage that we are to interpret the import of Genesis 2: 24. As it was in the case of divorce that 'from the beginning it was not so', so it is that in the matter of digamy or polygamy from the beginning it was not so. The indissolubility of the bond of marriage and the principle of monogamy are inherent in the verse. If this is its import, and Adam knew of the institution, then it would evacuate Genesis 2: 24 of meaning to suppose that Adam did not understand its implications.

THE ORDINANCE OF THE SABBATH

We read in Genesis 2: 2, 'And he (God) rested on the seventh day from all his work which he made'. The seventh day referred to here is unquestionably the seventh day in sequence with the six days of creative activity, the seventh day in the sphere of God's action, not the seventh day in *our* weekly cycle. In the realm of God's activity in creating the heavens and the earth there were six days of creative action and one day of rest. There is the strongest presumption in favour of the interpretation that this seventh day is not one that terminated at a certain point in history, but that the whole period of time subsequent to the end of the sixth day is the sabbath of rest alluded to in Genesis 2: 2. The contrast is between the work of creation and what is not the work of creation; and it must be borne in mind that the biblical concept demands that creation, in the sense of what is delineated for us in Genesis 1, must be restricted to the six days and not continued or resumed. It is in accord with this emphasis to regard the seventh day of rest as comprising all of the history that is not comprised in the six days. The considerations supporting this view may be conclusive and they are regarded as such by some careful and reverent scholars. But be this as it may, there are observations which must be made regarding God's rest.

(1) God's rest is not one of inactivity. God never ceased to be active in the universe which is his creative handiwork. To

this our Lord's own word is directly and significantly pertinent: 'My Father worketh until now, and I am working' (John 5: 17). (2) God's rest is cessation from one kind of activity, the specific kind of activity delineated for us in Genesis 1. God finished the work of creation, and he does not revert to it again. God's week, if we may use that term, is not a cycle, it is a once-for-all accomplishment. 'And the heavens and the earth were finished, and all the host of them. And on the seventh day God finished his work which he had made' (Genesis 2: 1, 2). (3) God's rest is the rest of delight in the work of creation accomplished. 'And God saw all that which he made, and behold it was very good' (Genesis 1: 31). This is expressly alluded to in Exodus 31: 17 in connection with God's sabbath rest, 'On the seventh day he rested and refreshed himself', and means surely the rest of satisfaction and delight in the completed work of creation.

When we come to Genesis 2: 3 the precise meaning is not as apparent as in the case of Genesis 2: 2. We read: 'And God blessed the seventh day, and sanctified it because that in it he rested from all his work which God created and made.' The question is: Does this refer simply to God's sabbath, or does it refer to a weekly day of rest in the cycle and sequences of our time? In Exodus 20: 11, in the fourth command of the decalogue, a similar formula is used: 'Wherefore the Lord blessed the sabbath day and sanctified it'. Here there can be no doubt that the blessing of the sabbath day and the sanctifying of it has direct bearing upon the seventh day in the weekly cycle ordained for man. This is the subject with which the commandment deals. Even in Exodus 20: 11 it is difficult to ascertain whether the sabbath day referred to is expressly the seventh day in the realm of God's activity or the seventh day in man's weekly cycle. But the significant feature of this verse is that, whichever interpretation we adopt, the sabbath of God's rest is the reason given for the sabbath of man's rest, the recurring seventh day of the week. And this would carry with it the inevitable inference that God blessed and sanctified the seventh day of our week precisely because he sanctified the seventh day in the realm of his own creative activity. If this is true in the case of Exodus 20: 11, the similarity of Genesis 2: 3 would lead to the conclusion that, in that verse also, reference is made to the reason why the seventh day of our week is sanctified and blessed by God.

In the transcendent realm of God's *opera ad extra*, on the grand plane of his creative action, he rested on the seventh day. God's mode of operation is the exemplar on the basis of which the sequence for man is patterned. There can be little doubt, therefore, that in Genesis 2: 3 there is at least an allusion to the blessing of the seventh day in man's week; and, when we compare it more closely with Exodus 20: 11, there is strong presumption in favour of the view that it refers specifically and directly to the sabbath instituted for man. This reference to the sabbath institution in Genesis 2: 2, 3 bears very intimately, therefore, upon the relevance and character of the ordinance which is given its most formal enunciation and definition in the fourth command of the decalogue, and we are compelled to make certain inferences and applications.

1. Since the action of God in creation has relevance quite apart from sin or redemption, we are bound to conclude that the sabbath institution would have had relevance to Adam in his state of innocence. While we have no way of knowing what period of time elapsed between the creation of Adam and his fall, and while we have no record of express revelation to Adam of the sequence, six days of labour and one day of rest, yet we have sufficient data to infer that, if Adam did as a matter of fact continue in his original state of integrity for a period of weeks, the institution of the sabbath would have applied to him. We know from Genesis 1: 14-19 that day and night, days, seasons, years were established ordinances and would have regulated Adam's life in this world from the outset. And if Adam had retained his integrity and had been confirmed in it, these ordinances would have continued to condition and regulate his life and activity. In the light of Genesis 2: 2, 3; Exodus 20: 11; 31: 17 we must also suppose that the archetypal pattern provided by God's own action in the realm of his own working and resting would have regulated Adam's labour and rest in the realm of his activity. How Adam had been informed, or how he would have been informed, we do not know. The most reasonable assumption is that the revelation to Adam took the form or would have taken the form of the data expressed for us in Genesis 2: 2, 3. But, in any case, it is contrary to analogy and sound reason to suppose that Adam, if he had retained his integrity, would not have known the pivotal

data of Genesis 1 and 2. Even after the fall Adam and his contemporaries must have known something of the creation narrative;
piety could not have existed on any other basis. How much more
necessary is this conclusion respecting Adam's knowledge if we
envisage a state of continued and confirmed integrity. It is inconceivable that Adam would have been ignorant of the fact
that in six days God made heaven and earth and on the seventh
day rested. In other words, the increase of knowledge would
necessarily have embraced information regarding creation and
the sequence in God's procedure. If so the pattern for man's life
implicit in that sequence must have been recognized by Adam.

2. We have found already that God's own rest on the seventh
day is not to be construed in terms of cessation from activity but
in terms of cessation from one kind of activity, the work of
creation. In like manner, the sabbath in man's week is not to be
defined in terms of cessation from activity, but cessation from
that kind of activity involved in the labours of the other six days.
Genesis 2: 2, 3 should itself guard us from the formalism which
was the error of pharisaism. Our Lord, when confronted with
this erroneous assumption, vindicated his working on the sabbath
by appeal to this consideration: 'My Father worketh until now,
and I work' (John 5: 17). Jesus is not here obliterating the rest
of the sabbath; he is not saying that the sabbath has been abrogated. He is vindicating the work he performed as consonant with
the rest of the sabbath precisely because the rest the sabbath requires is not the rest of inaction. Sabbath rest is not inactivity; it
is not unemployment, but employment of another sort from that
of the six days.

The sabbath institution, as it applied to Adam in his original
state of integrity, and as it would have applied to him in a state
of confirmed integrity, throws a flood of light upon the God-
centered character of the ethic which would have governed
Adam's behaviour. In fact it evinces the religious basis of that
ethic. The other creation ordinances, of course, would be a
constant reminder of his relation to, dependence upon, and responsibility to, God; they were divine mandates. But the ordinance of six days of labour and one of rest would have directed his
thought most pointedly to two things. First, it would advise him
that his life in this world was patterned after the divine example.

The reason for the cycle of labour and rest is that God himself followed this sequence. The governing principle of this ethic is not merely the will of God but conformity to the pattern of divine procedure. In this particular Adam was to be a son of the Father in heaven. Second, the cycle which this ordinance requires intimates that the rest, since it is not that of inaction and consists in activity contrasted with the labour of the other six days, must have its specific character in the rest of worship. Even in innocence man would have required time for specific worship. We are too ready to entertain the notion that religion in a state of sinless or confirmed integrity would have required no institutions as the medium of expression. Our conception of the piety of paradise becomes one of abstract, etherealized mysticism. This conception is not the conception which the data will bear out. There would have been a concreteness to life in paradise and likewise to the worship which paradise would have demanded. This is symptomatic of the kind of ethic which paradise exemplified. Unfallen man would need to suspend his weekly labours in order to refresh himself with the exercises of concentrated worship. It points to the concreteness of the ethic which integrity would have demanded and exemplified.

We may sum up our conclusions as follows. The weekly sabbath is based upon the divine example; the divine mode of procedure in creation determines one of the basic cycles by which human life here on earth is regulated, namely, the weekly cycle; this sequence of six days of labour and one of rest would have applied to Adam in the state of innocence and in a state of confirmed integrity in the event of successful probation; and the most reasonable supposition is that the revelation to Adam would have taken the form of the revelation we possess in Genesis 2: 2, 3. These conclusions place the whole question of the obligation of the sabbath institution in a perspective different from that frequently entertained. The argument commonly advanced is that the silence of Genesis on the matter of the sabbath indicates that there was no weekly sabbath in patriarchal times and that it was first instituted after the Exodus. Genesis is not silent. Genesis 2: 2, 3 proves that the sabbath is a creation ordinance and, as such, must have been known to Adam and his contemporaries. The silence of Genesis subsequent to Genesis 2: 2,

3 proves nothing as to the desuetude of the institution during patriarchal times, nor does it prove ignorance of the ordinance on the part of the patriarchs. But even if we suppose that the remembrance of this institution did pass away and that the patriarchs did not observe the weekly sabbath, it is no more difficult to explain this lapse from the creation ordinance than it is to explain the lapse from the principle of monogamy so clearly implied in Genesis 2: 24. It is precarious to base too much on silence. But even if the silence indicates declension, ignorance, and non-observance, this does not remove the creation ordinance nor does it disestablish its binding obligation.

THE ORDINANCE OF LABOUR

It is perhaps not sufficiently appreciated that the mandate respecting labour is implicit in the sabbath ordinance. The day of rest has no meaning apart from the background of labour. God's day of rest is the sequel to six days of creative activity and has no relevance in any other context. The sabbath institution implies labour; and its most significant feature in reference to labour is that it prescribes and defines, in terms of an established cycle, the extent of labour—six days of labour followed by one of cessation from that specific kind of employment which labour denotes. It is not, however, in the sabbath institution alone that the labour mandate was revealed to man. The Lord God put Adam into 'the garden of Eden to dress it and to keep it' (Genesis 2: 15). Here is explicit allusion to Adam's specific employment, and we must recognize that such labour is not a curse but a blessing. It finds its ground and sanction in the fact that man's life is patterned after the divine examplar established in the creation and formation of the universe which constitutes the realm of man's existence and activity.

That Adam's labour consisted in dressing the garden and keeping it informs us that it was highly worthy of man's dignity as created after the divine image to be employed in so mundane a task. This is eloquent warning against the impiety of despising and judging unworthy of our dignity the tasks which we call menial. And one cannot but suspect that the widespread tendency to take flight from agricultural and related pursuits springs from an underestimate of the dignity of manual toil and oftentimes reflects an unwholesome ambition which is the fruit of impiety. There is warrant for the judgment that economics, culture, morality, and piety have suffered grave havoc by failure to appreciate the nobility of manual labour. Multitudes of men and women, if they had thought in terms of this principle and had been taught in the home, in the church, and in the school to think in these terms, would have been saved from the catastrophe of economic, moral, and religious ruin because they would have been preserved from the vain ambition of pursuing vocations for which they were not equipped and which, on sober and enlightened reflection, they would not have sought. It is a fallacy to think, and it is one that has greatly impoverished the life of society, that culture cannot exist and flourish among manual toilers. It may well be that it actually does not exist and flourish among such. But, if so, it is because our thinking and our social structure have been to such an extent based upon and oriented to this false and pernicious premiss. And this premiss has embroiled us in a vortex from which only revolution in thought and practice will deliver us. Culture on a high level has been developed and can be developed concurrently with, and to a considerable extent through the instrumentality of, tasks which are not professional such as those of the farmer, the artisan, the tradesman, and the labourer. The Bible does not waste words. It tells us comparatively little respecting the employment of man as he was created. But in a few strokes it establishes a principle. And if, in the light of that principle, we examine our history, we discover how far astray from divinely instituted order have been the guiding principles of our civilization. All of this is but another index to the fact that man has fallen. In reality the marvel is that the labyrinth of our woes is not more complex and tangled than it is.

There is an indication in Genesis 1 and 2 of the variety which would have characterized the labours of mankind in the state of innocence, and would have characterized his labours in a state of confirmed integrity. The other mandates — the replenishing of the earth and subduing it — involved labour also. Even in the genial conditions which would have obtained in an uncursed earth it is not difficult to imagine the labour entailed in geographical expansion and the necessity of making adequate provision for sustenance and comfort in this process of expansion. But more significant in respect of labour is the mandate to subdue the earth. This means nothing if it does not mean the harnessing and utilizing of the earth's resources and forces. We are not to suppose that the earth is represented as offering resistance to man's dominion and that the subduing was to be that of conquering alien and recalcitrant powers. But the subduing of the earth must imply the expenditure of thought and skill and energy in bringing the earth and its resources under such control that they would be channelled to the promotion of certain ends which they were suited and designed to fulfil but which would not be fulfilled apart from the exercise of man's design and labour. In the sense in which Jesus spoke of the sabbath as made for man and not man for the sabbath, so we may say that the earth and its resources were made for man and not man for them; he was to exercise dominion over them, they were not to rule over him. The earth and its resources were to be brought into the service of his well-being, enjoyment, and pleasure.

The nature of man is richly diversified. There is not only a diversity of basic need but there is also a profuse variety of taste and interest, of aptitude and endowment, of desires to be satisfied and of pleasures to be gratified. When we consider the manifold ways in which the earth is fashioned and equipped to meet and gratify the diverse nature and endowments of man, we can catch a glimpse of the vastness and variety of the task involved in subduing the earth, a task directed to the end of developing man's nature, gifts, interests, and powers in engagement with the resources deposited by God in the earth and the sea. We must also take into account that the earth, untouched by the curse and the travail resulting from it, would have been perfectly congruous with the nature and endowments of man uncontaminated by sin and defilement and unhampered by the liabilities of sin's curse. And when we remember that the ultimate goal of man's creation and endowment, and of the creation and endowment of the earth as the sphere and platform of his employment, was not the cultivation of his powers and the cultivation of earth's resources for the promotion of his own good and enjoyment, but the magnifying of God's glory, then a vista of frontiers of employment opens to our vision. 'The earth is the Lord's and the fulness thereof.' The whole earth is full of God's glory. The chief incentive in subduing the earth and the chief end to be promoted by it would have been the discovery and exhibition of the manifold wisdom and power of God. We know how intriguing, even to godless men, is the scientific quest, and how untiring are their labours to discover the secrets of what they call nature. How incomparably more intriguing and defeatlessly rewarding would have been the quest of sinless man when, at every step of his path and in every detail of progressive understanding, the marvels of the Creator's wisdom, power, goodness, righteousness, and lovingkindness would have broken in upon his heart and mind, and every new discovery, every additional conquest, would have given cause afresh for the adoration, 'O Lord, how manifold are thy works! in wisdom hast thou made them all: the earth is full of thy riches' (Psalm 104: 24). We get a glimpse of the stupendous undertaking and the unspeakable glory of it all. We begin, perhaps, to understand a little of what culture should be. This is the culture that would have engaged and inspired man if he had been confirmed in his integrity. It would have been culture untiringly inspired by the apprehension of the Creator's glory and by the passion to apprehend and exalt that glory more. That our culture is so little inspired by that ideal is but proof that man has fallen. That any of this culture is found in the earth is proof of redemptive grace.

We must not forget that, back of all such employment and the cultural and religious advancement accruing from it, there is the express mandate in the form of commandment. Man would have pursued his task in obedience to God's command and in the awareness of God-given authority. We see how divine command casts the halo of sanctity over all the diversified involvements of his undertaking and undergirded him in the fulfilment of it. There is no conflict between the gratification of desire and the enhancement of his pleasure, on the one hand, and fulfilment of God's command on the other. Rather, the consciousness of compliance with divine command fortified and confirmed him in the propriety and piety of the pleasure enjoyed. It is a strange deflection of thought that leads students of biblical ethics to set up an antithesis between impulse arising from sense of duty and the impulse of love and delight. The tension that often exists within us between a sense of duty and wholehearted spontaneity is a tension that arises from sin and a disobedient will. No such tension would have invaded the heart of unfallen man. And the operations of saving grace are directed to the end of removing that tension so that there may be, as there was with man at the beginning, the perfect complementation of duty and pleasure, of commandment and love. The biblical ethic, as it would have been exemplified in a sinless world and as it is exemplified in redeemed humanity, knows no antithesis between duty performed in obedience to commandment and love as the fulfilment of law. 'Oh how love I thy law!' That would have been the constant refrain of man in confirmed integrity as he carried into effect the mandate to subdue the earth. That was the protestation of the second man, the Lord from heaven: 'I delight to do thy will, O my God; yea, thy law is within my heart.' And this is the harmony to which renewed man is restored: 'I delight in the law of God after the inward man.' It is this orientation that the biblical ethic establishes from the very outset, and it is only deflection from the biblical pattern of thought that would even suggest an antithesis between sense of duty and the spontaneity of delight and love.

Before closing our discussion of the ethics of primitive integrity there are two subjects which call for remark.

1. In connection with man's original state we must not overlook the relevance to our present interest of the prohibition respecting the tree of the knowledge of good and evil. This prohibition was the specific test of Adam's devotion and fidelity; his probation was concentrated in obedience to this prohibition. The resources of obedient disposition were placed under the most exacting demands in relation to this commandment. But, if so, it is surely because obedience to commandment is the way in which the utmost of devotion and fidelity is to be exemplified. The troth of love and faith is to be proven by obedience to commandment, and obedience is the principle of integrity. The general criterion of integrity, therefore, cannot be essentially different from that which is the supreme test of integrity.

It is eloquent corroboration of this observation that, after man fell and when God interrogated Adam as to his sin, the question is focused upon transgression of the commandment: 'Hast thou eaten of the tree, whereof I commanded thee that thou shouldest not eat?' (Genesis 3: 11). And when the curse was pronounced upon Adam the same emphasis appears: 'Because thou hast hearkened to the voice of thy wife, and hast eaten of the tree of which I commanded thee saying, Thou shalt not eat of it: cursed is the ground for thy sake' (Genesis 3: 17).

The fall of our first parents did not begin with the overt act of disobedience; it was preceded by a process of defection that culminated in it. But this process of defection was directed to the overt act, and the commandment was the criterion by which the process of defection was to be judged. Hence, when God interrogated Adam and executed the curse, it was transgression of the commandment that was thrust into the foreground and enunciated as the ground of condemnation. We may properly infer that transgression of commandment is the principle of sin and obedience to commandment the principle of integrity. Obedience to commandment is the subjective condition of virtue and commandment is the objective criterion. Disobedience to commandment is the subjective condition of sin and commandment its objective criterion.

2. The mandates given to man in his original state of integrity imply that confirmed integrity would have been followed by a long, drawn-out period of history. The probation prohibition was given in the context of a series of mandates and institutions and we must conclude that the purpose to be achieved by the probation commandment was not to fit man for translation to another realm in which these mandates and institutions would have had no relevance. Such a construction of the issue resultant upon successful probation would make mockery of the creation institutions and mandates. A successful probation would simply have confirmed man in the integrity by which he would be able to carry these mandates into effect and bring them to fruition. And so we must envisage the confirmation in knowledge, righteousness, and holiness as equipping Adam and his posterity for the continuous and successful discharge of all that was entailed in the creation ordinances and mandates. It is only in the unfolding temporal history with its cycles and sequences that we can understand the creation institution and appreciate the significance of Genesis 1: 14-19 with the alternations and sequences of day and night, seasons and years. In other words, we must not forget the

significance of time, with its successions and cycles, in the sinless state of unconfirmed integrity which actually existed, or its significance in that state of confirmed integrity which would have followed in the event of successful probation. What the ultimate eschatology would have been in this latter event we do not know. But it would not have been an eschatology without developments and achievements of temporal duration and succession. God himself followed a certain sequence in the creation and formation of heaven and earth—six days of creative activity and one day of rest. The significance of history for man is grounded in the significance of history for God himself in the realm of his creative and providential activity. The sequences which govern the creative order and the sequences which govern the life of man in that creative order are not originated or dictated by the new conditions which arose from sin, nor by the new conditions which the intervention of redemptive grace creates. And the limitations and restrictions which the sequences and cycles of temporal history impose are not the result of sin or the provisions of redemptive grace.

With the fall of man a new complex of conditions and circumstances entered which radically affected the life of man in this world. Because of the completely different situation we should expect, in the nature of the case, that new provisions would apply to man, provisions which could have had no relevance in a sinless state of either unconfirmed or confirmed goodness. We have a striking and instructive example of this at the very outset. Before the fall both Adam and Eve were naked and they were not ashamed (Genesis 2: 25). There were no emotions or sensations which would in any way suggest, far less dictate, the need or the propriety of clothing. The immediate sequel to their sin was that the eyes of them both were opened and they knew that they were naked, and they sewed fig leaves together, and made themselves girdles (Genesis 3: 7). This covering of themselves was apparently the instinctive reaction to the shame and fear which were the result of sin (cf. Genesis 3: 10). It is altogether reasonable to associate the covering of themselves with girdles with the same complex of emotion which induced our first parents to hide themselves from the presence of the Lord God among the trees of the garden, particularly the emotions of shame and fear, emotions which would never have invaded the human breast apart from sin and guilt. It is a signal fact in this connection that, later on, God himself clothed our first parents. By that action clothing is established as an institution and it has the force of a commandment. Hence we have an ordinance, adherence to which is required of man in his state of sin, which would have had no relevance in a state of sinless integrity. This illustrates and establishes a principle: not everything proper in a state of perfection is proper in a state of sin, and not everything proper in a state of sin would have been proper in a sinless state. We should expect, therefore, that numerous institutions divinely established for the regulation and direction of human conduct are institutions which are proper and necessary only because there is a state of sin and misery. Sin and the evils which follow in its wake affect the content of the ethic which God ordains for fallen man. We must beware of the tendency to discount the corruption of human nature. Many of the norms and canons which Scripture institutes are based on the premiss that human nature is depraved. If we do not entertain that assumption as one of the fundamental premisses of our thinking, we shall not be receptive to many of the features of the biblical ethic. The ethic the Bible institutes for man is not the ethic of a state of ideal perfection; it takes full account of man's sin and this is reflected in both the form and content of instituted law. It is undoubtedly this feature of biblical law that Paul has in view when he says that 'law is not made for a righteous man' (I Timothy 1: 9).

We might expect that the radical change in the human situation caused by the entrance of sin and its resulting miseries would have had the effect of abrogating, or at least modifying, the basic creation ordinances which had been given to man in his state of integrity. This, however, is precisely what we do not find. The creation ordinances of procreation, replenishing the earth, subduing the earth, dominion over the creatures, labour, marriage, and the sabbath are not abrogated. It is of paramount interest and significance to observe the ways in which the continuance of these ordinances is intimated and their sanctity preserved. Sometimes these ordinances are expressly enunciated; at other times they are implied. In the curses pronounced upon the woman and the man we might not expect to find any allusion to creation ordinances. But there is express allusion to two of these, the institutions of procreation and labour. The first appears in the curse upon the woman: 'I will greatly multiply thy pain and thy conception' (Genesis 3: 16). It is in connection with this ordinance of procreation that the curse upon the woman is to be peculiarly manifest. But there is no suspension or relaxation of the ordinance itself. In the curse upon Adam there is distinct allusion to the ordinance of labour. The circumstances under which man is to labour are radically altered; it is in connection with his daily toil that the curse upon him is to be acutely manifest. But he must still labour in order to gain for himself and his dependants the sustenance of life. 'In the sweat of thy face shalt thou eat bread' (Genesis 3: 19). Again in reference to procreation we have the repetition and intensification of this ordinance after the flood: 'And you, be ye fruitful and multiply; bring forth abundantly in the earth, and multiply therein' (Genesis 9: 7; cf. 1: 28). We have also the express indication of the way in which this ordinance was carried into effect; it was to be through marriage (Genesis 4: 1, 2, 17, 25; 5: 1-3). And in this we have certification of the continuance of the ordinance of marriage. In respect of the command to replenish the earth perhaps the most instructive episode certifying to us the continuance of the original mandate is the dispersion after the tower of Babel. In the building of the tower there was a variety of motives and intentions. But one feature of the design and of God's judgment upon it stands out distinctly. Mankind was bent upon localization of habitation and concentration of power. Whether by conscious intent to frustrate or by unwitting failure to carry into effect the original mandate to replenish the earth and subdue it, they were offering defiance to God's design and command. God intervened by judgment to circumvent the scheme which had as its purpose the defeat of the divine design and command, and in this dispersion of the nations is disclosed to us the sanctity which guarded the creation ordinance. That the sabbath institution had not been abrogated is established by the incorporation in the decalogue of the sabbath commandment.

These examples are sufficient to show that none of the basic ordinances which guided and directed the life of man in the state of original integrity were abrogated by the fall of man. Their obligation and sanctity remain inviolate. It is not saying too much if we maintain that these creation ordinances furnish us with what is central in the biblical ethic. These ordinances govern the life of man in that which is central in man's interest, life, and occupation; they touch upon every area of life and behaviour. The fall did bring revolutionary changes into man's life; yet these ordinances are still in effect and they indicate that the interests and occupations which lay closest to man's heart in original integrity must still lie close to his heart in his fallen state. Conditions and circumstances have been revolutionized by sin, but the basic structure of this earth, and of man's life in it, has not been destroyed. There is identity and continuity.

CHAPTER III

THE MARRIAGE ORDINANCE AND PROCREATION

THE first creation mandate mentioned in the Genesis narrative is that of procreation (Genesis 1: 28a).[1] This mandate is closely associated with the other institution which is the ordained means through which the command to procreate is brought to effect, namely, the ordinance of marriage. As we address ourselves to the examination of these two creation ordinances as they are fulfilled or desecrated in the unfolding history of the race, and as progressive revelation throws its light upon their character and implications, we shall deal with them together. We cannot think of the duty of procreation in abstraction from marriage. And we cannot think of marriage apart from the dignity and privilege of the procreative acts and processes which are bound up with it.

We have found already that Genesis 2: 23, 24 implies monogamy and that digamy or polygamy was a departure from the original institution and therefore, though suffered or tolerated under the Old Testament, was, nevertheless, a violation of God's instituted order. The first recorded deviation from the law of monogamy is the case of Lamech. 'And Lamech took unto him two wives' (Genesis 4: 19). The context suggests, to say the least, that the taking of two wives is co-ordinate with the other vices which appear so conspicuously in this case. It is admittedly difficult to determine precisely the import of the song to his two wives. But we have a confession of murder in any case, and there is also either boastful insolence, or murderous vindictiveness, or presumptuous arrogance. And we can scarcely suppress the inference that the reference to Lamech's digamy is for the purpose of intimating to us that his departure from monogamy goes hand in

The exercise of dominion over the earth and its creatures is referred to in Genesis 1: 26 but it is not expressed in the form of a mandate addressed to man. That is done in verse 28: 'and have dominion over the fish of the sea, and over the birds of the heavens, and over every living thing that moveth upon the earth.'

hand with these other vices and is intended to carry an indirect indictment of its wrong. As we shall see presently, the desecration of marriage is complementary to the vice of violence and oppression.

Contrary to a good deal of past and present speculation, we shall have to regard the marriages referred to in Genesis 6: 1-3 as marriages contracted between the godly and the ungodly, that the sons of God are not angels, or preternatural beings, but the children of God in the human family, and that the daughters of men are those from outside the line of the godly seed.[2] The judgment of God expressed in verse 3 indicates in unmistakeable terms the divine disapproval of mixed marriages even at that early stage of human history. The rampant iniquity described in the succeeding context cannot be dissociated from the evils which emanated from this violation of marital sanctity, and this violation must be regarded as ministering to the violence and oppression with which the whole earth was filled. There is the interaction of vice, and where the proprieties and sanctities that ought to govern the entrance upon marital relationship are discarded, the door is opened for the indulgence of the grossest and most violent vices. The children of God are the salt of the earth. When the interests of godliness do not govern the people of God in the choice of marital partners, irreparable confusion is the result and the interests, not only of spirituality, but also of morality, are destroyed. Here we have emblazoned on the story of this episode in the history of mankind the great principle that marital life is to be guided, not by impulse or fancy, but by considerations which conserve and promote the interests of godliness. It is the Old Testament counterpart of the New Testament principle that Christians should marry only 'in the Lord'.

We discover, therefore, that the exercise of the procreative impulse and compliance with the divine command to be fruitful are not to be given unrestricted and indiscriminate scope. The institution of procreation is circumscribed. It is only within the marital bond that a man is to know a woman, and only his wife may he know. And since the marital bond is monogamous, only with one wife may a man enter into conjugal intercourse. Furthermore, in the choice of a marital partner we are not to be guided by impulse

[2] See Appendix A, pp. 243ff.

or fancy, but by those considerations which conserve and promote the interests of godliness. When we correlate these guiding principles we can see how far-reaching are the restraints. Procreation is the divine institution and the procreative impulse is native to man. But the interests of godliness must be paramount in the discharging of the duty and the satisfying of the impulse. Godliness is the governing principle. This means that in the exercise of so basic an impulse as that of sex, and in the fulfilment of so basic an institution as that of procreation, the biblical ethic is shown to have a religious root and religious motivation. No aspect of the biblical ethic is regulative of conduct apart from the fear of God and the promotion of that fear among men.

We have striking examples in patriarchal times of the recognition of the sanctity which guarded the institution of procreation. Undoubtedly the most signal instance is the profound sense of the demands of chastity in the case of Joseph. When plied with alluring and persistent temptation to violate the sanctity of conjugal intercourse he said: 'How can I do this great wickedness, and sin against God?' (Genesis 39: 9). In the face of such sensitivity and nobility of character we must infer that in patriarchal circles there was an intense cultivation by both precept and practice of the sanctity of sex and of the proprieties by which its urges are to be regulated. Chastity in its grandeur is written across the history of Joseph. The inculcation of the demands of chastity must have been a feature of patriarchal religious instruction. And the religious motivation is patent. Joseph did not say, 'How shall I violate the trust my master has reposed in me?' Nor did he say, 'How shall I be party to your marital infidelity and violate the trust your master has reposed in you?' But he did say, 'How can I do this great wickedness, and sin against God?' Integrity is grounded in and impelled by the fear of the Lord.

We may not condone the deceit of Jacob's sons towards Hamor and Shechem, nor the ruthless revenge of Simeon and Levi (Genesis 34: 13, 25, 26). Instruments of cruelty were in their habitations (cf. Genesis 49: 5, 6). But we cannot fail to appreciate the indignation and deep sense of violated honour which Jacob's sons entertained when the purity of their sister Dinah had been desecrated by Shechem the son of Hamor. We rightly detect the accents of a highly developed ethic when we read, 'Now Jacob heard that he had defiled Dinah his daughter; and his sons were with his cattle in the field: and Jacob held his peace until they came ... And the sons of Jacob came in from the field when they heard it; and the men were grieved, and they were very wroth, because he had wrought folly in Israel in lying with Jacob's daughter; which thing ought not to be done' (Genesis 34: 5, 7). Chastity was not a virtue peculiar to Joseph; it has its background in the patriarchal tradition of a well-recognized ethic guarding the sanctity of sexual relationship.

That this tradition was not confined to the Abrahamic family is evident from the case of Abimelech, king of Gerar, when he took Sarah, Abraham's wife (Genesis 20: 2-18). God reproved Abimelech: 'Behold, thou art but a dead man, because of the woman whom thou hast taken; for she is a man's wife' (verse 3). Abimelech's defence resided in his ignorance of the fact that Sarah was Abraham's wife and this was why he could plead: 'in the integrity of my heart and the innocency of my hands have I done this' (verse 5). God recognized his plea as valid (cf. verse 6). But the implication of his plea is that, if he had known, he could not have taken her in the integrity of his heart and with a blameless conscience. And this implies that he was fully aware of the wrong of taking another man's wife and therefore aware of the sanctity guarding the marital relation. To speak proleptically, he recognized the sanctity of the seventh commandment. It is ironical indeed that Abimelech should have to reprove Abraham for misconduct in concealing the fact that Sarah was his wife, particularly since Abraham thought that it was the absence of the fear of God in Gerar that made it necessary for him to resort to this means of self-protection. But the episode shows how acute was the sense of sanctity respecting marriage outside the circle of the covenantal revelation concentrated in Abraham and his seed.

As indicative of the measures taken in the patriarchal period to prevent the dangers and liabilities arising from mixed marriages we have the steps taken by Abraham to ensure that his son Isaac would not take a wife of the daughters of the Canaanites (Genesis 24: 2-4), and also the charge given by Isaac to Jacob: 'Thou shalt not take a wife of the daughters of Canaan. Arise, go to Padan-aram, to the house of Bethuel thy mother's father; and take thee a wife from thence of the daughters of Laban thy mother's brother' (Genesis 28: 1, 2). Although Rebekah had probably another motive which she had concealed from Isaac when she said to him, 'I am weary of my life because of the daughters of Heth: if Jacob take a wife of the daughters of Heth, such as these, of the daughters of the land, what good shall my life do me?' (Genesis 27: 46), yet undoubtedly she spoke the truth respecting her concern for Jacob's marriage. For we are told that Esau's Hittite wives 'were a grief of mind unto Isaac and to Rebekah' (Genesis 26: 35). There is scarcely room for question that, when Rebekah spoke so disparagingly to Isaac of the daughters of Heth, she had particularly in mind Esau's wives and, though the urgency of her protestation to Isaac was prompted by the need of having Jacob away from the rage of Esau, there was also the deepest concern that Jacob, as the one in whom the covenant promise was to be fulfilled, should not be drawn into the entanglements of Hittite marital alignment.

In surveying the history of divine revelation respecting the marriage ordinance we have thus found a series of restrictions which more closely define the sphere within which the procreative impulse may be exercised in pursuance of the procreation mandate. We now come to another series of proscriptions which imply further delimitation. They are those laws of the Pentateuch which prescribe that marriage is not to be within certain degrees of consanguinity and affinity (Leviticus 18: 6ff.; 20: 11-21; Deuteronomy 22: 30; 27: 20-23).[3] We may not discount the difficulties of interpretation which arise in some of these instances, particu-

---

[3] The expression 'uncover the nakedness' (עֶרְוָה גִּלָּה) has reference to sexual intercourse. In Ezekiel 16: 36 (cf. vv. 35, 37); 23: 18 it is used of the sexual intercourse involved in whoredom, that is to say, of extra-conjugal intercourse, even though it is possible in these cases that the whoredoms referred to are those of idolatry. Of course, extra-conjugal intercourse with persons specified in these passages in Leviticus and Deuteronomy is forbidden. Such sexual intercourse would have the additional guilt of being not only fornication or adultery, but incestuous fornication or adultery. But that these ordinances have reference to marriage is also apparent, and there can be no doubt but that the main purpose is to prohibit marriages within these degrees of consanguinity and affinity. This is shown by Leviticus 18: 18; 20: 14, 21. The expression 'take a wife' indicates that more is involved than an act

(continued on p. 50)

larly those connected with Leviticus 18: 16, 18.[4] Nor should we suppress the questions which arise in connection with the marriages of Abraham and Jacob in relation to these Mosaic provisions. But these difficulties in particular cases do not remove or obscure the general principle of these Mosaic ordinances, namely, that marriage within certain degrees of consanguinity and affinity was forbidden. And the import of most of these prohibited degrees is quite obvious.

What is of particular interest to us is that this principle of prohibited degrees is enunciated in the New Testament and applied to the ethic governing Christian conduct. Sometimes appeal is made in this connection to the case of Herod and Herodias. But this is not as conclusive as it might appear. John the Baptist could have reproved Herod for violation of Old Testament law, even though that law would have had no relevance under the New Testament. There is undoubtedly one feature of John's reproof that is significant, namely, that he recognized the Old Testament law in question as applicable to Herod. And that fact may have far-reaching implications for the universality of obligation inherent in the corresponding Old Testament prohibitions. There

[4] See Appendix B, pp. 250ff.

---

sexual intercourse (cf. also Leviticus 20: 17). Besides, in Leviticus 20: 20, 21 the consequence of uncovering the nakedness of an uncle's wife or a brother's wife is that 'they shall die childless'. In these cases the penalty was not that of death but that the parties should die childless, a consequence which surely has in view the marital relationship of the persons concerned. Cf. E. Neufeld: Ancient Hebrew Marriage Laws (London, 1944), p. 192: 'The prohibition, then, is one against sexual intercourse with a specified class of individuals which, a fortiori, must make marriage between these persons illegal, as only by sexual intercourse could the marriage finally be consummated. Whether there was any distinction between extra-marital and intra-marital relations in the mind of the lawgiver it is impossible to say. The expressions, however, are used with a laxity which leads one to assume that no clear differentiation between the two was under consideration, and that the law was directed against incestuous intercourse as much as against incestuous marriages.' David R. Mace: op. cit., p. 153, says: 'The word "take" occurs twice (Leviticus 18: 18; 20: 17), and in the first instance certainly seems to imply marriage with the woman. Elsewhere the phrase used is 'to lie with', which normally implies a single act of sexual intercourse. Nevertheless there is nothing which distinguishes these prohibitions from the other incestuous ones where marriage appears to be understood; so we may conclude that it is to be assumed throughout.'

is, however, another incident in New Testament history and teaching that puts beyond question the perpetual sanctity of the principle of prohibited degrees. It is the case of the incident at Corinth and Paul's teaching in relation to it (I Corinthians 5: 1ff.). 'It is actually reported that there is fornication among you, and such fornication as is not even among the Gentiles, that one of you hath his father's wife.'[5] The woman in question here is undoubtedly the step-mother.[6] In Leviticus 18: 7, 8 distinction is made between uncovering the nakedness of 'thy mother' (verse 7) and uncovering the nakedness of 'thy father's wife' (verse 8). Hence Paul is dealing with a case which falls into the category of that forbidden expressly in Leviticus 18: 8; 20: 11; Deuteronomy 22: 30; 27: 20.

This fact, that it is the step-mother who is in view, shows more pointedly the relevance to the New Testament ethic of the prin-

[5] There are questions of the rendering and interpretation of verse 1 which do not particularly concern the main question in which we are now interested.

[6] In Leviticus 18: 7, 8 the LXX as well as the Hebrew makes clear the distinction between a uterine mother and a step-mother. With reference to the latter it says: ἀσχημοσύνην γυναικὸς πατρός σου οὐκ ἀποκαλύψεις and is careful to distinguish between this as uncovering the shame of his father (ἀσχημοσύνη πατρός) and uncovering the shame of his mother (ἀσχημοσύνη μητρός). With reference to the 'father's wife' we do not find the statement 'she is thy mother' (μήτηρ γάρ σού ἐστιν) as in Leviticus 18: 7 with reference to the uterine mother. There is therefore the clear distinction between the uterine mother and the step-mother. This kind of impurity is that which had been committed by Reuben (Genesis 35: 22) when he lay with Bilhah his father's concubine. That this was considered a grievous offence before the time of Moses is apparent from Genesis 49: 4. Jacob calls it 'defiling the couch' of his father (cf. Ezekiel 22: 10; Amos 2: 7). This instance would evince that the prohibition of Leviticus 18: 8 would apply to a father's concubine (cf. II Samuel 16: 21, 22) as well as wife, and that if a father had more wives than one the prohibition would apply to all of them; they would all fall into the category of what we call step-mother, except, of course, the uterine mother dealt with in Leviticus 18: 7. There need be no question, therefore, that, when Paul speaks in I Corinthians 5: 1 of γυναῖκα τοῦ πατρός, the person in view is to be identified in terms of Old Testament usage, particularly that of the LXX. There is no ground for supposing that he means the uterine mother (cf. Neufeld: op. cit., pp. 195f.).

On the Talmudic interpretations see The Babylonian Talmud, tractate Sanhedrin, Chap. VII. In the Soncino Press translation (London, 1935) see particularly Sanhedrin I, pp. 363ff.

ciple or principles which underlie the Old Testament prohibitions.[7] In the case of a step-mother there was no blood relationship; the marriage was not therefore within a degree of consanguinity but merely of affinity. If the incident had been concerned with a degree of consanguinity such as a mother or sister, we might be disposed to argue that the incest was so blatant and so obviously repulsive to human instinct that we should fully expect the New Testament to frown upon it. But since the case is clearly within the category of affinity and not of consanguinity the bearing of the Mosaic prohibitions in their entirety upon the ethic of the New Testament is more apparent. The severity of the condemnation which Paul pronounces upon this marital conjunction, and his reference to it as a sin which is not even current among the Gentiles, rest upon the assumption that marriage within such a degree of affinity was a gross violation of divine law universally applicable to the marital relationship. If this is true in respect of a certain degree of affinity, how much more must marriage within certain degrees of consanguinity be prohibited? We are forced to conclude that the prohibited degrees of Leviticus 18 are assumed to be in force under the New Testament. Admittedly, here in I Corinthians 5, we have only one instance. But it is the type of instance that carries far greater weight in support of the conclusion than would other instances of the Mosaic prohibitions. In the ethic of the New Testament there are degrees not only of consanguinity but also of affinity within which marriage is forbidden. The kind of degree of affinity is illustrated in I Corinthians 5. It would be wholly unreasonable to think that marriage of a man and his step-mother is the only prohibited degree of affinity. In the nature of the case there must be others. To discover what they are we must go to the Mosaic revelation. I Corinthians 5: 1ff. points us concretely to Leviticus 18: 8; 20: 11; Deuteronomy 22: 30; 27: 20. It is unquestionably in these same contexts that we are to find our answers to the other question which the New Testament ethic itself requires us to ask: What are the degrees of consanguinity and affinity within which marriage is prohibited? These pentateuchal passages not only inform us of the prohibited degrees; they also provide the limits within which we are to con-

[7] See Appendix C, pp. 257f.

fine prohibition.[8] The disposition has been widespread to add to the list of prohibited degrees. But this tendency is but an example of the iniquity of human thought when it seeks to be a legislator. After all, when we examine the Mosaic provisions and compare them with the restrictions which ecclesiastical and political

[8] It is understood, of course, that in line with the position taken in Appendix B the present writer makes allowance for extension beyond those specifically mentioned in the pentateuchal passages in terms of the principles implicit in the degrees expressly prohibited; that is to say, extension in terms of the degree of kinship exemplified in the cases specified. What is being opposed is the tendency to extend the prohibitions to degrees of kinship which find no analogy whatsoever in the prohibited degrees of Leviticus 18. One notable example is that of prohibiting the marriage of first cousins. Whatever may be said against marriage within such a degree of relationship on biological or eugenic grounds, there is no warrant from Scripture for such prohibition, not to speak of the prohibition within degrees farther removed, as in some ecclesiastical canons.

For an outline of the history on this question of prohibited degrees cf. *Kindred and Affinity as Impediments to Marriage* (London, 1940), being the report of a commission appointed by the Archbishop of Canterbury in 1937. This survey shows the *reductiones ad absurdum* to which arbitrary extensions have led. On Archbishop Parker's table of kindred and affinity see pp. 41-45; cf. also *The Canon Law of the Church of England* (London, 1947), pp. 126f.

On the present position of the Church of Rome see *Codex Iuris Canonici Pii X Pontificis Maximi* (Rome, 1918), Canons 96, 97, 1042-1044, 1076, 1077. For an exposition of these canons see Francis X. Wahl: *The Matrimonial Impediments of Consanguinity and Affinity* (Canon Law Studies, Number 90), Washington, 1934. Cf. also Joseph J. C. Petrovits: *The New Church Law on Matrimony* (Philadelphia, 1921), pp. 222-272; George Hayward Joyce: *Christian Marriage* (London, 1948), pp. 507-569.

As representative of the Protestant position at the time of the Reformation cf. Calvin: *Opera* (Brunswick, 1882), Vol. XXIV, 659-667, Vol. XXVIII, 61-64; in English see *Commentaries on the Last Four Books of Moses* (C. T. S., Grand Rapids, 1950), Vol. III, pp. 96-108.

On the customs of various peoples and tribes cf. Westermarck: *op. cit.*, pp. 82-239; James G. Frazer: *Totemism and Exogamy* (London, 1910), Vol. IV, pp. 71-169. It is of interest to note the prevalence of exogamic prescriptions. Westermarck says that 'among peoples unaffected by modern civilization the exogamic rules are probably in the large majority of cases more extensive than among ourselves' (p. 101). This fact only underlines the liberality of the biblical principles in contrast with human sentiment and custom.

On the law in the several States in the U.S.A. cf. Geoffrey May: *Marriage Laws and Decisions in the United States* (New York, 1929), especially the chart on page 477.

tradition would impose, it is not the severity of the Mosaic provisions that impresses us but their liberality. We may not take from God's law. When we do we open wide the way of licence. We may not add to God's law. When we do we arrogate to ourselves God's prerogative and we pervert the perfect law of liberty.

In this Pauline passage (I Corinthians 5: 1ff.) there is also an indication of New Testament law as it is to be distinguished from Old Testament law. It must be noted that Paul does not allow, nor does he give any charge in terms of, the sanction by which this sin was penalized in the Old Testament. In the Old Testament the death penalty was provided for this sin (Leviticus 20: 11). Paul fully recognizes the sin but he says nothing of this specific sanction. Instead he prescribes the ecclesiastical censure of excommunication: 'deliver such a one unto Satan for the destruction of the flesh' (I Corinthians 5: 5). In this silence respecting the Old Testament sanction and in the imposition of ecclesiastical censure we discover a principle by which we are to be guided in the interpretation and application of Old Testament norms of behaviour which are of abiding obligation. The New Testament recognizes the permanent validity and obligation of a law which had been expressly enunciated in the Old Testament; there is no alleviation of the gravity with which the violation of this law is esteemed. The gravity of the offence is esablished by the fact that the extreme of ecclesiastical censure is pronounced upon it. But the sanction by which the gravity of the offence was recognized and penalized in the Old Testament economy is revoked. The sanction has been changed from the corporeal to the spiritual, a change which, by its very nature, underlines the gravity of the offence and therefore the abiding sanctity of the law violated by it.

It is this same line of thought and procedure that we find, for example, in the case of adultery. The law of Moses did not provide for divorce in the case of adultery; it required death for the adulterer and the adulteress. Our Lord instituted divorce as the proper recourse for the innocent spouse who had been wronged by adultery on the part of the other. By implication our Lord abrogated the death penalty for adultery. But in the abolition of the death penalty the sin of adultery is not relieved of any of its heinousness as a violation of God's law. It is precisely because the spirituality of the law and the wickedness of its violation are more fully revealed that the abrogation of the penal sanction takes place.[9]

These instances establish a principle for our understanding and guidance when we recognize, on the one hand, the abiding sanctity of law that had been promulgated in the Old Testament and, on the other, the abrogation of the Old Testament sanction. The abolition of the Old Testament penalty in no way interferes with the permanent sanctity of the precept itself. It is the enhanced emphasis upon the sanctity of the precept that makes possible the abrogation of the corporal penalty.

In what we call the sermon on the mount our Lord deals explicitly with the sanctity governing the marital relation and with the sanctity of sex relations. His teaching is introduced in terms of the seventh commandment: 'Ye heard that it was said, Thou shalt not commit adultery' (Matthew 5: 27). The contrast which he institutes when he adds, 'But I say to you that every one who looks upon a woman to lust after her hath committed adultery with her already in his heart' (verse 28) is the contrast between the teaching of the scribes and Pharisees, who had confined adultery to the overt act, and his own teaching to the effect that the commandment has reference to the lascivious desire of the heart as well as to the outward act. The pivot of Jesus' indictment is the clause, 'to lust after her'. The thought is that to fix one's eyes on a woman with lewd and lascivious desire is adultery of the heart. It needs to be noted, however, that what Jesus exposes as adultery of the heart is not merely the intent of committing adultery with the woman concerned. The verb 'to lust after' does not have the strength of expressing the design to seduce the woman and to pursue her to that end. That could be and no doubt would be the sequel in certain cases. But this is not the force of what Jesus says. He does not say, 'in order to commit adultery with her' (πρὸς τὸ μοιχεῦσαι αὐτήν) but simply, 'in order to lust after her' (πρὸς τὸ ἐπιθυμῆσαι αὐτήν). It is the lustful desire upon which our Lord places his finger of reproof, and not merely the later development of seductive design and then, perchance, the further development of seductive solicitation. Our Lord's

[9] For a fuller treatment of our Lord's teaching on divorce cf. John Murray: *Divorce* (Philadelphia, 1953).

indictment is far more penetrating and scrutinizing. What he condemns as the adultery of the heart is the adulterous desire, even though, for many reasons of restraint, this desire may not express itself in seductive designs or outward solicitations to the adulterous act. In Calvin's words, 'This teaches us also that not only those who form a deliberate purpose of fornication, but those who admit any polluted thoughts, are reckoned adulterous before God. The hypocrisy of the papists is too gross and stupid, when they affirm that lust is not a sin, until it gain the full consent of the heart' (*Comm. ad loc.*). What Jesus is doing here in reference to sex purity is precisely what he had done earlier in this discourse in reference to the sanctity of life (Matthew 5: 22). He is showing that violation of these sanctities is registered first of all in the most rudimentary inclinations and emotions. And we may well be reminded, 'him that is without sin, let him cast the first stone'.

In reference to the sanctity of sex as the sanctity which guards the marriage institution and the proper exercise of the procreative function it is necessary to make the necessary distinctions. The line of demarcation between virtue and vice is not a chasm but a razor's edge. Sex desire is not wrong and Jesus does not say so. To cast any aspersion on sex desire is to impugn the integrity of the Creator and of his creation. Furthermore, it is not wrong to desire to satisfy sex desire and impulse in the way God has ordained. Indeed, sex desire is one of the considerations which induce men and women to marry. The Scripture fully recognizes the propriety of that motive and commends marriage as the honourable and necessary outlet for sex impulse. What is wrong is the earliest and most rudimentary desire to satisfy the impulse to the sex act outside the estate of matrimony. It is not wrong to desire the sex act with the person who may be contemplated as spouse if and when the estate of matrimony will have been entered upon with him or her. But the desire for the sex act outside that divinely instituted and strictly guarded sanctuary which God has reserved for the man and his wife alone is wrong; and it is from this fountain of desire that proceed all the evils by which the sanctity of sex is desecrated.

The terms used in this passage from the sermon on the mount are those that refer to adultery in the specific sense, that is, sexual aberration on the part of a married person. The term, 'hath committed adultery' is not the generic term for sex impurity. It would be quite proper, therefore, to think of Jesus as focusing attention upon the desire that is specifically adulterous as more pointedly illustrating the general principle. This does not mean, however, that other forms of sexual aberration do not come within the scope of our Lord's condemnation. By implication every form of lascivious desire is reproved as fornication of the heart. But our Lord exposes the sin of sexual uncleanness by concentrating attention upon lust as it may express itself in lustful desire for another man's wife or, at least, the lustful desire of a married man for a woman who is not his wife. The iniquity of sex lust is advertised by concentrating attention upon that form which more conspicuously and expressly exposes its wickedness.[10]

The importance which our Lord attached to the sanctity guarding the marriage ordinance and the gravity with which he estimated its violation are evidenced by the fact that it is in connection with this question that we have one of the most conspicuous examples of the exercise on his part of the legislative authority vested in him as the Messiah. In the exercise of this authority he abrogated, as we have already noted, the Mosaic provisions regarding divorce; by implication he abrogated the Old Testament sanction by which divorce was penalized; and he instituted divorce for the cause of adultery. Nothing could emphasize his jealousy for the sanctity of the marriage bond more than his abrogation of the concession granted by Moses out of deference to the hardness of men's hearts, and nothing could underline his assessment of the desecration perpetrated by marital infidelity more than the fact that he regarded this sin as the *only* reason why a man might *put away* his wife and a wife her husband.

There is another aspect of our Lord's teaching respecting marriage that must not be overlooked. It is his teaching in answer to the disciples when they said, 'If the case of the man be so with his wife, it is not expedient to marry' (Matthew 19: 10). Jesus' answer was: 'Not all are able to receive this saying, but those

[10] *Cf.* Joseph Addison Alexander: *The Gospel according to Matthew Explained* (New York, 1873), p. 141. 'The extension of the doctrine here laid down to other cases besides breaches of the marriage vow is not to be secured by tampering with the words, but by parity of reasoning, and by observing the extensive application of the principle involved.'

to whom it is given. For there are eunuchs who were born such from their mother's womb, and there are eunuchs who were made eunuchs by men, and there are eunuchs who made themselves eunuchs for the sake of the kingdom of heaven. He that is able to receive it let him receive it' (Matthew 19: 11, 12). What Jesus apparently means when he says that 'not all are able to receive this saying' is that not all are able to act upon the principle stated by the disciples to the effect that it is not expedient to marry. That is to say, not all are able to refrain from marriage; only 'those to whom it is given', namely, those who have the gift of continence and therefore of celibacy. Jesus proceeds to deal with such and enumerates three classifications. There are some who have been born that way. There are others who have been placed under that necessity by the force of circumstance which is not of their own making or choosing, by virtual compulsion. There are others who, though not born as celibates and though not compelled to be such by force of circumstance imposed by others, nevertheless voluntarily choose to be celibates for the sake of the kingdom of heaven. In the case of this last group we are not to reckon them as devoid of sexual urge and emotion, but as endowed with the gift of continence and therefore as able to practise celibacy in the interests of serving more effectively the kingdom of God. Jesus' concluding word, 'he that is able to receive it let him receive it', is undoubtedly directed to this abstinence from sexual intercourse and therefore from marriage.

Considerable difficulty has been encountered with Paul's statement, 'I wish that all men were even as I myself' (I Corinthians 7: 7) and similar statements to like effect in the same context. We should bear in mind that Paul's teaching has its counterpart in our Lord's own teaching. When Jesus says, 'he that is able to receive it let him receive it', he is enunciating the same thought as that of the apostle when he wrote that 'it is good for a man not to touch a woman' and that 'each man has his own proper gift of God, one after this manner and another after that' (I Corinthians 7: 1, 7). Where there is the gift of continence, Paul is saying, a person may remain unmarried and act upon the general principle of the disciples' statement, 'It is not expedient to marry'.

It is worthy of special note that our Lord does not lay down a law of celibacy. The starting point for his teaching on this occasion is the formulation of the disciples, 'It is not expedient to marry'. They did not say, 'It is unlawful to marry', and neither does our Lord. He is not applying the category of 'ought' or of 'ought not'. In this respect, as we shall see later, our Lord's teaching is identical with that of the apostle. Neither our Lord nor the apostle lays down a law to the effect that to marry would be sinful or that to refrain from marriage would be sinful. There is no law of the expedient. Marriage is not an obligation for all; there are good and noble reasons why one may be celibate. It is for each one carefully to consider what he is given and what he is able to receive; he must consider that to which God has called him in respect of this particular relationship. Our Lord's teaching does, however, establish a law that is invariable in its obligation and application. If celibacy is the path imposed by circumstance, or voluntarily chosen in the interests of God's kingdom, then abstinence from sexual intercourse is the indispensable condition. In terms of our Lord's teaching the notion of intercourse in a state of celibacy is unthinkable. The word 'eunuch' which Jesus uses presupposes the exclusion of sexual conjunction. Our Lord's ethic respecting marriage and the sex act means that celibacy and the indulgence of the sex act are contradictory and that a vow of celibacy and the practice of intercourse outside the marital bond would be a monstrous travesty of the most elementary ethic of sex relationship.

Anyone cursorily acquainted with the Epistles of Paul knows that the most difficult questions posed by the Pauline teaching arise in connection with I Corinthians 7. The whole chapter, with the exception of the few verses 17-24, is devoted to matters concerned with marriage and even they are not unrelated to the main concern of the chapter.

The subject was not initiated by the apostle himself. The Corinthians had written to him on the question. It is difficult to determine precisely the problems posed for Paul in the letter or letters concerned. But his answer does disclose their general character. It does not concern us to be able to reconstruct the precise content of the communication or communications; this would be a futile undertaking.

When Paul says at the outset that it is good for a man not to touch a woman, we are not to infer that it is bad to touch a woman. This would be plainly inconsistent with the succeeding context; and to make such an assumption betrays a falsely ascetic bias. But the apostle means more than that it is expedient, or profitable, or advantageous, not to touch a woman. To use Edwards' terms, it is 'morally beautiful', or Meyer's, it is 'morally salutary'.[11] It is not inconsistent with the highest demands of the Christian ethic; to refrain from marriage on the proper considerations is perfectly consonant with the demands of the kingdom of God. Celibacy must not be impugned as unworthy of the high calling of God in Christ Jesus and no stigma is to be attached to the single state when it is followed out of consideration for high and noble ends.

The expression Paul uses, 'not to touch a woman', is a euphemism for joining oneself to a woman in sexual union (cf. LXX Genesis 20: 4, 6; Ruth 2: 9; Proverbs 6: 29). The kind of sexual union in view is determined by the context. Paul is not reflecting on the question of illegitimate sexual intercourse; in such an event he would have said much more than 'it is good for a man not to touch a woman'. He would have condemned it unsparingly as fornication or adultery. Neither is Paul dealing with the sexual relations of those who are already married; he is not saying 'it is good for married persons to practise complete abstinence from the marriage bed'. That would contradict what he demands in the succeeding context. He is dealing simply and solely with the question of initiating and consummating the conjugal relation. It is good, he says, for a man to be in such control of his body and of his sex urges that it is not necessary for him to enter upon the conjugal relation. He unfolds the reason for this judgment later on in this chapter.

Having established that principle that it is perfectly good, perfectly consistent with divine vocation and devotion to Christ, for a man to remain celibate, it becomes equally necessary to take account of the reasons why a man may marry or must marry. 'But on account of the fornications let each man have his own wife, and let each woman have her own husband' (verse 2). The plural 'fornications' points very likely to the prevalence at Corinth of

[11] The references are to T. C. Edwards and Heinrich Meyer in their respective commentaries *ad loc.*

fornication, and it is in view of that situation that the exhortation is given, 'let each have his or her own spouse'. The principle enunciated in verse 1, therefore, is not the only one applicable in human life. While true and applicable in the circumstances in which it may properly operate, it is not an absolute and universally binding principle. Under certain conditions marriage is imperative. Paul does not say, 'each person *may* have his or her spouse', but 'let him have' and 'let her have'. When the alternative is the peril, or tragedy, of fornication, there is no escape from the obligation to marry. In verse 9 Paul is perhaps even more pointed: 'But if they do not have continence let them marry'. The imperative is to be given its full force, and he adds, 'For it is better to marry than to burn'. Incontinence requires marriage, for marriage is the divinely instituted outlet for the sexual urge. And marriage, though it entails many trials, burdens, cares, anxieties, and distractions, is nevertheless better than the distraction caused by burning.

The burning to which Paul refers is the flame of sexual passion. Two remarks are necessary in order to guard the apostle's thought from misunderstanding. First, there is no condemnatory insinuation to the effect that such burning is sinful; Paul is simply taking account of the fact that the sexual urge is in some persons particularly potent and insistent. Second, Paul distinguishes between sex desire and sex burning. In other words, the strength of the term 'to burn' is to be noted. Calvin's remark is pertinent: it is one thing to have heat, it is another thing to burn.[12] Paul does not say, or mean, that it is better to marry than to have sexual desire, for such weakening of the term 'to burn' would set up an inadmissible contrast and would amount to nonsense. If burning meant simply sexual desire, then it would mean that marriage is the cure for sex desire and would terminate it. Obviously that is not the apostle's intent. When we take into account the strength of what is implied in burning, namely, consuming passion, then there is a valid contrast and marriage is viewed as relieving this consuming and distracting passion. It is better to marry than to be laid waste by the consuming flames of sex passion.

[12] *Comm. ad loc.* His exact words are 'aliud est uri, aliud sentire calorem'— 'it is one thing to burn, it is another to feel heat'.

Having thus established the necessity of marriage under certain conditions the apostle now proceeds to deal with the obligations and proprieties which regulate marital relations (verses 3-6). 'Let the husband render to the wife her due, and in like manner also the wife to the husband' (verse 3). He is referring to the conjugal debt, the marital act, and insists that there is to be mutual liberality in this matter. Again we have the imperative. In verse 4 Paul states the ground of this mutual liberality; neither man nor wife has exclusive right to his or her body. They are one flesh; therefore the one spouse does not have the exclusive mastery or authority so as to have the right unilaterally to withhold from the other when the other properly desires or solicits the conjugal act. This does not, of course, exclude the moderation, restraint, delicacy, and modesty which ought to regulate the marital relations of the spouses; but it does explicitly forbid the onesided resistance which has too frequently marred and disrupted marital relations. The iniquity of this resistance and failure to co-operate in the use of the conjugal act becomes all the more reprehensible when it puts on the garb of piety. Then it becomes contemptible piosity.

When the apostle continues, 'Do not defraud one another' (verse 5), that is, 'Do not withhold yourselves from one another', he is simply propounding in a negative way what he has stated positively in verse 3. The reason for this is immediately forthcoming. The prohibition is introduced in order to delineate the conditions under which there is legitimate exception. There are three conditions under which the conjugal act may be suspended: (1) It must be by mutual consent: unilateral denial is forbidden. Onesided withholding would be inconsistent with the provisions set forth in the two preceding verses. (2) It must be for a season, therefore not perpetual. The proprieties of marriage are violated and one of its main purposes defeated by perpetual continence. It is apparent that a vow of continence in the married relation is an impiety of which Scripture knows nothing. (3) It must be for the purpose of prayer on the part of the spouses. The prayer in view here cannot be the regular and ordinary exercise of prayer which ought to be a constant feature of the believer's life; it must refer to a special exercise of prayer and in that respect resembles periods of fasting for special reasons and to special ends. These three reasons are co-ordinate and there is no suggestion or allowance that the abstinence may take place under one of these conditions in isolation from the others.

The temporary character of the abstinence envisaged in the foregoing circumstances implies that when the season is ended there must be the resumption of the use of the conjugal act. But Paul adds this requirement and does not leave it to inference: 'and be together again'. This coming together again has reference to sexual union and the separation presupposed need not be anything more than the abstinence from the sex act.

The particular reason that Paul gives here for this resumption of the use of the conjugal act, namely, 'lest Satan tempt you on account of your incontinence', does raise an exegetical difficulty, though not one which in any way perplexes the perspicuity of the preceding verses. Does this consideration, Satan's temptation, assign the reason why the spouses should resume the conjugal act or does it give the reason why they should refrain for a time in order that, without distraction, they might give themselves to prayer? That is to say: Does this clause referring to Satan's temptation go directly with the preceding clause or does it go with the exceptive clauses? The latter possibility is not to be summarily dismissed. If it were the correct interpretation the thought would run as follows. On account of the fornications each man is to have his own wife and each woman her own husband. Within the marital relation the spouses are to be free and liberal to each other in the discharge of the conjugal debt; they are not to withhold themselves from each other. But bear in mind that the use of the marital act is not the only purpose to be served by marriage. There are the broader obligations of piety which must not be overlooked. If these other obligations are discounted, Satan will take advantage of you. Constant and unrelieved indulgence in the sex act may have a debilitating effect, and your moral and spiritual resources may thus be weakened. Hence it is necessary to give yourselves to special seasons of prayer in order to be reinforced with that spiritual strength requisite for the resistance of Satan's temptations. Do not allow your incontinence to sap your spiritual resources and thus provide Satan with the opportunity to tempt you to sin. This interpretation makes good sense and the warning is true and necessary.

But there are good reasons for adopting the other interpretation, namely, that the clause in question goes directly with the preceding clause and states the reason why the spouses should resume the use of the conjugal act.

(1) Incontinence is stated by the apostle to be the ground of Satan's temptation. The most apparent force of such a statement would be that incontinence is that which Satan lays hold upon to lead into sin; it is the handle he uses for seducement. Now, incontinence would not conveniently denote that indulgence in the marital act which would have to be interrupted for a season. Incontinence is not regarded as sinful. When a person allows his or her incontinence to constrain to illegitimate sexual intercourse, then there is sin. And, of course, excessive indulgence in the sex act within the marital bond would be sin; excess is always sin. But Paul does not call excessive indulgence in the sex act incontinence in this passage or elsewhere.[13] Incontinence is simply the mastering sex urge that leads the person to the divinely instituted outlet for its satisfaction. In a word, there is no warrant for supposing that the incontinence of which Paul speaks is excessive indulgence in the sex act, an indulgence from which the interests of piety would require abstinence for a season.

(2) The thought that the removal of the legitimate outlet for the sex urge will provide Satan with the occasion to tempt to sin fits exactly into the situation which the apostle contemplates. Paul takes full account of the potency of the sex urge; he knows full well that when spouses refrain from one another the sex impulse is liable to become so insistent that the spouses may readily succumb to illegitimate measures of relief. Hence it is better to be together again and use the divinely appointed means of satisfaction. Paul was jealous for the recognition of the honour-

---

[13] Continence is not to be equated with self-control. Under certain conditions self-control will require abstinence from the sex act and, outside the marital bond, self-control demands complete abstinence from the sex act. But the person who exercises full self-control in this matter may not have the gift of continence and hence must marry in order that his incontinence may receive its legitimate outlet. And the married person who is temperate in the exercise of the marital act with his spouse is nevertheless incontinent. His incontinence requires him to use the marriage bed, but he is not intemperate. It seems to the present writer that Cecil De Boer in his book *The Ifs and Oughts of Ethics* (pp. 369ff.) has failed to make this distinction and his discussion is consequently to that extent confusing.

ableness and proper use of the marriage bed. At Corinth false ascetic views were very likely prevalent; it is certain that fornication was rampant. It is this latter sin, so often going hand in hand with false views of the conjugal relation, that the apostle is jealous to prevent. He knows human weakness, he knows the prevalence of the sex vice, and he is jealous that the divine ordinance be honoured and the divinely instituted means of preventing sexual aberration and sensuality fully utilized. We must appreciate the sustained emphasis: on account of the fornications let each one have his or her own spouse; let each render to the other the conjugal debt; do not withhold yourselves from each other (except under specified conditions); be together again. Do not allow Satan to take advantage of your incontinence and steal a march on your weakness. Let the marital act be honoured. It is as if Paul had said, 'Let marriage be had in honour among all and let the bed be undefiled, for whoremongers and adulterers God will judge' (Hebrews 13: 4).

(3) It must be observed that the main emphasis of verse 5 is contained in the two clauses, 'do not withhold yourselves from one another' and 'be together again'. The exceptive clauses are the exception and they are distinctly subordinate. It is unnatural, to say the least, to relate the concluding clause to anything else than the main burden of the verse. It is the withholding that Paul is jealous to prevent and it is surely that withholding that he conceives of as giving Satan the opportunity to seduce to sin.

The sustained interest of the apostle in the proper use of the marriage bed and his demand that spouses should recognize and discharge their obligations to each other in this regard expose, perhaps more pointedly than any other part of Scripture, the false prudery, oftentimes very hypocritical, of the thinking and practice which has gained currency within professing Christian circles. Any notion to the effect that the marital act tends to a lowering of the spiritual temperature and is not compatible with the highest demands of Christian devotion is one that, from its inception, is an assault upon the handiwork and institution of God. It is no wonder that the apostle elsewhere should characterize the prohibition of marriage as a doctrine of demons (I Timothy 4: 1, 2). The false asceticism which has come to expression in the demand for a celibate clergy springs from a bias that has no affinity with the Christian ethic and is antithetical to the whole spirit of the biblical revelation. Perhaps the most blatant attempt to throw the halo of a false sanctity around this anti-biblical direction of thought is the dogma of the perpetual virginity of the virgin Mary. The whole interest of this tenet is the thought that it would be inconsistent with the holiness of the virgin to suppose that she had sexual relations with her husband Joseph after the birth of Jesus. The fact is that biblical holiness would have dictated marital relations with her husband, and to suppose that she did not have such would be a grave reflection upon her character. Our high esteem for the character of the virgin as a woman saved by grace and sanctified by the Spirit demands that we deny her perpetual virginity. Perpetual virginity would put her in the category of a wretch, and our respect for her nobility and piety will have none of it. To be a good woman she must have had these normal marital relations, and the most natural and reasonable supposition is that the brothers and sisters of our Lord were the offspring of Mary and Joseph after the birth of Jesus the Christ. We thus see how baneful is the deflection of thought and attitude which casts any reflection upon the honour and purity of the marital act. It was just that pernicious ethic with bag and baggage of demonic propaganda that the apostle Paul resisted. He did so with vehemence, and it comes to eloquent expression in that concluding clause of I Corinthians 7: 5, 'lest Satan tempt you on account of your incontinence'. Paul is propounding the doctrine that marriage and the marital act are safeguards against the deceit and seduction of Satan. Both the asceticism and the sensuality of Corinth underlined and advertised for the apostle the dignity and nobility of the divine institution.

It might seem that the repeated imperatives of verses 2-5 and 9, which we have just considered and which we have found to be so significant, are deprived of a great deal of their force by the terms of verse 6: 'But this I say by way of concession, not by way of commandment'. What does Paul have in mind as spoken only by way of concession? The question turns on the antecedent of the word 'this'. How much of the foregoing context is included? Some interpreters hold that it refers to verses 2-5 so that all Paul's injunctions respecting marriage in these four verses are said by permission and not by commandment. It should be understood, if this view is adopted, that the imperatives of the preceding verses are not thereby so weakened as to be of no effect as imperatives. It is easy to see that the imperatives, and the corresponding obligations which they enunciate, could still have force once certain conditions are presupposed as existing. So Paul would be saying, in effect: It is not a commandment that every man should have his own wife and every woman her own husband. Let it be distinctly understood that this is not an unconditional obligation, and therefore it is not a commandment. However, there are two qualifications. (1) Rather than succumb to fornication it is necessary to marry; marriage is the only alternative where there is incontinence. (2) Once the marital relation has been entered into certain obligations respecting the marital debt ensue. We thus see that full allowance is made both for the idea of concession and for the imperatives which obtain under certain conditions. Paul did not retract the mandatory elements of verses 2-5 and 9 when he said that to marry was a permission, not a commandment.

There are good reasons for this interpretation of verse 6. (1) If the antecedent of 'this' in verse 6 is restricted to verse 5 as a whole or part of verse 5, then there are decided objections. It is true that the exception of verse 5, namely, withholding for a season for the purpose of prayer, could be regarded quite properly as a concession and not as a commandment. But there is a syntactical difficulty here. This exception is subordinate in verse 5 and not the main subject. Hence it would be difficult to see how it could be the antecedent of verse 6. There would need to be more specification of the subject of verse 6 if this were to hold. If we take the whole of verse 5 to be the antecedent, this is syntactically reasonable. But then we meet with an exegetical objection that is really insuperable. The main burden of verse 5 is that spouses must discharge the conjugal debt—they may refrain for a season but then, with the expiration of that period and the fulfilment of the end in view, they must come together again. The main injunctions of verse 5 therefore (comprehending all of the verse except the exception) cannot be merely by permission or concession. In the situation in which verse 5 is relevant the injunctions are expressly mandatory. (2) Verse 7 stands in very close relation to verse 6. We need but read them together to detect this. Now in verse 7 Paul is dealing with the whole question on which he gives his verdict in verses 1-6. He states first his own preference and then the general principle which applies to every individual. The first part of verse 7 is distinctly reminiscent of the principle stated in verse 1: 'it is good for a man not to touch a woman'. The second part of verse 7 contemplates the whole situation dealt with in verses 1-6, a recognition that there is a diversity of gift from God. Since verses 6 and 7 stand in such close relation, it is necessary for verse 6 to have in view a much broader context than is provided by verse 5 alone. (3) The idea of concession accords very naturally with verse 2 in relation to verse 1. While it is good for a man not to touch a woman, yet, because of the fornications, a concession has to be made. Verse 2 is a concession to the exigencies of the case and consequently all that follows to the end of verse 5, though mandatory in the exigencies contemplated, is nevertheless subsumed under the circumstance of verse 2, and the imperatives of the intervening verses come into operation only if and when the necessity mentioned in verse 2 obtains.

The sum of the whole passage would then be: In order to prevent fornication let marriage be had in honour, its uses fully appreciated, and its obligations discharged. Within the married state let both spouses be mutually faithful and benevolent. But not every one is required or charged to be married; it is good for a man not to be married. Some have the gift of continence and in such cases marriage is not mandatory. Hence what has been said in respect of the necessity of marriage is not a universal command; it is a permission that provides for the legitimacy of marriage and its necessity in certain contingencies but it falls short of a commandment.

We shall be in a better position to understand Paul's statements in verse 7 after we have considered verses 25-40. In verse 7 he sums up the whole situation respecting the question of marriage and sets forth the principle which is virtually a reiteration of our Lord's in Matthew 19: 11, 12.

The aspect of the marriage problem which is introduced in I Corinthians 7: 25 is one that for us is much more difficult because it is not so directly relevant to the practical exigencies of our every-day experience, and we are not familiar with some of the customs and practices which are presupposed in this passage. Paul is discussing the question of virgins and their relation both to suitors and parental guardians. To say the least, our western customs do not conveniently assist us in assessing the precise question with which the apostle deals.

At the outset he makes clear that he has no commandment of the Lord in reference to this matter and therefore the judgment which he proceeds to give is one which he is constrained and warranted to give as one who obtained mercy of the Lord to be faithful. It is well to observe that here the apostle is not expressing precisely the same contrast as he drew earlier in verses 10 and 12. In that instance the contrast was between the revelation given by the Lord in the days of his flesh and that given by the apostle himself in the exercise of his apostolic authority and inspiration. As far as normative character is concerned there is, of course, no difference between the word spoken by the Lord and that spoken by the apostle in the exercise of apostolic inspiration. In verse 25, however, he is not contrasting the legislative pronouncements of the Lord given in the days of his flesh, and the legislative pronouncements given from the Lord through the apostle. The distinction here is between *commandment* and what is *not commandment*. That is to say, on the question with which he is now going to deal there is no divine *legislation* in the form of precept or prohibition —'I have no commandment from the Lord'.

In evaluating this distinction it is necessary to make certain reservations and qualifications. (1) We are not to suppose that there are no precepts of the Lord in the ensuing passage (verses 25-40); there are several. In verse 27, 'Art thou bound to a wife? seek not to be loosed', and in verse 39, 'A wife is bound for so long a time as her husband lives', are examples of binding principles of God's law. All that this distinction means is simply that the burden of what Paul is going to say respecting the question of virgins is not in the category of binding legislation. (2) The judgment of the apostle is in the category of advice or counsel as distinguished from commandment—'I give advice as one having obtained mercy of the Lord to be faithful'. Interpreters frequently suppose that the advice here given is nothing more than the well-considered opinion of the apostle on a subject respecting which there is not only no divine commandment but also no divine counsel; that, as far as the divine mind or will on this question is concerned, there is no light whatsoever and that the apostle was simply giving his own opinion as a wise and faithful servant of Christ, an opinion to be respected on that account but not one invested with inspired or authoritative sanction.[14] It is this view that I am constrained to dispute. The inspiration of this passage is not merely that of providing us with an authentic transcript of what the apostle thought. We shall have to regard it as counsel which bears the imprimatur of the Holy Spirit and therefore divinely validated and inspired as counsel. It is the counsel of the Holy Spirit given through the instrumentality of the apostle. The reason for coming to this conclusion is the terms of verse 25 and of verse 40. When Paul says, 'I think that I also have the Spirit of God', he is not expressing mere opinion. This is a way of appealing to the authority of the Holy Spirit. And when he says that he gives advice as one having obtained mercy of the Lord to be faithful, he is surely thinking of more than reliable and well-considered judgment on his part. He is thinking rather in terms of the office that had been entrusted to him and of which he speaks at greater length in I Timothy 1: 12, 13. He means that he is entrusted with the commission of faithfully declaring the mind of the Lord. Here we have not simply an authentic transcript of the apostle's judgment but an authentic registering of counsel given by the apostle in the exercise of apostolic commission and authority. It was judgment registered in the official discharge of that office which he marvelled had been entrusted to him and in

[14] Cf. F. Godet: *Comm. ad loc.* 'Hence it follows that Paul does not give the counsel immediately to be mentioned in virtue of his apostolic authority, but as a simple Christian. The words are very instructive, as showing with what precision he distinguished apostolical inspiration from Christian inspiration in general, making the former not only the highest degree, but something specifically different from the second. He thus, with a consciousness perfectly assured, traced the limit between what he had directly received by way of revelation, with a view to his *apostolic* teaching, and what he himself deduced from Christian premises by his own reflections, as any believer may do under the guidance of the Spirit' (Eng. Trans. by A. Cusin, Edinburgh, Vol. I, p. 368). Many other commentators do not adopt this distinction between apostolic authority and Christian judgment but recognize that Paul here is giving counsel in terms of his apostolic commission, yet they do not appear to appreciate, at least not sufficiently, the implications of the counsel given in the exercise of apostolic authority and inspiration.

which it was his supreme concern to be faithful. (3) If the judgment of the apostle bears the imprimatur of the Holy Spirit and is the mind of the Lord, we have an important principle here illustrated, namely, that on certain questions which are of deep concern to us the Lord has not given to us law, but only counsel or advice. On certain details of life and behaviour the Lord has not bound us by *law* to one course of action rather than another. If we follow one course rather than the other we have not sinned, because we have not transgressed law.

Admittedly it may be difficult for us to appreciate this distinction. But the difficulty does not excuse us in evading the plain force of what the apostle says, and it is well for us to readjust our way of thinking if the distinction is not familiar or congenial. Furthermore, the distinction is similar to that between the obligatory and the expedient, a distinction basic to the biblical ethic. There is always the tendency to invest with the sanction of law certain courses of action which considerations of expediency may dictate. Consequently, courses of action against which there is no law are liable to be branded as wrong because they contravene the prescriptions of expediency. This is a tendency which must be resisted. Expediency knows no law, and when expediency is erected into law the sphere of liberty is invaded and confusion of conscience results. It is a distinction of similar import that the apostle makes in this chapter.

The counsel which Paul gives is stated expressly: 'I think therefore that this is good on account of the present distress, that it is good for a man thus to be. Art thou bound to a wife? seek not to be loosed: art thou loosed from a wife? seek not a wife.' The reason given for this counsel—the present distress—has given much trouble to expositors. Is this distress to be taken generically as 'the distress which exists for every Christian at all times', as Grosheide says,[15] or is it to be regarded as specific and therefore of some particular distress of that period in the history of the early church? It seems that the latter alternative is more acceptable and that the apostle has in mind some distress of direct relevance at that time or in the immediately impending future. Why should we not identify this distress as the woes and tribulations which

[15] F. W. Grosheide: *Commentary on the First Epistle to the Corinthians* (Grand Rapids, 1953), p. 175.

our Lord himself predicted would occur in that generation? Why should we not associate it with the tribulation of which our Lord said that 'then shall be great tribulation such as was not from the beginning of the world until now' (Matthew 24: 21)? We must believe that the apostle was well aware of our Lord's predictions and warnings and would discover in the distresses of his own time the anticipations, at least, of that tribulation which was to reach its climax in the destruction of Jerusalem.[16]

There is, of course, no objection to our giving to the word of the apostle a broader application and one that will have relevance to our own time as well as to the apostolic age. But this is by way of application in terms of principle rather than by way of interpretation of the denotation of the apostle's term 'the present distress'. We can readily associate the words, 'The time is shortened: and it remains that both those who have wives be as those who have not, and those who weep as those who weep not', with the same distress. The shortness of the time can have reference to the shortness of the interval between the present and the full realization of the tribulation. Or it can refer to the shortness of inter-adventual time. In the New Testament perspective the inter-adventual period is short, however long it may be from our historically oriented viewpoint: it is the consummation of the ages, the last time; the night is far spent and the day is at hand. This datum of New Testament teaching bears closely upon life in this world and upon marriage in particular. We are always to view the present life in all its interests and details in the perspective of Christ's advent. We may never allow our occupation with things ephemeral and temporal to engross us to such an extent that we shall lose sight of the fact that soon those who have wives will be as those who have not. 'For the fashion of this world is passing away' (verse 31). The eschatological perspective should always characterize our attitude to things temporal and temporary. Our outlook is one of this world and not of the age to come if our relation to temporal associations and ties is one of absorption to the exclusion of things eternal.

It is in this perspective that the advice of the apostle is to be interpreted and evaluated. Concretely, his counsel is to the effect

[16] Cf. e.g., Charles Hodge: *An Exposition of the First Epistle to the Corinthians*, ad loc.

that virgins should remain unmarried. The reason is stated by the apostle in a variety of ways but it is summed up in the consideration that the unmarried person is in a position to give more unencumbered devotion to the kingdom of God and to the cause of holiness. In a word, the unmarried cares for the things of the Lord.

We would be ready to think that considerations of undistracted devotion to the Lord would constitute any action which would interrupt or interfere with such unencumbered and concentrated devotion a sinful act and one of disloyalty to Christ. But this is exactly what Paul does not say. He says the opposite and he says it repeatedly. 'But if thou dost actually marry, thou hast not sinned, and if the virgin marry, she has not sinned' (verse 28). 'He does not sin: let them marry' (verse 36). 'But this I say for your own profit; not that I may cast a snare upon you, but for that which is seemly, and that ye may wait upon the Lord without distraction' (verse 35). It is clear from such statements that the counsel of the apostle is not for the purpose of binding believers to celibacy; nor does his counsel carry the implication that, if it is not followed, the persons have thereby sinned. Hence the care for the things of the world, predicated of the married man in verse 33 and of the married woman in verse 34, does not involve any ethical condemnation as if the care in view were sinful. In the married state such mutual concern for each other on the part of the spouses is required. The contrast between care for the things of the world and care for the things of the Lord is a contrast between the undivided, concentrated devotion to the things of the Lord, which the unmarried exemplify, and the distribution of interest and concern which must, in the nature of the case, characterize married persons. The latter must pay more attention to things which are of a temporal and temporary character. Furthermore, the terms are not absolute but comparative; it is not to be thought that the married person has no concern for the things of the Lord. What we have is simply a relative appraisal of interests.

In verses 36-38 the question that has tended to make interpretation difficult is the identity of the person who stands in such a relation to a virgin that she is called 'his virgin' (verse 36) or 'his own virgin' (verses 37, 38), and who gives her in marriage or gives her not in marriage in accordance with the determinations of his own will. Is this the virgin's father or is it the virgin's suitor? The latter alternative would appear to be in better accord with certain details, as, for example, that of having no necessity and having power over his own will; he has the gift of continence and is therefore not placed under the necessity of contracting marriage with the virgin whom he loves and with whom he stands on relations of warm friendship. But however appealing such a view can be in construing certain features of the passage there is at least one cogent reason for thinking that the person in mind is the virgin's father (or foster guardian). It is that the verb used to denote the action of the person in view is not that of 'marrying' but of 'giving in marriage' and therefore one that is uniformly distinguished from 'marrying'.[17] If the person in view were the suitor who may marry the virgin, then he would not be spoken of as giving her in marriage but as marrying her. And so we should have to read verse 38, not as it actually is, but thus: 'Wherefore also he who marries his own virgin does well, and he who does not marry her will do better'. Since that is not the language of Paul, and since the term he does use is exactly that suited to the action of the virgin's father, namely, 'giving in marriage', we must suppose that the person in view is the virgin's father. The virgin's suitor or fiancé is presupposed in the passage— the father gives his daughter in marriage to a man. And when it is said in verse 36, 'let them marry', those in view are undoubtedly the marrying parties, namely, the virgin and her suitor. But the suitor is not the chief personage in this passage; it is the virgin's father. How then are we to construe his relations and his actions in regard to his daughter?

The same kind of counsel is given in reference to 'giving in marriage' on the part of the virgin's father as was given earlier to the virgin herself in reference to marrying. This fact that the same pattern is followed in respect of the counsel given may surprise us. Nevertheless the case is such that the virgin's father is conceived of as exercising certain prerogatives in terms of which he also must decide what is more or less profitable for his own virgin daughter. The father must make the same relative appraisal

---

[17] *Cf.* Matthew 22: 30; 24: 38; Mark 12: 25; Luke 17: 27; 20: 34, 35. Apparently γαμίζω does not occur in the LXX.

which we found earlier. Since marriage entails encumbrances which interfere with unrestrained and uncurtailed devotion to the Lord, it is well to refrain from marriage. Hence the virgin's father may, on the basis of this consideration, refuse to give his daughter in marriage. If he gives her in marriage he does not sin; the virgin may marry her suitor (verse 36); this is the only legitimate verdict in the premises on which the whole passage proceeds. And if the father gives her in marriage he does well (verse 38). But here again 'counsel' comes into operation; 'he who does not give her in marriage will do better' (verse 38; *cf.* verse 37).

The apostle speaks in this connection of a necessity or lack of necessity which constrains the father to a certain course of action. What is this necessity? Apparently it is the necessity which rests upon the virgin herself and which the father duly and properly takes into account. If the virgin daughter has passed the bloom or flower of her age and she feels the constraint or necessity of marriage, then the father may consider himself as acting in an unbecoming, perhaps shameful and perilous, manner with reference to his daughter if he refuses to give her in marriage. In such an event let the father give her in marriage and let the virgin and her suitor marry; the father has done what is proper and no sin is entailed for any of the persons concerned (verse 36). But if this necessity does not arise and the father is resolved in his own mind and will to keep his daughter in her virgin state, then the father is at liberty to do so. He does not sin; rather he does well (verse 37); in fact he does better than if he had given her in marriage (verse 38).

We might think that the father in this case is given the right of rather arbitrary and wilful action. We must bear in mind, however, that the father is not conceived of or represented as judging and acting arbitrarily in this matter. He is represented as giving due consideration to the age and state of mind of his daughter. If she is under the constraint of the marital urge, in that respect placed under a necessity, the father may consider himself as behaving in an unbecoming manner if he places her under prohibition. Though Paul does not expand on the psychological processes in this case, yet it is apparent that full scope is given for the consideration of the virgin's necessities, and the father is assumed to give due and full consideration to these factors.

However, if there is no such necessity as that with which we have been dealing, the father may resolve to refuse to give his daughter in marriage. The harshness that might appear to us to be inherent in this determination on the father's part is relieved by the consideration that the counsel of the apostle in this whole context, for the reasons he has given, is to the effect that a virgin is more blessed and more useful in the promotion of the kingdom of God if she remains unmarried. It is that premiss that the father is assumed to resolve and act upon in this case, and it must also be remembered that there is no warrant in this passage for interference on the part of the father with the demands of incontinence.

It might appear, and it has been alleged to be the case, that Paul's conception of marriage is on a low level, that he represents the avoidance of fornication as the only reason for marriage, and that he had become the victim of a false asceticism when he said, 'I wish that all men were even as I myself' (I Corinthians 7: 7). Certain considerations must be kept in mind if Paul's teaching in I Corinthians 7 is not to be set in a wrong perspective and made the occasion of caricature.

1. Paul does not provide us in I Corinthians 7 with his whole view of marriage. Two salient facts should immediately advise us of this. (a) In Ephesians 5: 22-33 Paul deals at some length with the nature and obligations of marriage, and we shall not find anywhere in Scripture a higher conception of the sanctity and dignity of the marriage ordinance. So high is his conception of the married relation that he staggers us by the analogy he institutes: 'For this cause a man will leave his father and mother and shall be joined unto his wife, and they two shall be one flesh. This mystery is great, but I speak to Christ and to the church' (Ephesians 5: 31, 32). (b) In I Timothy 5: 14 he says: 'I will therefore that the younger women marry, bear children, keep house, give none occasion to the adversary to speak reproachfully'. However we might reconcile this with the various counsels of I Corinthians 7: 25-40, it is quite obvious that our interpretation of Paul is truncated if we do not take this passage into account.

2. The high conception of marriage set forth in Ephesians 5: 22-33 does not mean that every person should be married. This diversity in human endowment and vocation Paul deals with

expressly in I Corinthians 7. And Paul's treatment in this Epistle is in line with what we have found to be the teaching of our Lord (Matthew 19: 11, 12). The Christian life involves in many cases choices between things which are good in themselves and the choice in such instances is dictated by intelligent evaluation of the circumstances, of the gifts God has given us, and of the calling to which he has called us. This applies to marriage also, and we are forced to recognize that there are considerations arising from the claims of the kingdom of God for which a man or woman may resign the privileges and joys of the married estate. To view it from another angle, he or she may consider the cares and concerns incident to marriage as impediments to the discharge of a particular vocation to which he or she is convinced Christ has called. Each person must give prudent and conscientious consideration to the question of the gift God has bestowed upon him. This is what Paul says without any ambiguity: 'But each one has his own gift from God, one after this manner, another after that' (I Corinthians 7: 7).

3. We may not discount or underestimate the fact that marriage is the divine provision for the sex impulses with which God has endowed us. These impulses are not ignoble; they are implanted by God, ingenerated in our nature. Since God had created man with these sex instincts, there would have been an imperfection in God's creation if he had not made provision for the satisfaction of these impulses. It is not in line with biblical thought to underestimate the motivation and urge to marriage arising from the sex impulse in the more restricted sense of desire for the sexual act. There is a wholesome candour about the way in which Paul develops and applies that truth. His treatment is a protest against the false asceticism which has too frequently been entertained, practised, and propagated in connection with the sexual urge. Ironically enough this asceticism lies close to the grossest kinds of sexual indulgence.

4. When Paul says that he wished that all men were even as himself and in that respect placed under no necessity to marry, he is not an unrealistic dreamer. It is easy to retort: if everyone were to follow Paul's example or desired wish, what would become of the human race or of the church of Christ? But such an objection is pedantic in the extreme. This statement on the part

of the apostle is surely a rhetorical way of expressing the intensity of his desire for unencumbered preoccupation with the interests of the kingdom of God. It is not that he conceived of it as possible or feasible that all should remain celibate. He forthwith takes account of the opposite—'each one has his own gift from God'. But this rhetorical expression evinces the ardour of his zeal for the kingdom of the Lord and Saviour and it is a reminder of the great truth that there are eunuchs who have made themselves eunuchs for the sake of the kingdom of heaven. So urgent were the demands of the gospel, so pressing was the need for undistracted labour to promote it in the world, that Paul could wish all believers free from the distracting cares of the married state in order that they might without hindrance devote their energies and talents to the defence and promotion of the gospel.

CONCLUDING OBSERVATIONS

We have been following the course of the history of progressive revelation in reference to the first institution regulative of human thought and conduct with which revelation as deposited in the Scripture confronts us. It is that of procreation and fruitfulness (Genesis 1: 28). We have found that there is no suspension of this institution but rather repeated emphasis upon it. The entrance of sin into the world radically affected the conditions under which it was to be exercised but, however aggravated these conditions of curse and travail are, they do not remove the obligation to be fruitful and multiply: they rather intensify the necessity or the urge to its exercise. Indeed it is the tendency to abuse the instinct and impulse to the procreative act that makes the necessity of marriage all the more urgent.

We find that the supervention of redemptive and saving grace upon the ruin of sin sanctifies and ennobles the procreative act. We have sustained emphasis upon the blessing which God bestows upon the faithful observance of this institution. 'I have gotten a man from the Lord', said the first mother on the occasion of the first birth, at least presumably the first birth. And the psalmist expresses it when he says: 'Lo, children are the heritage of the Lord: and the fruit of the womb is his reward . . . Happy is the man that hath his quiver full of them: they shall not be ashamed, but they shall speak with the enemies in the gate' (Psalm 127: 3, 5).

In the New Testament we have the sanction of the Lord himself when he says of little children, 'Of such is the kingdom of heaven' (Matthew 19: 14). And by Paul in I Corinthians 7: 3-6 we have the intimation that there is to be no aspersion cast upon the sexual act; he enjoins the free exercise of it to the full extent compatible with sobriety and the interests of God-fearing living. Married persons are not to withhold themselves from each other except by mutual consent for a season that they may give themselves to prayer and then they must be together again lest Satan tempt them by reason of their incontinence.

Even when spouses are not one in the Lord, there is to be no restraint in the discharge of conjugal debt. The forces of redemptive grace are not suspended when one spouse is an unbeliever; greater is he who is in the believer than he who is in the unbeliever. The offspring is sanctified in the believer (I Corinthians 7: 14). The divine institution is intact even in this anomalous relationship. The obligations incident to it are not in the least degree relaxed and the promises of God's covenant grace to the believer are not in any degree abbreviated or retracted. It is still true: 'Let the husband render unto the wife her due: and likewise also the wife unto the husband' (I Corinthians 7: 3).

The marital institution is sanctified by the forces of redemptive grace to such an extent that it is made one of the main channels for the accomplishment of God's saving purpose in the world. It is in the bosom of the Christian family that the nurture which the Lord himself provides is administered. Believing parents are simply the instruments of the nurture which the Lord exercises. Of this our Lord in the days of his flesh gave a concrete example when he took the little children into his arms and blessed them and said, 'Of such is the kingdom of God'. He has given us in this a token of what he does continuously through the instrumentality of the Christian family by the efficacious operations of his grace in the hearts and lives of little infants who are the partakers of his covenant grace.

This institution, however, is not one of indiscriminate procreation. In the history of revelation there is a series of proscriptions which defines and delimits the sphere or relation within which the procreative institution exists and the procreative act exercised. This series of proscriptions we shall now review.

1. It is only within the marital relation that the procreative institution and its demand have relevance (Genesis 2: 23, 24). This is enunciated at the very outset. Among all the other animate creatures man did not find a mate which answered to his nature and needs. This has reference to his sexual nature and needs, as well as to other considerations, and in principle points to the abomination, later expressly condemned as such, of sexual relations with any other species of animate being.

2. The marital institution is that of monogamy. This is implicit in Genesis 2: 23, 24 and this passage is authoritatively interpreted for us in that way in the New Testament, our Lord himself being one of the authoritative interpreters to this effect. The seventh commandment is of far-reaching relevance in this regard. The ten commands obviously enunciate the elementary and basic principles regulative of human conduct. The seventh word intimates that the law which restricts the sexual act to the married relationship is one which belongs to the substrate of that conduct which is consonant with the holiness of God and our responsibility to him. The sexual act is a sanctuary sacred to the man and his wife alone. For any person to invade that sanctuary but man and wife is a desecration that violates one of the elementary canons regulative of human life and behaviour. It is for man with wife and wife with man exclusively, and this applies to homosexual as well as heterosexual aberration.

3. The third limitation is that the monogamous relation itself is to be directed by the demands of ethics and piety. It is to be in the interests of promoting piety and of maintaining the line of demarcation between the godly and the ungodly. This is the chief lesson inscribed in the episode recorded in Genesis 6: 1-3. It is the principle summed up by Paul in three words 'only in the Lord'— μόνον ἐν Κυρίῳ (I Corinthians 7: 39). It is one way of expressing the principle which appears in other respects also that marriage and its entail of responsibilities are organically related to higher ends than the mere satisfaction of the sex impulse. As will be noted presently, even when the satisfaction of the sex instinct is given its full place of honour and propriety in connection with marriage there is even then the governing principle of piety as that which occupies the place of paramount concern.

4. The fourth principle of restriction is that marriage within

certain degrees of consanguinity and affinity is forbidden. There is not only the confinement of the field of choice by moral and religious criteria, but also the restriction arising from family ties. The relationships specified in Leviticus 18 and 20 are relationships outside the field of legitimate choice and the New Testament indicates that these prohibited degrees apply to its ethic as well as to the Old.

5. The fifth and final principle could be expressed in a variety of ways. It can perhaps be most adequately expressed as the principle that marriage is a specific calling of God and is not the calling of all without exception or distinction. Celibacy or virginity is a gift of God and therefore the calling of the person thus gifted. In contemplating marriage there are precedent considerations. Each person must deliberately and intelligently determine for himself the course of action to which God has called him and, in recognition of the paramount claims of the kingdom of God, determine the alternative which he is to follow. In the concrete this is the question of the gift which one possesses; it is this gift that is the index to us of our calling from God. In a word, entrance upon the marital status is to be for the believer not an act of blind, impetuous impulse or fancy but an act dictated by rational, deliberate decision in the light of the criterion by which God enables us to judge, the gift given us by God or the gift withheld from us. Marriage, as the institute of procreation, is not in the category of involuntary reaction to physical stimuli, but is ever to be contracted and its purposes and responsibilities fulfilled in full recognition of the governing principle of all thought, intention, and conduct—whatsoever we do we are to do to the glory of God. And this means that the act of marriage, with its entail of obligations and privileges, comes within the sphere of intelligent and responsible action dictated by the sum-total of relevant revelatory considerations.

CHAPTER IV

THE ORDINANCE OF LABOUR

IN the biblical revelation the first allusion to the institution of labour after the fall of man is in the curse pronounced upon Adam (Genesis 3: 17-19). It should be noted that the curse is not the curse of labour; it is the pain and hardship connected with labour and the frustration that man will encounter by reason of the curse upon the ground. We find this echoed in the words of Lamech, the father of Noah, when, on the birth of the latter, he said: 'This same shall comfort us concerning our work and toil of our hands, because of the ground which the Lord hath cursed' (Genesis 5: 29). The significant feature for our present interest is that, notwithstanding the curse, there is still to be the fruit of labour; Adam would still eat bread. Labour and its appropriate reward are not abrogated.

Examples of compliance on the part of Adam's sons with the demands of this institution appear in the case of both Cain and Abel. 'And Abel was a keeper of sheep, but Cain was a tiller of the ground' (Genesis 4: 2). The development of the arts in the history of the family of Cain indicates the commendable extent to which the human family, notwithstanding widespread degeneration, had been constrained to pursue the mandate of labour and to subdue the earth. Every indication is to the effect that toil was a pervasive feature of life in this world, that such toil had a variety of form from the outset, and took on increasing multiformity with the development of the race. We should not be surprised, therefore, to find in the case of Noah sufficient resource and aptitude to be able to build the ark; nor should we be unprepared to read that after the flood Noah began to be an husbandman and planted a vineyard (Genesis 9: 20). The curse pronounced upon Canaan for the ignoble conduct of Ham, the curse of abject servitude, and the blessing upon Shem and Japheth are not unrelated to the institution of labour. The curse consists in the aggravated conditions under which labour is to be conducted.

When we arrive at the period of the three patriarchs, Abraham,

Isaac, and Jacob, we read of the riches of Abraham, the toil of Jacob in Padan-aram, and the wealth of Esau. The Scripture casts no reflection upon the riches accumulated in these instances. Wealth as the fruit of toil, or as an inheritance from the toil of others, carries no dishonour. Isaac's blessing upon Jacob included, 'God give thee of the dew of heaven, and of the fatness of the earth, and plenty of grain and new wine' (Genesis 27: 28); and Esau's own wealth was in fulfilment of the blessing, 'Behold, of the fatness of the earth shall be thy dwelling' (Genesis 27: 39).

It is this background that places in proper perspective more than one of the precepts of the decalogue. If we think, for example, of the fourth commandment, it should not be forgotten that it is the commandment of labour as well as of rest. 'Six days shalt thou labour, and do all thy work' (Exodus 20: 9). If we will, we may call this an incidental feature of the commandment. But it is an integral part of it. The day of rest has no meaning except as rest from labour. It is rest in relation to labour; and only as the day of rest upon the completion of six days of labour can the weekly sabbath be understood.

The stress laid upon the six days of labour needs to be duly appreciated. The divine ordinance is not simply that of labour; it is labour with a certain constancy. There is indeed respite from labour, the respite of one whole day every recurring seventh day. The cycle of respite is provided for, but there is also the cycle of labour. And the cycle of labour is as irreversible as the cycle of rest. The law of God cannot be violated with impunity. We can be quite certain that a great many of our physical and economic ills proceed from failure to observe the weekly day of rest. But we can also be quite sure that a great many of our economic ills arise from our failure to recognize the sanctity of six days of labour. Labour is not only a duty; it is a blessing. And, in like manner, six days of labour are both a duty and a blessing. If this principle were firmly established in our thinking, then the complications and hypocrisies often associated with the demand for a five-day week would not have so readily afflicted our economy, and moral degeneration would not have proceeded at the pace we have witnessed.

The New Testament teaching respecting the institution of

labour is pointed and explicit. It goes to the root of the question when it indicts idleness as impiety. When Paul enjoins the Thessalonian believers to withdraw themselves from every brother who walked disorderly and not after apostolic tradition (II Thessalonians 3 : 6), we might think that what he has in view is false doctrine, such as John had in mind when he wrote: 'If any one comes unto you, and brings not this teaching, receive him not into your house, and give him no greeting: for he that gives him greeting partakes in his evil deeds' (II John 10, 11). Or we might think that Paul had in view some such sin as adultery, or fornication, or idolatry, or extortion, as in I Corinthians when he says, 'I wrote unto you not to keep company, if any man that is named a brother be a fornicator, or covetous, or an idolater, or a reviler, or a drunkard, or an extortioner; with such an one no, not to eat' (I Corinthians 5 : 11). Such sins as these would undoubtedly fall under the ban which Paul prescribes for the Thessalonians. But our too frequent loose thinking and false charity receive a jolt when we discover that the particular kind of disorderliness that the apostle has in mind in this case is that of idleness along with its companion vice of being a busybody. 'For we hear of some that walk among you disorderly, that work not at all, but are busybodies' (II Thessalonians 3: 11). We might be disposed to think that the judgment of the apostle passes the bounds of mercy and charity when, with reference to this vice of idleness, he writes, 'For even when we were with you, this we commanded you, If any will not work, neither let him eat' (verse 10). And the severity of the apostle's judgment reaches its climax when he says that 'if any provides not for his own, and specially for his own household, he has denied the faith, and is worse than an infidel' (I Timothy 5: 8; cf. verses 13-16). But the implications are unmistakeable. It is a mark of the faith of Jesus, an index to the integrity and equity which are the fruits of the Spirit of Christ, that we labour to earn our livelihood and provide for those who by reason of kinship are dependent upon us. The ethic of the New Testament, sanctioned by nothing less than command in the Lord Jesus Christ, is that we work with quietness and eat our own bread (II Thessalonians 3: 12). When our thought is governed by this ethic idleness is seen to be iniquity and reaches the proportions of enormity when it puts on the garb of piety and considers labour incompatible with the demands of communion with God. Only a spurious mysticism can entertain such a conception, and it is then pre-eminently that the indictment is most applicable, 'such an one has denied the faith, and is worse than an infidel' (I Timothy 5: 8).

It is this same kind of rebuke that our Lord administered to the Pharisees and scribes when he charged them with hypocrisy: 'Full well do ye reject the commandment of God, that ye may keep your own tradition' (Mark 7: 9). What our Lord had in mind was the open breach of the fifth commandment in deference to the tradition that a man was relieved of the necessity of giving support to his father and mother if that wherewith he would have assisted them was given to God. They had made void the word of God by their own tradition (cf. verse 13). It is the spurious religiosity that substitutes the supposed dedications of religious devotion for the concrete and practical duties of divine ordinance. In Paul's terms the way of godliness is that children should 'learn first to show piety to their own family and to requite their parents: for this is acceptable in the sight of God' (I Timothy 5: 4).

This criterion of the Christian ethic strikes not only at conspicuous idleness; it strikes also at the sloth, the laziness, which is too frequently the vice of professing Christians. It strikes at the dissipation of time and energy of which we all must plead guilty. The principle that too often dictates our practice is not the maximum of toil but the minimum necessary to escape public censure and preserve our decency. As we think of the extent to which this attitude has pervaded thought and practice, we get some insight of the degeneracy into which our abandonment of biblical canons of thought has led us. It is openly discernible in industry. But so far has our thinking diverged from the biblical patterns of thought on the divine institution of labour, and to such an extent has the concern for ease and entertainment come to prepossess us, that sloth and lassitude have invaded the most sacred vocations. How may we expect the social and economic structure to be permeated with the conception of the obligation, the dignity, and the pleasure of honest and conscientious labour if the church itself shows so little of blood, sweat, and tears in fulfilling its vocation? Paul the apostle took account of the danger that widows might become parasites on the church of God.

'Honour widows that are widows indeed,' he enjoined. 'But she that liveth in pleasure is dead while she liveth'; and he would have no such reproach mar the benefactions of the church (I Timothy 5: 3, 6, 7). But what shall we say when the ministers of the Word become parasites and bear the reproach of being dead while they live indolently and delicately?

The institution of labour underlies the whole question of human vocation. We need to appreciate here anew the principle which was reflected upon earlier in connection with celibacy and marriage. What path of life each individual is to follow in reference to this basic interest of life is to be determined by the proper gift which God has bestowed, and this is the index to the divine will and therefore to the divine call. In connection with the specific kind of labour in which each person is to engage we find this same kind of sanction. Each person's labour is a divine vocation. Our Protestant reformers felt called upon to give particular emphasis to this phase of biblical teaching. 'It is to be remarked', wrote Calvin, 'that the Lord commands every one of us, in all the actions of life, to regard his vocation. For he knows with what great inquietude the human mind is inflamed, with what desultory levity it is hurried hither and thither, and how insatiable is its ambition to grasp different things at once. Therefore, to prevent universal confusion being produced by our folly and temerity, he has appointed to all their particular duties in different spheres of life. And that no one might rashly transgress the limits prescribed, he has styled such spheres of life *vocations*, or *callings*. Every individual's line of life, therefore, is, as it were, a post assigned him by the Lord, that he may not wander about in uncertainty all his days . . . It is sufficient if we know that the principle and foundation of right conduct in every case is the vocation of the Lord, and that he who disregards it will never keep the right way in the duties of his station. He may sometimes, perhaps, achieve something apparently laudable; but however it may appear in the eyes of men, it will be rejected at the throne of God; besides which, there will be no consistency between the various parts of his life. Our life, therefore, will then be best regulated, when it is directed to this mark; since no one will be impelled by his own temerity to attempt more than is compatible with his calling, because he will know that it is unlawful to transgress the bounds assigned him. He that is in obscurity will lead a private life without discontent, so as not to desert the station in which God has placed him.'[1]

It is the consciousness of divine vocation in the particular task assigned to us that will imbue us with the proper sense of responsibility in the discharge of it. The New Testament lays peculiar stress on the God-oriented motivation and direction of all our toil. This is, of course, a specific application of the governing principle of all of life—'whether therefore ye eat, or drink, or whatsoever ye do, do all to the glory of God' (I Corinthians 10: 31). 'For none of us lives to himself, and none dies to himself: for if we live, we live to the Lord, and if we die, we die to the Lord' (Romans 14: 7, 8). But the specific application to the sphere of labour receives particular emphasis. There is good reason for this. When labour involves drudgery, when the hardship is oppressive, when the conditions imposed upon us are not those which mercy and justice would dictate, when we are tempted to individual or organized revolt, when we are ready to recompense evil on the part of our master with the evil of careless work on our part, it is just then that we need to be reminded, 'whatsoever ye do, do it heartily as to the Lord and not to men, knowing that from the Lord ye shall receive the recompense of the inheritance. Ye serve the Lord Christ' (Colossians 3: 23, 24).

It is in the context of this exhortation that the apostle lays his finger upon the cardinal vice of our labour: we do it to please men. 'Servants, obey in all things them that are your masters according to the flesh; not with eye-service as men-pleasers, but in singleness of heart, fearing the Lord' (Colossians 3: 22; cf. Ephesians 6: 5-8). Men-pleasing takes multiple forms, and with these forms is linked as great a variety of vice. Even when the most satisfactory work is performed, and even though great pleasure may be derived from the doing of it out of consideration for man, either as master or simply as appraiser of our handiwork, even then both motivation and performance violate the first principle of labour, 'with good will doing service, as unto the Lord, and not unto men' (Ephesians 6: 7), however much higher in the scale of human values such service may be as compared with work poorly done. It is this principle that puts all eye-service

[1] *Inst.* III, x, 6 as translated by John Allen.

and men-pleasing in the category of sin.[2] The most sacred vocation on earth, the proclamation of the Word of God by the spoken or written word, is prostituted to the worship of men rather than dedicated to the praise of God if it is guided by the criterion of passing muster before men. And it will not receive the recompense of the inheritance; it does not serve the Lord Christ (*cf.* Colossians 3: 24). We are reminded of the word of our Lord respecting those who may at the last protest, 'Lord, Lord, have we not prophesied in thy name, and in thy name have cast out demons, and in thy name have done many mighty works?' and to whom he will profess, 'I never knew you: depart from me ye that work iniquity' (Matthew 7: 22, 23). And as we descend in the scale of human values, is it not a well-recognized fact that the bane of much workmanship is that the workman worked well only when he was under the eye of his master or supervisor? It is the same vice that explains the lack of pleasure in work; labour is boredom and about all that is in view is the pay-cheque. This evil that turns labour into drudgery is but the ultimate logic of eye-service and men-pleasing. Perhaps the most tragic result of all is the way in which eye-service betrays moral judgment. If we seek to please men, then, in the final analysis, it is expediency that guides conduct. And when expediency becomes the rule of life, obedience to God loses both sanction and sanctity and the workman is ready to be the accomplice in furthering ends which desecrate the first principles of right and truth and justice. God-service is the first principle of labour, and it alone is the guardian of virtue in all our economic structure.

It is this same principle of God-service that must guide our thinking as we deal with other aspects of the ordinance of labour. One of the most complex questions of our modern situation is that of the relation of master to servant and servant to master, often referred to as the relations of capital to labour. It is not simply in our modern age that this question is complex. It was an issue of grave concern in other ages and particularly in apostolic times. We have many intimations in the New Testament of its concern with what we may call the labour question. In dealing

[2] Though the doing out of wrong motivation is sin, it does not follow that the doing should therefore be suspended. The ploughing of the wicked is sin. But it is more sinful not to plough.

with the biblical ethic it would be a denial of the relevance of the
New Testament data as well as of the sufficiency of Scripture to
think that Scripture does not provide us with the principles which
should guide both theory and practice on the question of labour.
We may attempt to deal with some of these.

The New Testament does not cast any aspersion or suspicion
upon riches as such any more than does the Old. It would be
foolhardy to say that Scripture is against capitalism. It is true
that the severest kind of condemnation rests upon ill-gotten
gain. Perhaps the most trenchant censure is that of James: 'Go
to now, ye rich, weep and howl for your miseries that are
coming upon you. Your riches are corrupted, and your garments
are moth-eaten, your gold and silver are rusted, and their rust
shall be for a witness against you and shall eat your flesh as
fire. Ye have heaped up treasure in the last days. Behold, the
hire of the labourers who have mowed down your fields, which
is of you kept back by fraud, crieth: and the cries of them who
have reaped are entered into the ears of the Lord of Sabaoth.
Ye have lived in pleasure on the earth, and been wanton; ye have
nourished your hearts in a day of slaughter. Ye have condemned,
ye have killed the just; and he doth not resist you' (James 5: 1-3).
But the rich in view, it is quite apparent, are the fraudulent and
extortionary rich, the cruel, the sumptuous, the voluptuous,
the extravagant, who grind the faces of the poor. That James
did not consider riches as in themselves the mark of such vices
is shown by his appeal to Job in the same context as one whose
character was to be emulated and whose latter days of riches
and wealth were in this instance the proof that the Lord is
pitiful and of tender mercy.

The Bible consistently warns against and condemns the vices
which are the snares of the rich. 'How hardly shall they that have
riches enter into the kingdom of God' (Mark 10: 23). And our
Lord underlined this truth when he added, 'it is easier for a
camel to go through the eye of a needle than for a rich man to
enter into the kingdom of God' (verse 25). It is not without
significance, therefore, that Paul should write, 'Ye see your
calling, brethren, that not many wise after the flesh, not many
mighty, not many noble are called' (I Corinthians 1: 26). And

when he writes to Timothy it is altogether consonant with the witness of Scripture in general that the charge to the rich should be in terms of their characteristic sins and of the virtues which their riches make peculiarly appropriate and necessary as the fruits of the Spirit of grace. 'Charge them that are rich in this world that they be not highminded, nor have their hope set upon the uncertainty of riches, but upon God who giveth us richly all things to enjoy; that they do good, that they be rich in good works, that they be bountiful,[3] ready to communicate, laying up in store for themselves a good foundation against the time to come, that they may lay hold on the true life' (I Timothy 6: 17-19). The New Testament fully apprises us of the dangers incident to wealth and it is unsparing in its condemnation of the vices which so frequently beset the rich. In the same context Paul warns us that 'the love of money is the root of all evils' and that those who have set their hearts on riches 'fall into temptation and a snare and into many foolish and hurtful lusts, such as drown men in destruction and perdition', that some, who coveted after riches, 'have been led astray from the faith and have pierced themselves through with many sorrows' (I Timothy 6: 9, 10). How could it be otherwise? We are at the heart of the biblical ethic. The lust for wealth is covetousness, and covetousness is idolatry. And not only are we at the heart of ethics; we are at the heart of religion. Godliness is not a way of gain (cf. I Timothy 6: 5). Religion is not a living.[4] Religion is trust in God and its fruit, the opposite of covetousness, is contentment. 'Godliness with contentment is great gain . . . and having food and raiment, we shall be therewith content' (I Timothy 6: 6, 8).

The evils of capitalism are not to be spared. Perhaps few weaknesses have marred the integrity of the witness of the church more than the partiality shown to the rich. The church has compromised with their vices because it has feared the loss of their patronage. Its voice has been silenced by respect of persons and discipline sacrificed in deference to worldly prestige. James

[3] This is E. K. Simpson's rendering of εὐμετάδοτος (The Pastoral Epistles, London and Grand Rapids, 1954, p. 90).

[4] In reference to the final clause of I Timothy 6: 5, E. K. Simpson says, 'Counting religion a living is of course the correct version of the final clause' (ibid., p. 84).

in his Epistle does not spare this evil that has afflicted the church and disrupted the unity and communion of the saints. 'My brethren,' he says, 'have not the faith of our Lord Jesus Christ, the Lord of glory, with respect of persons. For if there come into your assembly a man with a gold ring in goodly apparel, and there come in also a poor man in vile clothing, and ye have respect to him that weareth the goodly apparel, and say, Sit thou here in a good place; and ye say to the poor man, Stand thou there or sit under my footstool; have ye not then made distinctions among yourselves and have become judges of evil thoughts?' (James 2: 1-4). Respect of persons! It has warped the judgment of judges and equity could not enter. It has also invaded the sanctuary of God's house, and the vices of the rich—highmindedness, oppression, voluptuosity, worldliness—have enjoyed immunity from censure and the rich themselves a patronage of 'distinction' which has brought into the church itself the reproach of worldliness.

The abuse of riches and the abuses of the rich do not, however, make wealth evil. The economic structure presupposed in the teaching of the New Testament as well as of the Old is one in terms of the distinction between rich and poor. And it is apparent that this distinction is recognized not simply as a providential fact which the application of biblical principles would in due time eliminate, but as a distinction compatible with the divinely instituted order of society. When Paul, for example, enjoins that the rich should not be highminded nor have their hope set on the uncertainty of riches (I Timothy 6: 17), he does not insinuate to the least degree that it was evil to possess these riches. He proceeds to inculcate the virtues which the rich should exhibit, virtues appropriate to the abundance of their earthly possessions, that 'they do good, that they be rich in good works, that they be ready to distribute, willing to communicate' (verse 18). And he reminds the rich that it is God 'who gives us richly all things to enjoy' (verse 17). Riches are not evil; they are God's benefactions. We are, therefore, to put our hope in him as the bountiful giver, not in the riches themselves—they are uncertain because they are at the disposal of God's sovereignty and in the exercise of the sovereignty by which he dispensed them he can also take them away.

It is simply a fact that God has not ordained equality of distribution of gift or possession. And because this is so, it is impossible to put equality into effect. Some are more capable of increasing their possessions; they are more provident, diligent, in-
dustrious, progressive. Are we to suppose that the qualities which
make for the development of natural resources are to be dis-
couraged? Are we to engage in a levelling process that will secure
uniformity and make all conform to a stereotyped average? How
absurd would be the attempt, and how futile! Equality is not a
fact of God's providence, and it is not a rule to be practised in the
order he has instituted; diversity is a fact to be recognized and
the rule to be followed. Liberty itself must take account of
inequality. Unequal distribution of wealth is indigenous to the
order God has established and to the natures with which he has
endowed us.

The Scripture enunciates the basic principles which should
guide the mutual relations of master and servant. Perhaps the
central principle is that 'the labourer is worthy of his hire'
(Luke 10: 7; I Timothy 5: 18; cf. Matthew 10: 10; I Corinthians
9: 14). The Old Testament has its distinct stipulations to this
same effect. 'Thou shalt not oppress thy neighbour, nor rob him:
the wages of a hired servant shall not abide with thee all night
until the morning' (Leviticus 19: 13; cf. Deuteronomy 24: 14, 15).
In terms of principle, wages are to be paid and they are not to be
withheld longer than is reasonable or equitable. In direct address
to masters the same is expressed in the charge, 'Masters, render
unto your servants that which is just and equal' (Colossians 4: 1).
Here the necessity of wages is implied, but the emphasis rests
upon the obligation that wages be proportionate to the service
rendered. The Scripture does not specify in detail what proportionate and equitable compensation is. The New Testament
writers were fully aware of the variety and complexity obtaining
in connection with employment, and it would not be in harmony
with the analogy of Scripture to enter into specifications of this
sort. But the Scripture says enough to establish justice and
equity as the governing principle. And when it says that it has
said much. There are two considerations which bring to light
the far-reaching implications of this provision.

First, it would be easy for us to think that what is to govern compensation is simply and solely contract between employer and employee. And, presumably, the parable of the householder might be appealed to in support of this view (Matthew 20: 1-16). It is to be admitted that compensation in agreement with contract may be perfectly proper and equitable. But it is easy to see that, if this were the governing principle of compensation, the grossest injustices could arise, as they have arisen. Contract can be the instrument of grievous oppression. The labourer can be compelled to agree to a contract that will reward him a meagre pittance of adequate compensation simply because the alternative is to be without any labour or reward. Has not history exemplified the frequency of that abuse? Contract can be a proper method of employment and compensation. But it is only an incident; it does not itself determine what the adequate compensation is. How grand and noble is the governing principle of Scripture! 'Masters, render unto your servants that which is just and equal.' And while justice and equity may sometimes use the way of contract to protect their provisions, yet contract may just as often be the means of violating, with the semblance of fairness indeed, the very requirements of justice. Justice is the royal law of liberty.

The second consideration that brings to light the far-reaching implications of equity as the governing principle of compensation is the fact that, when the New Testament was written, slavery was common and was presupposed in the instructions given to masters and servants. Much debate has surrounded the subject of slavery and a great deal of eloquence has been enlisted on both sides of the question.[5] There can be no debate as to its

[5] *Cf.* for the argument in support of the intrinsic wrong of slavery William E. Channing: *Slavery*, written in 1835 (*Works*, Boston, 1897, pp. 688-743); Francis Wayland: *The Elements of Moral Science* (Boston, 1839), pp. 208ff.; William Whewell: *The Elements of Morality, including Polity* (London, 1845), Vol. I, pp. 344-368; John Wesley: 'Thoughts upon Slavery' in *Works* (London, 1878), Vol. XI, pp. 70ff.; *cf.* Vol. XIII, p. 153. On the other side of the question, to wit, that slavery and slave-holding are not wrong under all conditions, *cf.* Charles Hodge: *Essays and Reviews* (New York, 1857), pp. 473-511; James Henley Thornwell: *Collected Writings* (Richmond, 1881), Vol. IV, pp. 379-436; R. L. Dabney: *The Practical Philosophy* (Kansas City, 1897), pp. 403-416. See also Appendix D, pp. 259ff.

prevalence when the New Testament was written, and it is just as obvious that the apostles did not engage in a crusade against the institution as such. If the institution is the moral evil it is alleged to be by abolitionists,[6] if it is essentially a violation of basic human right and liberty, if slave-holding is the monstrosity claimed, it is, to say the least, very strange that the apostles who were so directly concerned with these evils did not overtly condemn the institution and require slave-holders to practise emancipation. If slavery *per se* is immorality and, because of its prevalence, was a rampant vice in the first century, we would be compelled to conclude that the high ethic of the New Testament would have issued its proscription. But this is not what we find. It seems hardly enough to say that the New Testament quietly establishes the principles which would in due time expose the iniquity of the institution and by their irresistible force stamp it out.[7] If it is the evil it is stated to be, we should expect more.[8] The apostles were not governed by that kind of expediency; they openly assailed the institutions of paganism that were antithetical to the faith and morals of Christianity. What could

[6] In accordance with common usage the designation 'abolitionists' is employed in the more generic sense to include those who maintained the intrinsic wrong of slavery even though they were opposed to the propagandists who pleaded for immediate emancipation and who in the United States came to be known as 'the abolitionists', particularly after 1831, in distinction from all others. The methods of such 'abolitionists' were not only deplored by those who were pro-slavery in their sentiment, not only by those who, though favouring emancipation, did not plead the intrinsic wrong of slavery, but also by many who strenuously maintained that slavery was essentially a violation of human nature and its rights, as for example, W. E. Channing (*cf. op. cit.*, pp. 747ff.). On the different theories respecting slavery in the United States see Lewis G. Vander Velde: *The Presbyterian Churches and the Federal Union 1861-1869* (Cambridge and London, 1932), pp. 134ff.

[7] *Cf.* Channing: *op.* cit., p. 723: 'Slavery, in the age of the Apostles, had so penetrated society, was so intimately interwoven with it, and the materials of servile war were so abundant, that a religion preaching freedom to the slave would have shaken the social fabric to its foundation, and would have armed against itself the whole power of the state. Paul did not then assail the institution. He satisfied himself with spreading principles which, however slowly, could not but work its destruction.' With a different emphasis and from another viewpoint see Jac. J. Müller: *The Epistles of Paul to the Philippians and to Philemon* (Grand Rapids, 1955), p. 190.

[8] On the attitude of Christ and his apostles *cf.* for an expanded treatment, Charles Hodge: *op. cit.*, pp. 480ff.

be more outright and severe than the denunciation quoted above, 'Go to now, ye rich, weep and howl for your miseries that are coming upon you' (James 5: 1). And, without doubt, the economics of that day were to a large extent bound up with the evils that were the occasion for such denunciation. The apostles were not afraid to upset an economic *status quo* when it violated the fundamental demands of equity.

The facts with which we are confronted require us to hesitate before we indulge in wholesale condemnation of the institution of slavery as such. The line of thought required by the silence of Scripture, on the one hand, and its positive teaching, on the other, is to appreciate the distinction between the institution and the abuses to which it has been subjected and which have frequently been concomitant. The New Testament deals explicitly with the latter and is overt in its denunciation of them. If it had said nothing more than 'Masters, render unto your servants that which is just and equal', it would have laid the axe at the root of the tree of these abuses. Paul enjoins both bond and free that they are to do service with good will 'as unto the Lord and not unto men'; but he immediately subjoins, 'And, ye masters, do the same things unto them, forbearing threatening, knowing that he who is both their Master and yours is in heaven, and there is no respect of persons with him' (Ephesians 6: 8, 9). Nothing could have confronted the masters of the bond as well as of the free with the iniquity of oppression, inequity, and mercilessness more than to be reminded of the account that will be given to the Lord of all, with whom there is no respect of persons. Paul is reiterating what Job had preached long before: 'If I have despised the cause of my man-servant or of my maid-servant, when they contended with me; what then shall I do when God riseth up? And when he visiteth, what shall I answer him? Did not he that made me in the womb make him? And did not one fashion us in the womb?' (Job 31: 13-15). These are the considerations that dictate right behaviour; and when they are woven into the texture of human relationships they insure that we 'do justly, and love mercy, and walk humbly with our God' (Micah 6: 8).

It is this jealousy for that which is just and equal, for the recognition that there is no respect of persons with him who is the Lord of all, without the proscription of slave-holding or slave-service, that constrains the conclusion that it is at the point of distinction between slavery and its abuses that the ethic of the New Testament is to be discovered. Much of the apparent cogency of the argument against slavery itself has been derived from the justice of the condemnation of the abuses so frequently associated with it. But exposure of the wrongs of abuse does not touch the question of the legitimacy of bond-service itself.

If we regard the prophetic deliverance of Noah with respect to Canaan, 'A servant of servants shall he be unto his brethren' (Genesis 9: 25), as implying bond-service for Canaan—it would be difficult to think otherwise—then this is the first overt allusion to slavery in the Scripture. It is apparent that it is a curse upon the sin perpetrated by Ham. It could be contended, therefore, that slavery is an evil consequent upon sin and not compatible with ideal conditions. Of course it is a curse arising from sin, an evil that sin carries in its wake. But this obvious fact does not make the practice intrinsically wrong. There are many institutions which are evils emanating from sin; they are instituted to put into effect the curse upon sin. Capital punishment is an evil consequent upon sin, as will be shown in Chapter V, but it is a divine institution, and constituted authority must carry it into effect. Many of the functions of the civil magistrate are necessitated by the fact of sin. Prisons are evils resulting from sin but it is not wrong to have prisons. No penal institution is compatible with ideal conditions.[9] But the inescapable fact is that we do not live in a world of ideal conditions. So, again, the argument drawn from the curse upon Canaan does not touch the question of the intrinsic wrong of slavery.

If bond-service is justifiable under certain conditions, what is to be our definition of that which is legitimate? The exponents of abolitionism have been wont to contend that slavery means the property of man in man, and the distinction between the inalienable personality and freedom of man and the impersonality of things is thus obliterated. Man, it is said, does not have property

[9] In using capital punishment and prisons as illustrations we are not taking the position that slavery is in the same category as a penal institution. The point being illustrated is simply that an institution which stems from the fact of sin is not necessarily sinful.

in man and therefore slavery is a violation of human personality, of its intrinsic rights and privileges. If we were to concede the propriety of this definition of slavery, we must exercise some restraint before we admit the conclusion drawn from it. Is it not true that, in certain respects, there is, in other institutions, the property of man in man? The prime example is that of marriage. It cannot be denied that the man has property in his wife and the wife in her husband. To deny this is to contradict the basis of marriage that the two become one flesh. And is there not also in the family the property of the parents in the children, a property which cannot be violated by others or even by the children themselves? Indeed, the glory of marriage and of the family as institutes of God is the very fact of the property which one has in another. And to a lesser extent it may be said that the state has some property in its citizens. There is here, also, the fact of corporate entity; and the corporate entity does not exist in abstraction from the individuals who compose that entity. In these relationships of marriage, family, and state, individuality and personality are not obliterated by the property which one has in another. When rightly conceived and regulated there is not even tension between the fact of property of man in man, on the one hand, and individual personality on the other. Indeed it is in these relationships that personality develops and achieves its ends. Hence, if the definition of slavery is the property of man in man, we are not to suppose that this *ipso facto* brands slavery as wrong. If it be objected that these other instances do not provide precise parallels, the argument is not that they are exact parallels, but simply that they exemplify the principle of the property of man in man sufficiently to expose the fallacy of cavalier appeal to the wrong of such property.

It is not to be conceded, however, that slavery involves the property of man in man. At least, we may not concede the propriety of such a definition and take our starting point from it. The fact appears to be, rather, that slavery is the property of man in the *labour* of another.[10] And when we adopt this as our definition and starting point, who is to say that property in another person's labour is not proper under certain conditions? This arrangement may be, in fact, a benign and merciful way of

[10] *Cf.* Thornwell: *op. cit.*, p. 414.

securing from another the obligation he owes. We may think of the person who has become deeply involved in debt to another. Are we to say that it is improper for the creditor to have property in the debtor's labour until that debt is defrayed? In many cases this would be much more merciful to the debtor than the ways provided for in our allegedly advanced civilization. And, if we bear in mind the principles that *must* govern the relation of master to servant, it is a method that involves exacting demands for the creditor. It is not difficult to envisage other situations in which property in another man's labour may be quite feasible. It does not affect the main question at issue whether the person who is placed in the position of bond-service is subjected to it voluntarily or involuntarily. A man could voluntarily choose servitude for good reasons, or he might be forced into it if exigencies required it. It is not to be taken for granted that slavery is *per se* involuntary servitude.[11]

When we view slavery from this angle of property of one man in the labour of another, the institution is relieved of the appearance of monstrosity which it is liable to carry for us moderns. The property of some men in the labour of others and the property of institutions in the labour of those who are associated with them we cannot get rid of. The employer has property in the labour of his employees; the presence of contract does not eliminate this fact. Once the contract is entered into, the employee is *bound* to perform the labour contracted. The state has property in the labour of the citizens. In this case it is not by contract; it is a necessity inherent in the institution. Sometimes large numbers of the citizenry are *compelled* for lengthy periods of time to render full-time service to the state under conditions far more stringent, and involving far more danger to life and property, than the conditions under which slaves may be called upon to serve their masters. It is not necessary to multiply examples. Property in our labour on the part of others is a fact of our social structure. And we must not be naïve enough to think that we can abstract our labour from our persons. If another has

---

[11] It would not appear that men like Dabney and Thornwell make sufficient allowance for voluntarily chosen bond-service. We have the most striking example of this in the Old Testament provisions (Exodus 21: 5, 6; Deuteronomy 15: 16, 17).

property in our labour there is an extent to which, or an aspect from which, this must be viewed as property in our persons.[12] And we know quite well that this is no violation of our being, personality, right or privilege. It is a necessity of our nature and of the social organization of the human race. There is no need to think that the property of another in our labour or, to that extent, in the person of the one involved in bond-service as such, is a violation of what is intrinsic to personality, and we are able to see the reserve of the New Testament as dictated by the principles of which the Scripture is the charter.

If the foregoing position is correct then we can see how the institution of slavery and the recognition of its legitimacy as such bring to light the far-reaching implications of equity as the governing principle of compensation. When the New Testament says, 'Masters, render unto your servants that which is just and equal', it has slave-holders in mind as well as the masters of free men (*cf.* Ephesians 6: 8, 9). And this means that bond-servants are to be compensated for their labour in proportion to the service rendered. The principle 'The labourer is worthy of his hire' is not suspended. This places the slavery which the New Testament recognizes in an entirely different perspective from what the word 'slavery' is liable to connote to us. We are ready to construe slavery as the unrestricted right of the master to the service of his slave, that the slave has no rights, these rights being completely submerged in the property that the master has in his labour and, to that extent, in his person. This is a complete misconception; it is not the slavery the New Testament accepts as a licit *status quo*. If that conception of the involvements of slavery was entertained in the apostolic age, and undoubtedly it was to a considerable extent, it is that conception that the New Testament plainly condemns. James was unsparing in his

[12] Those who define slavery strictly in terms of property of one in the labour of another do not take sufficient account of the way in which property in labour involves, to some extent, property in the person. These same writers, however, have thoroughly exposed the fallacy of the argument that slavery involves property in man as if he were a thing. They have safeguarded the distinctions which arise from the unique and distinguishing nature of man. Slavery as such does not mean that the slave is the chattel of his master. The nature of that which is owned determines the character of the ownership and the use made of it by the owner.

denunciation. Paul attacks the root of the evil in the injunctions we have referred to. Slavery encumbered by such misconception and abuse the New Testament unequivocally assails as a violation of the Lordship of Christ and of the equity which he, as the King of righteousness, demands. The Old Testament forbade man-stealing and prescribed the death penalty for such wrong-doing. 'And he that stealeth a man, and selleth him, or if he be found in his hand, he shall surely be put to death' (Exodus 21: 16). Paul classifies men-stealers with murderers, fornicators, liars, and false swearers. The Bible gives no quarter to this kind of traffic in the souls and bodies of men. But it is the severity of Scripture in reference to such desecrations of right that makes all the more significant its reserve in regard to the property of one man in the labour of another. It is ours to make the necessary discrimination so that our judgment will reflect the Scripture itself and guard its perfection and sufficiency.

But though slavery as the property of one man in the labour of another is not intrinsically wrong, it does not follow that we ought to seek to perpetuate slavery. Though the Scripture exercises an eloquent reserve in refraining from the proscription of the institution, and though it does not lay down principles which evince its intrinsic wrong, nevertheless the Scripture does encourage and require the promotion of those conditions which make slavery unnecessary. The Scripture as redemptive revelation, furthermore, is calculated to promote conditions under which slavery would be *wrong*. Though under certain conditions slavery is not wrong, it does not follow that slavery is right under all conditions. And if the conditions under which slavery is legitimate are entirely eliminated, then, of course, it would not be proper to continue it. It is in this connection that the distinction implicit in the foregoing analysis needs to be underlined. Many have taken the position that, although slavery is not openly condemned in the New Testament, yet it lays down principles which imply the intrinsic wrong of slavery and that these principles were allowed to work out in due time their logical consequence. If this were the case then the Scripture, by good and necessary consequence, would establish the intrinsic wrong of slavery; and the only difference would be that, instead of express statement, the Scripture does this by necessary implication. It is this position that has been controverted above for the reason that I know of no Scripture teaching to support this inference. But it may and must be said that Scripture is intended to promote and establish *conditions* which eliminate slavery.[13] This is, no doubt, the reason why the abolition of slavery followed in the wake of Christianity. The Protestant Reformation, for example, witnessed great advance in this respect. There was economic advancement as well as moral and religious. And these conditions in due time brought an end to slavery. For such development we must be profoundly grateful.[14]

An illustration of this distinction, though not in all respects parallel, is that Christianity requires the promotion of conditions in which capital punishment would no longer be necessary. As redemptive revelation Scripture is intended and calculated to promote these conditions. Whenever such conditions prevail it would not only be unnecessary but wrong to inflict capital punishment. If there were no murderers, there would be *de facto* no death penalty for murder. Or, to change the illustration, if there were no crimes, it would be unnecessary and wrong to have prisons. It is this type of situation we must have in view when we deal with slavery. The world has made more progress,

[13] *Cf.* the provisions of Leviticus 25: 39-46 as bearing upon this by way of analogy.

[14] Although Scripture does not support the thesis that slave-holding is intrinsically wrong under all conditions and circumstances, yet anyone imbued with the sensitivity which biblical principles create cannot but regard as notorious and execrable infamy the traffic by which slavery oftentimes came to exist and was continued, particularly the crime associated with the Negro slave trade. There is undoubtedly a close connection between the evangelical revival in England in the eighteenth century and the crusade conducted by William Wilberforce and the 'Clapham Sect', culminating in the abolition of the slave trade in 1807 and the emancipation act of 1833 (*cf.* Ernest Marshall Howse: *Saints in Politics: The Clapham Sect and the Growth of Freedom*, Toronto, 1952, pp. 138-165). The thesis that slavery is not intrinsically wrong does not in the least justify the 'gigantic evils' frequently accompanying the institution. That the conscience of men had been aroused to the disgrace of these evils is the fruit of the gospel. It is just these evils that the Scripture itself unsparingly condemns, as was shown above. But the line of distinction between right and wrong in respect of this question we must not obliterate. We do no honour to Christianity when we fall into this confusion. Here, as elsewhere, the line of distinction between right and wrong is not a chasm; it is a razor's edge.

ostensibly at least, in creating the conditions which eliminate the necessity or propriety of slavery than it has in eliminating the conditions which make capital punishment or prisons mandatory. Lamentably so. If the world had heeded the gospel of redemption, conditions would have been radically different. And we must not be so naïve as to think that the conditions for the discontinuance of slavery are as far advanced as we are ready to believe. Sometimes the methods taken to end slavery have demonstrated how backward the world has been in developing the conditions favourable to the decease of the institution. But be this as it may, a good deal of progress has been made in creating conditions unfavourable to the continuance of slavery. And surely our gratitude to God should be profound.

When we recognize not only the fact of slavery but its legitimacy under certain well-defined conditions, then we are able to understand the uniform witness of the New Testament: 'Servants, obey in all things your masters according to the flesh' (Colossians 3: 22; cf. Ephesians 6: 5; Titus 2: 9; I Peter 2: 18). It is to be admitted that the charge to obey would not be irrelevant or improper even if slavery were intrinsically wrong; it is not difficult to see the reasons why the New Testament writers would have refrained from advocating insurrection as the way of rectifying the evil and why they would have pleaded the opposite of a sit-down strike. But in view of what we have found already, it is not in that light that we are to understand the charge to obey. It is within the sphere of what is admitted to be a legitimate relationship that slaves are enjoined to be obedient to their masters. The master-servant relationship is a divine institution, and the duties of servants to masters as well as of masters to servants are to be performed out of conscience toward God. These obligations arise from the master-servant relationship whether servants are bond or free; in virtue of the authority which the master possesses there is no difference in respect of the divine sanction by which obedience on the part of servants is required. It is *in the Lord* that obedience is rendered. 'Servants, be obedient . . . with fear and trembling, in singleness of your heart, as unto Christ' (Ephesians 6: 5; cf. Colossians 3: 22, 23; I Peter 2: 18, 19). And this applies not only to believing masters, not only to the good and gentle, but also to the unbelieving and froward (*cf.* I Peter 2: 18-20; I Timothy 6: 1, 2). The bond-servant who labours heartily as unto the Lord is the Lord's freeman and the servant who is free is Christ's bond-servant (*cf.* I Corinthians 7: 22).

The notion of obedience implies voluntary, hearty, and cheerful performance of the master's will. We may speak of involuntary service, but not of involuntary obedience. The obedience that is enjoined upon servants is obedience in its true and proper connotation because it is rendered to masters 'as unto Christ' (Ephesians 6: 5). It is obedience, therefore, with all the qualities which distinguish *obedience* from coerced, involuntary, formal compliance with the master's directions; obedience is not merely subjection. The New Testament stresses this in unmistakeable terms—'doing the will of God from the heart; with good will doing service, as unto the Lord, and not unto men' (Ephesians 6: 6, 7); 'whatsoever ye do, do it heartily, as unto the Lord, and not unto men' (Colossians 3: 23). This concept gives to the labour of the bond-servant an entirely different complexion; when the forces of redemptive grace were brought to bear upon slaves and bore fruit in the recognition of the lordship of Christ, the whole attitude of the slave to both labour and master was transformed. We could not conceive of a more revolutionizing force in the direction of reforming economic conditions than this transformation of the bond-servant's psychology. And no consideration is more relevant to our modern labour situation, from whatever angle it may be viewed, than the necessity of having the labourer imbued with this attitude of soul. In this precise connection it is above all else the redemptive principle. Its widespread absence is our basic economic ill.

The implications of obedience for the freeman are no less significant. We must not become so absorbed in the questions that pertain to slavery that we discount, or overlook, the demand for obedience as it applies to the free. That Paul, for example, has the free in view as well as the bond is apparent from Ephesians 6: 8 (*cf.* I Corinthians 7: 21, 22). A freeman is not, of course, bound to the service of one man as the bond-servant may be. But when he undertakes to serve a master the obligation of obedience ensues. The important consideration here is that it is not the fact of bond-service that grounds the necessity of obedience. It is grounded in the master-servant relationship howsoever that relationship may have come to be constituted; it is the authority vested in the master by divine ordinance that makes subjection mandatory. Here again we have a principle of the biblical ethic that has far-reaching consequences. If. the order which is established on Christian principles is to be maintained, some radical thinking will have to be done in terms of this principle. There are few things more distasteful to modern man than subjection to *authority* and the demand for *obedience* to authority. *Obedience* to God or man, the keeping of the commandments of God or man, runs athwart his conception of freedom. Too often it is not because he has a well-defined conception of freedom that is alien to objective authority; it is because he has lost touch with the moorings of honesty, integrity, industry. He is out to do the least he can for the most he can get. He does not love his work; he has come to believe he is very miserable because of the work he has to do. Labour is a burden rather than a pleasure. And so a whole complex of psychological factors makes the principle of obedience utterly alien to his way of thinking, feeling, and acting. Applying the thought psychologically, 'truth has fallen in the street, and equity cannot enter'. We are not saying that this temper is universal. But is there any possibility of denying its prevalence? And if the Christian revelation is relevant to all areas of life, if it is relevant to the relations of man to man, if it is relevant to the relations of employer to employee in particular, are we not compelled to conclude that, if there is to be the preservation of an economy imbued with Christian principles, or the reformation of our economy in terms of the benign influences emanating from the redemptive revelation and grace which Christianity embodies, then labour must embrace and appreciate the first element of *its* obligation, 'Servants, obey in all things your masters according to the flesh'. If obedience with its correlate of hearty, willing, cheerful performance is not relevant as the first principle of the servant's relation to his master in the consciousness that he owes this service *in the Lord*, if it is not relevant for the labouring man of the present hour, then there is no purpose in maintaining that the Bible is regulative of theory or practice in our modern economy; biblical directives would have to be esteemed obsolete.

In the master-servant relationship the demand on the master for that which is just and equal, that he may do justly and love mercy, and the demand for obedience as unto the Lord on the part of the servant point the direction in which development must be sought. The Bible does not work out for us all the details of this development. It leaves open the field in which the guiding principles are to be applied; it takes account of the profuse diversity there will be in conditions and circumstances. But these principles are determinative, and they are the conditions apart from which inequity is sure to be the result. These principles are the law of the Lord. The law of the Lord is perfect and in keeping of it there is great reward. The Bible is the charter of justice and liberty, of truth and equity.

Any person sensitive to justice and mercy will be gratified at the correction of many iniquities that not so long ago were the reproach of labour conditions. Great strides have been made in rectifying the injustices and ameliorating the hardships under which the labourer had to serve. Even if we deplore the methods sometimes used to achieve these ends, and even though we may never grant that in such instances the end justified the means, we cannot but be grateful for the results. And there is much scope for further improvement. Yet there is evidence that we are heading at a disquieting pace for reversal of what we must call the biblical economy. If we have not arrived we are on the verge of arriving at the mastery of labour, and that means the tyranny of labour. There is and has been the tyranny of the employer; that is the abuse of God-given authority. But when we have the tyranny of the servant, then we have the complete reversal of divine order. The need for warning is clamant. The tyrannies of communism are not far removed, and who with his eyes open can fail to dread the tyranny to which the labouring man no less than others will be subjected in the slavery of a communistic régime. Our complacency, our lack of vigilance, our failure to prize the simple yet exacting principles of Scripture regarding the relation of master and servant, of employer and employee, our readiness to dismiss these guiding principles as obsolete, have put us on the way to this other kind of slavery. And if we get to the terminus of that road, the slavery of the first century will be tame in comparison. Greece and Rome had their free men. Totalitarian collectivism has no free men. The ethic of the New Testament is one of obligation; it requires obedience; it recognizes authority which is of divine origin and institution. It is an ethic of law. But it is the law of liberty because it is the law of God and 'God alone is Lord of the conscience, and hath left it free from the doctrines and commandments of men, which are, in any thing, contrary to His Word; or beside it, if matters of faith, or worship'.[15]

[15] *The Westminster Confession of Faith*, XX, ii.

CHAPTER V

THE SANCTITY OF LIFE

IN the prelapsarian revelation there is no overt reference to the sanctity of life, but there is eloquent indirect allusion. The implication of the threat pronounced upon the eating of the forbidden fruit (Genesis 2: 17) is that the dissolution of man's life is the wages of disobedience and therefore unnatural and abnormal. Death is not the debt of nature but the penalty upon sin. Any interference with the tenure of life can obtain only where the abnormal conditions arising from sin exist. There is no intimation in this period of revelation whether it would ever be proper, under the abnormal conditions created by sin, for one man to take the life of another; that is, we are not informed that one man might properly be the active instrument in executing the death penalty upon another. Such knowledge would be irrelevant. The purpose of the threat of death was to inhibit man from committing the trespass which would have created these abnormal conditions.

In the unfolding of human history and of divine revelation we do not have to wait long to find a clear indication of the sanctity attaching to man's life and of the wrong involved in the taking of one man's life by another. It is noteworthy that, next to the sin of our first parents, the first recorded sin is that of Cain, which had its issue in the murder of his brother Abel. It is apparent that the passions from which the ruthless act proceeded were those of anger and envy (Genesis 4: 5-8). God's disapproval and condemnation are plainly expressed in the sequel. 'The voice of thy brother's blood crieth unto me from the ground. And now cursed art thou from the ground, which hath opened its mouth to receive thy brother's blood from thy hand' (Genesis 4: 10, 11). The similarity of the curse upon Cain to the curse pronounced upon Adam for the original sin is apparent, but perhaps more striking is the difference. There is an intensification of the curse. In the case of Adam the ground was cursed for his sake (Genesis 3: 17); in the case of Cain he was cursed from the ground, or more cursed than the ground that opened its mouth to receive his brother's blood. In the words of Keil and Delitzsch, 'Defiance grows with sin, and punishment keeps pace with guilt'.[1] In this episode the sanctity of life and God's judgment on any wanton and malicious assault upon it are clearly established. Perhaps more arresting in this connection is the halo of sanctity which God places around the life of Cain himself. The Lord 'appointed a sign for Cain, lest any finding him should smite him', and said, 'whosoever slayeth Cain, vengeance shall be taken on him sevenfold' (Genesis 4: 15). Life is so sacred that even the life of the murderer is to be respected; it is not to be wantonly or ruthlessly taken away. Crime is not to be punished by crime; the life of the murderer is not to be taken in the way of violence or thirst for blood after the pattern of the murderer's own crime.

Without doubt, it is this providential protection afforded Cain that Lamech later on appealed to when he said, 'If Cain shall be avenged sevenfold, truly Lamech seventy and sevenfold' (Genesis 4: 24). This is the appeal of presumption and arrogance, whether it be interpreted as the vengeance which he himself resolved to execute or as the vengeance which he expected God to execute. In either case, notwithstanding the audacity and arrogance of it, his boast does show how deeply seated in the tradition of the Cainite family had become the recognition of the seal of protection placed around the life of Cain. The abuse to which the sanction was subjected shows the tenacity with which the fact was remembered and to some extent appreciated.

As we proceed in the history of the human family we find that the depravity of the human heart manifested itself to such an extent in the violation of this sanctity that the indictment against the human race becomes epitomized in the charge of 'violence'. Before the flood we are told that the wickedness of man was great in the earth, that all flesh had corrupted their way upon the earth, and that the earth was filled with violence (Genesis 6: 5, 11, 12). And the result was the destruction of the race with the exception of eight persons. It is the irony of man's perversity and the proof of God's veracity that the desecration of life's sanctity should be visited with the judgment of dissolution: 'I will destroy man whom I have created from the face of the

---

[1] C. F. Keil and F. Delitzsch: *Biblical Commentary on the Old Testament* (Eng. Trans.), Vol. I, Grand Rapids, 1949, p. 113.

ground' (Genesis 6: 7). It is against this background that the post-diluvian institutions take on significance.

It is signal evidence of God's grace that the indictment respecting the depravity of man's heart that 'every imagination of the thoughts of his heart was only evil continually' (Genesis 6: 5), depravity which filled the earth with violence and therefore with the desecration of life's sanctity, should be given later on as the *reason* why the Lord would not again curse the ground with a flood and destroy all living as he had done (Genesis 8: 21). The reason is stated to be that 'the imagination of the heart of man is evil from his youth'. The import surely is that God's covenant of perpetual forbearance and mercy (Genesis 9: 8-17) is necessitated precisely because of the deep-seated and native depravity of man's heart; it is God's grace alone that explains the preservation of man, not any change in the native perversity of the thought of his heart. Symptomatic and confirmatory of this grace of God is the fact that the institutions which guarded and promoted the new order instituted after the flood are institutions which have as their purpose the maintenance and furtherance of life. The wages of sin is death; the destruction of the flood demonstrated this concretely and conspicuously. ·After the flood, in accordance with God's covenant and in pursuance of it, the Lord manifested his grace in making provision for the safeguarding and enhancement of life as the antithesis of death.

These provisions are exemplified in three institutions—the propagation of life (Genesis 9: 1, 7), the sustenance of life (Genesis 8: 22; 9: 2b, 3), and the protection of life (Genesis 9: 2a, 5, 6). As particularly relevant to our present topic we shall focus attention upon the third of these, the protection of life. 'And the fear of you and the dread of you shall be upon every beast of the earth, and upon every fowl of the heavens . . . And surely your blood for your souls will I require; at the hand of every beast will I require it: and at the hand of man, at the hand of every man's brother I will require the life of man. Whoso sheddeth man's blood, by man shall his blood be shed: for in the image of God made he man' (Genesis 9: 2a, 5, 6).

It may not be strictly accurate to speak of these provisions simply in terms of the protection of life. Perhaps the chief emphasis is upon the punitive, and there must not be any suppression of the sanction that belongs intrinsically to retribution as a dictate of justice apart from any accessory considerations. This lies on the face of the reason given for the exaction of the death penalty, 'for in the image of God made he man'. Nevertheless there is without doubt in this passage the underlying thought of the safeguards by which the life of man is to be protected; the retributive sanctions have the effect of discouraging and inhibiting invasions upon the sanctity of man's life.

The protection afforded man is twofold: first as respects man in relation to animals (9: 2a, 5a); second as respects man in relation to man (9: 5b, 6). As respects man in his relation to animals there is a striking contrast between what is portrayed in Genesis 2: 19, 20 and that in Genesis 9: 2a, 5a. In the former there is no hint of fear or dread; the picture is one of confidence and submission. In the latter the need for protection against danger is presupposed and is secured by the fear and dread instilled in the animals. It is difficult to determine the precise purpose of the slaughter of the animal which has killed a man through its ferocity (9: 5a). But the requirement does accentuate the sacredness of human life, and it prepares us for what follows respecting the death penalty to be executed upon the murderer.[2]

As respects man in his relation to man the main question in this passage is whether the clause, 'by man shall his blood be shed' is a statement of fact or a command. As far as construction is concerned it could be either.[3] If the clause is simply a statement of fact, the thought is that divine retribution will take its course and will sooner or later catch up with the murderer; he that takes the sword will perish with the sword. God's providence will insure this outcome even though the human agent of execution will not necessarily be prompted by the motive or intent of bringing to effect the divine law of retribution.[4] There are considera-

---

[2] Calvin: *Comm. ad* Genesis :5:9 'In saying that he will exact punishment from animals for the violated life of men, he gives us this as an example. For if, on behalf of man, he is angry with brute creatures who are hurried by a blind impetuosity to feed upon him; what, do we suppose, will become of the man who, unjustly, cruelly, and contrary to the sense of nature, falls upon his brother?' (Eng. Trans. by John King, C.T.S., Grand Rapids, 1948, pp. 294f.).

[3] יִשָּׁפֵךְ could be Jussive as well as Imperfect Niphal of שָׁפַךְ.

[4] *Cf.* Calvin: *Comm. ad* Genesis 9: 6.

tions which favour the other interpretation, namely, that here a charge is given to man to execute the death penalty.

(1) If the text of verse 5b were simply, 'the blood of him who sheds the blood of man I will require', then the thought could well be that God will require it and will order it so in the movements of his providence. But the terms of the text, 'at the hand of man, at the hand of man's brother will I require the life of man', point definitely to a requirement laid upon the man's brother, that is to say, that God will require the retribution to be executed by another who is called the man's brother. (2) The final clause in verse 6, 'for in the image of God made he man', when taken in conjunction with the *requirements* expressed in verse 5, is most naturally interpreted as providing the reason why man is to inflict the death penalty upon the murderer. It would not be impossible to regard it as stating the reason why God orders it to fall out this way in the arrangements of his retributive providence. But since verse 6 follows upon the stipulation of verse 5b, we should expect verse 6b to enunciate the reason for this requirement rather than the reason for what, as a matter of fact, is not overtly mentioned in the passage as a whole. (3) The later provisions of the Pentateuch respecting manslaughter distinctly require that the murderer be *put to death* and that he be put to death at the hand of the avenger of blood (*cf.* Numbers 35: 16-21). We may conclude therefore that it would be quite contrary to the analogy of Scripture, as well as to the natural force of the whole passage, to regard Genesis 9: 6 as anything else than a charge given to man to execute the death penalty, and that verse 6b enunciates the reason why this extreme penalty is to be exacted.

Another question that arises in connection with verse 6 is whether the concluding clause states the reason why man should be given the authority to execute the death penalty or why the death penalty should be exacted. On the first alternative the thought would be that the image in which man is created and the consequent authority with which he is invested warrant the exercise of this prerogative. On the other alternative the stress falls upon the heinousness of the offence; an assault upon man's life is a virtual assault upon the life of God. So aggravated is this offence that the penalty is nothing less than the extremity. It must be said that both of these interpretations are in accord with the context. In favour of the first it may be said that the emphasis placed upon the requirement that each man's brother should exact the penalty may be regarded as carried over to verse 6 for the purpose of reinforcing man in the discharge of this obligation by reminding him of the prerogative that belongs to him in terms of the image of God in which he was created. In favour of the second alternative is the consideration that the clause in question does provide the answer to the insistent question: Why is such an extreme penalty exacted for the shedding of blood? Furthermore, it is more feasible to take the concluding clause of verse 6 as more directly related to what immediately precedes, namely, that the blood of the murderer is to be shed. The first view appears to load the thought that it is by *man* that the blood of the murderer is to be shed with more weight than the sequence and emphasis of the clauses warrant.

In either case, however, the accent falls upon the divine image in man as the rationale of the execution of the death penalty. Whether the fact of God's image in man is the reason why man is charged to take the life of another, or whether it is the reason why life is taken, we must perceive that the institution of capital punishment is grounded in the fact that the divine image constitutes man's uniqueness. And we cannot deny that, in this ordinance, capital punishment is established as the retribution to be meted out to the person who wantonly and wilfully takes the life of his fellow. When we ask about the perpetuity of this institution, no consideration is more pertinent than this: the reason given for the exacting of such a penalty (or, if we will, the reason for the propriety of execution on the part of man) is one that has permanent relevance and validity. There is no suspension of the fact that man was made in the image of God; it is as true today as it was in the days of Noah. To this must be added the observation that, in respect of our relations to men, no crime is as extreme and, as concerns the person who is the victim, none is as irremediable, as the crime of taking life itself. Furthermore, in no other instance of biblical jurisprudence is the reason for the infliction of a penalty stated to be that man is made in the image of God. That consideration is reserved for this particular crime and for the sanction by which it is penalized. The institution of capital punishment for murder is, therefore, in a different category from those other provisions of the Pentateuch in which putting to death was required for many other offences. Not only do the time and circumstances of the institution differ; the reasons which underlie the sanction in this case are radically different. We have good reason, therefore, for maintaining that the institution is of permanent obligation.

Of the ten words of the decalogue it is the sixth, 'Thou shalt not kill', that is based upon and enunciates the principle of the sanctity of life. The commandment is the brief and concrete way of formulating this principle which had been recognized and applied long before Sinai. In our modern context the translation 'Thou shalt not kill' needs to be guarded against misinterpretation. The commandment is not in the general terms of prohibiting the putting to death of another, as our word 'kill' might suggest. The term used in the commandment is the specific one to denote what we call murder. What is in view in the prohibition is violent, wilful, malicious assault upon the life of another. The Mosaic revelation, which had the decalogue at its centre, prescribed the death penalty for a great many offences, and the sixth commandment could never have been understood as prohibiting the infliction of death as retribution for certain sins. Any argument against capital punishment based upon the sixth commandment does not have even the semblance of plausibility; it could be used only by those who abstract the sixth commandment from the total context in which it appears.

That the sixth commandment has in view wilful and premeditated assault upon human life is made clear by the merciful provisions of the Pentateuch itself in providing cities of refuge to which the manslayer might flee. These cities of refuge were not for the purpose of affording asylum for those guilty of murder. They were established so that the manslayer might flee thither until he could stand before the congregation for judgment; and the congregation was given well-defined criteria by which to distinguish between the manslayer who was a murderer and the manslayer who slew his neighbour unwittingly, without hatred or intent of harm. In the latter case the congregation was to deliver the manslayer out of the hand of the avenger of blood and grant him the protection of the city of refuge, whereas in the former case the manslayer who was a murderer was to be put to death at the hand of the avenger of blood (*cf.* Numbers 35: 9-28). These criteria clearly indicate the lines along which the prohibition of the sixth commandment is to be interpreted. And they also show beyond all doubt that the sixth commandment is not to be interpreted as in any way abrogating the institution of capital punishment; they confirm its sanction and propriety. It is the sanctity of human life that underlies the sixth commandment. But it is that same sanctity that grounds capital punishment.

It is in the light of these principles that we are to view the power of the sword vested in the civil magistrate. It is a strange turn of thought which causes some who espouse an evangelical view of Holy Scripture to fail to appreciate the implications of the biblical teaching that the powers that be are ordained of God to bear the sword and execute wrath upon evildoers (*cf.* Romans 13: 1-7; I Peter 2: 13-17). It is true, of course, that all punishment is evil; for all punishment is the wages of sin. But it does not follow that the execution of the evil which consists in punishment is *per se* sinful. If this were so then God himself would commit sin in executing wrath, a blasphemous thought. And it cannot be gainsaid that God appoints agents who are the instruments in the execution of his wrath. Oftentimes, indeed, he ordains instruments for the execution of his wrath who unholily and wickedly fulfil his holy and righteous purpose (*cf.* Isaiah 10: 5-14). But God also appoints ministers with the commission to be the executors of punishment with the result that they are obliged to put the penalty into effect. It is this kind of appointment that the civil magistrate has received; he is responsibly the minister of God. He is not only the means decreed in God's providence for the punishment of evildoers—something that may be said of every instrument, however bad, which executes the divine retribution—but he is God's instituted, authorized, and pre-scribed instrument for the maintenance of order and the punish-ment of evildoers.

This conception of the magistrate's authority, so distinctly enunciated in the biblical passages cited above, reveals the weak-ness of the pacifist contention. Paul says that the civil magistrate is the minister of God, an avenger for wrath upon him who does evil, that he attends upon the service committed to him, and that it is for this reason that, out of conscience toward God, we must be in subjection. It is as the avenger of evildoing and in pursuance of that function that he bears the sword (Romans 13: 4-6). And Peter puts the matter no less clearly when he says that governors are sent by the Lord for vengeance on evildoers (I Peter 2: 14). The sum of this teaching is that, when the civil magistrate executes just judgment upon the crimes committed within the sphere of his jurisdiction, he is executing not simply God's decretive will, he is not merely the providential instrument of God's wrath, but he is actively fulfilling the charge committed to him, and it would be a violation of God's preceptive will not to do so. And what is true in respect of his prerogative within his domain applies also to any attempt from without, by aggression or otherwise, to upset the order of justice and peace which it is his commission to maintain. When one state, for example, unjustly wages war on another, resistance on the part of the state which is the victim of aggression is nothing more than the application of the same principle in terms of which the civil magistrate executes justice upon the violators of equity, order, and peace within his own domain. By what kind of logic can it be maintained that the magistrate, who is invested with the power of the sword (Romans 13: 4), may and must execute vengeance upon evildoers within his domain but must sheath the sword of resistance when evildoers from without invade his domain? When he resists this attempt from without to disrupt the order which it is his duty to maintain, he must do this by his appointed agents, the forces which are armed with the sword. To plead pacifism or non-resistance under such conditions is to annul the New Testament teaching that the civil magistrate is sent by the Lord to punish and suppress evildoing and to maintain the order of justice, well-doing, and peace. The institution of civil government is not totalitarian. But within its own well-defined sphere of jurisdiction it exists for the maintenance and promotion of well-being that we may lead a quiet and peaceable life (cf. I Timothy 2: 2). In a word, it is for the purpose of preserving and promoting 'life'. It is the principle of the sanctity of life that undergirds this institution, and its punitive functions no less than the more positive find their sanction in that sanctity.

The sanctity of human life resides in the fact that man was made in the divine image. This sanctity underlies the prohibition of murder, and it validates and necessitates capital punishment for the crime of murder. A close relation exists between the law of God, as it pertains to the preservation and taking of life, and the redemptive provisions of grace. What does redemption secure? No one word sums it up better than the word 'life'. Our Lord said, 'I came that they may have life, and may have it abundantly' (John 10: 10); 'And I give to them eternal life, and they shall never perish, and no one shall snatch them out of my hand' (John 10: 28). The sum of the gospel is that grace reigns 'through righteousness unto eternal life through Jesus Christ our Lord' (Romans 5: 21). It is quite unnecessary to multiply the evidence; it is all-pervasive in the New Testament. Sin has brought death; redemptive grace brings life. And this life consists in fellowship with God (cf. John 17: 3). It will reach its consummation when the last enemy—death—will be destroyed and the people of God will enjoy the full fruition of participation in Christ's resurrection life, 'when this corruptible will have put on incorruption and this mortal will have put on immortality' (I Corinthians 15: 54). It is the sanctity of life that gives meaning to the redemptive process in all its phases. Life is forfeit by sin, and redemption is the redemption of forfeit life. God is not the God of the dead but of the living, and therefore those to whom he is God and who are his people must attain to the resurrection of the dead, to the fulness of life as heirs of God and joint-heirs with Christ (cf. Mark 12: 27; Philippians 3: 11; Romans 8: 17). It is not merely forfeit life that has been redeemed but forfeit life has been redeemed unto the securing and bestowal of life in the highest reaches of blessing and privilege conceivable for created beings; it is the life of the adoption.

Only in this light can we properly appreciate the relevance and application within the kingdom of Christ and of God of the divine institutions by which the sanctity of life was expressed and guarded. In terms of commandment the sanctity of life is expressed in the words, 'Thou shalt not murder'; in terms of sanction the penalty is expressed in the institution, 'whoso sheddeth man's blood, by man shall his blood be shed'. These commands do not lose their relevance in the kingdom of God in this world.

As we shall see in a later chapter, no word of Scripture bears upon the interpretation and application of the sixth commandment with more force than the teaching of our Lord in Matthew 5: 21-26. But many other passages in the New Testament establish the same truth. Perhaps none of these arrests our attention more than the word of John. 'Every one who hates his brother is a murderer, and ye know that no murderer hath eternal life abiding in him' (I John 3: 15). Murder is the fruit of hatred and hatred is the principle of murder. Hatred is the law of death—'he who does not love abides in death' (verse 14). Love is the law of life. The antithesis makes it impossible for murder and eternal life to cohabit in the same person. Paul's word is to the same effect: 'Owe no man anything, but to love one another: for he that loveth his neighbour hath fulfilled the law. For this, thou shalt not commit adultery, thou shalt not murder, thou shalt not steal, thou shalt not covet, and if there is any other commandment, it is summed up in this word, in this, thou shalt love thy neighbour as thyself' (Romans 13: 8, 9). The sixth commandment, like the others, is one of the concrete ways in which the summary commandment of love is exemplified. 'Love worketh no ill to his neighbour' and must therefore be governed by, and manifest itself in, 'all lawful endeavours' to preserve and promote the life of others as well as our own. And James, when he makes his appeal to the commandment, 'Thou shalt love thy neighbour as thyself', and calls it the 'royal law', adduces the sixth commandment to illustrate that in which the transgression of this 'royal law' as the 'law of liberty' consists. 'Now if thou dost not commit adultery, but dost commit murder, thou art become a transgressor of the law' (James 2: 11). As all are aware, James is jealous for the works of faith as the credentials of our justification. The judgment of God, he is saying in effect, brings our works as well as our faith within its purview. And this judgment of God has its criterion. James tells us what it is: 'So speak ye and so do as those who will be judged by the law of liberty' (verse 12). Of that law of liberty he had just cited two examples, one of which is the sixth commandment. It is the royal law of liberty that transgression of this commandment desecrates, and it is this same law that compliance fulfils. There is no tension for James between the general and the particular, between generalization and detail. If we offend at one point we are guilty of all (*cf.* verse 10). The sixth commandment in its negative particularity is the test of our conformity to the law of God's kingdom and it is, with the other precepts of like particularity, the criterion of God's judgment. It is the law of life, of love, of liberty; it is the law of the King. Again we see emblazoned on this commandment the sanctity of life, and man's life is sacred because it is after the likeness of God's. And how could the sanctity of life, as enunciated in the sixth commandment, cease to have relevance in that kingdom which is one of life because it is one of love, and righteousness, and peace, and joy in the Holy Spirit?

Is there evidence to show that the ordinance of capital punishment is applicable in the order which the New Testament has introduced? In the Old Testament we found that it is correlative with the sixth commandment and is based upon the same principle which the sixth commandment embodies, namely, the sanctity of life. We have also found that the reason given for the execution of capital punishment is a reason that has permanent validity; man is made in the image of God and assault upon man's life is assault upon the life of God. The sin of murder does not become any less heinous under the New Testament; it gathers greater proportions with the increase of revelation respecting the sanctity of life.

It is conceivable that the progress of revelation would remove the necessity for the penal sanction. This is the case with the death penalty for adultery. And the same holds true for many other penal sanctions of the Mosaic economy. Does the same principle apply to the death penalty for murder?

In answer to this question it is necessary to keep in mind two considerations: (1) the specific character of the sin of murder and its peculiar gravity, (2) the time and circumstance in which capital punishment for murder was instituted. In reference to the first we must take into account the fact that, of all the sins which are concerned with our relations to our fellowmen, murder is the capital sin. As a violation of the summary commandment, 'Thou shalt love thy neighbour as thyself', it is in a unique category because, as far as this world is concerned, there is no way of being reconciled to the victim of our wrong-doing, no way of remedying the breach, no way of securing his forgiveness. As far as our relations to the victim are concerned, murder is an irremediable sin. Furthermore, the gravity of this offence is emphasized by the fact that only in this case is the divine image in man pleaded as the reason for the penalty inflicted; assault upon man's life is assault upon the life of God 'for in the image of God made he man'. In reference to the second consideration the ordinance of capital punishment was instituted at the epochal stage in human history when there was, as it were, a new beginning. There is a note of universality analogous to the institution of animal food and the covenant of perpetual preservation (Genesis 9: 3, 8-17). For these reasons it should cause no surprise if this ordinance should stand apart from the other ordinances of the Mosaic economy which involved the death penalty for other kinds of sin. There is an unquestionable uniqueness attaching to the sin and to the reason for the infliction of the penalty, and, to say the least, this uniqueness would demand hesitation before we apply to this ordinance the abrogation which we find in the case of the death penalty for other sins under the Mosaic economy. With these considerations in view we are in a better position to examine the New Testament evidence.

First of all, we do not have in the New Testament anything pertaining to this institution that is parallel to what must be interpreted as our Lord's abrogation of the death penalty for adultery. Our Lord instituted divorce for adultery (Matthew 5: 31, 32; 19: 9); by implication he abrogated the Mosaic death penalty.[5]

Secondly, the teaching of the New Testament regarding the power and use of the sword as the prerogative of the civil magistrate carries with it express warrant for the infliction of death. To suppose that the sword (Romans 13: 4; cf. I Peter 2: 14) can be restricted to lesser forms of punitive infliction and does not imply the extreme penalty is to go in the face of that which 'the sword' properly and obviously symbolizes.[6] This passage

[5] See above, p. 16f.

[6] It is well expressed by F. A. Philippi: 'But this passage certainly contains a *dictum probans* for the position that even the N.T., instead of abolishing,

(continued on p. 120)

(Romans 13: 4) therefore distinctly implies that to the civil magistrate is given not only the power but, as the minister of God, the right, the authority, to use the sword for the infliction of death as the penalty for crimes which merit this retribution. If we were to attempt to draw up a catalogue of such crimes we would encounter difficulty. But one thing is plain; in terms of biblical teaching the one crime that is placed beyond all question as falling into this category is that of murder. The right of the sword implies at least one crime for which death may be inflicted. That one crime, if there should be only one, is the crime of murder. This, above all others for the reasons given, warrants and demands the *jus gladii*.

In the third place, the apostle Paul, who penned Romans 13, in his defence before Festus said, 'If therefore I do wrong and have committed anything worthy of death, I refuse not to die' (Acts 25: 11). Here we have a few eloquent facts. (1) Paul recognized that there were crimes which were worthy of death. How many or how few he considered worthy of such a penalty we do not know. But the biblico-theological background of Paul's thought would have settled for one beyond all question, the crime of murder. (2) Paul protests that he would not offer resistance to the infliction of the death penalty if he had been worthy of it. Paul's conscience was so attuned to the demands of justice that he would plead no deviation from rectitude even though he himself were to be the victim of its demand. And he would not plead deviation in the case of another, because Paul's ethic was governed by the command, 'Thou shalt love thy neighbour as thyself'. (3) Implicit in Paul's protestation is his recognition that some authority had the right to put to death.

---

expressly ratifies the right of governors to inflict the penalty of death; for while the sword stands here as a symbol of government, punitive authority in general, it describes that authority precisely in its uttermost expression as *jus gladii* in the proper sense of the word. It is therefore perfectly absurd, when the apostle applies to the culminating form of the punitive authority of rulers an expression whose historically and juridically fixed signification cannot for a moment be called in question, to wish to assert that he denied to authority the right of exercising that which the sword *properly* symbolizes; comp. Matthew xxvi. 52; Revelation xiii. 10; and respecting the actual exercise of the *jus gladii*, Acts xii. 2' (*Commentary on St. Paul's Epistle to the Romans*, Eng. Trans. by J. S. Banks, Edinburgh, 1879, Vol. II, p. 299).

What authority he considered as invested with that right, whether the Roman government only or the Jewish people through the Sanhedrin,[7] it does not concern us now to try to determine. It is sufficient to know that Paul assumed the right to exist and that he would not appeal from a judgment to execute the death penalty if he had been guilty of a crime warranting it.

We can scarcely overlook this same kind of conscientious regard for, and sensitivity to, the demands of justice in the penitent thief upon the cross when he replied to the other male-factor's railing: 'And we indeed justly; for we receive the due reward of our deeds: but this man hath done nothing amiss' (Luke 23: 41). His recognition of just retribution for crime is consonant with the transformed state of mind which his prayer addressed to the Lord himself evinced. It is an eloquent index to the nobility of thought which sainthood carries with it; not only is it wholly diverse from the ranting and railing of the impenitent thief, but it has no affinity with the sentimentality that knows little of the sanctity of life or of justice.

We have sufficient evidence, therefore, for the conclusion that the institution of capital punishment is not abrogated in the New Testament but that it is one of the prerogatives of that civil magistracy which is an ordinance of God and therefore one of the respects in which we must needs be subject not only for wrath but also for conscience sake. The perpetuity of this sanction accentuates the gravity of the offence involved in

[7] On the moot question whether the Sanhedrin had authority in Paul's time to pronounce and execute the death penalty cf. Emil Schürer: *A History of the Jewish People in the Time of Jesus Christ* (Eng. Trans., Edinburgh, 1890), Div. II, Vol. I, pp. 187f.; Sidney B. Hoenig: *The Great Sanhedrin* (Philadelphia, 1953), pp. 88f.; Alfred Edersheim: *The Life and Times of Jesus the Messiah* (New York, 1910), Vol. II, pp. 556f., 569f. Undoubtedly the chief priests and the whole Sanhedrin sought to put Jesus to death and condemned him to be worthy of death (Matthew 26: 59, 66; Mark 14: 55, 64; Luke 22: 71; John 19: 6, 7) and Pilate said to the chief priests and officers 'Take him yourselves and crucify him: for I do not find any crime in him' (John 19: 6). Yet in answer to a similar reply on Pilate's part the Jews said, 'It is not lawful for us to put any man to death' (John 18: 31). The question is then simply that of the right of putting the death penalty into effect. On the question of responsibility, as distinct from the authority to put into execution, cf. N. B. Stonehouse: 'Who Crucified Jesus?' in *The Westminster Theological Journal*, V, 2, pp. 137-165.

murder. Nothing shows the moral bankruptcy of a people or of a generation more than disregard for the sanctity of human life. And it is this same atrophy of moral fibre that appears in the plea for the abolition of the death penalty. It is the sanctity of life that validates the death penalty for the crime of murder. It is the sense of this sanctity that constrains the demand for the infliction of this penalty. The deeper our regard for life the firmer will be our hold upon the penal sanction which the violation of that sanctity merits.

CHAPTER VI

THE SANCTITY OF TRUTH

'WHAT is truth?' said Pilate. The irony of his question is that truth, 'the truth', stood before him. The tragedy of Pilate's bewilderment was the complete absence of comprehension regarding the stupendous character of the Person whom he had delivered to be crucified. Pilate's vacillation and his readiness to be directed by expediency rather than by justice show that he was not 'of the truth'. 'Everyone who is of the truth heareth my voice', said Jesus (John 18: 37). There was tension in Pilate's mind because he had some sense of justice. But 'the truth' he did not know, and truth did not command his judgment.

Pilate's question is inescapable and none is more basic. If the question is to be oriented properly it must, first of all, take the form, 'What is the truth?' Our Lord's answer to Thomas, 'I am the way, the truth, and the life' (John 14: 6) points the direction in which we are to find the answer. We should bear in mind that 'the true' in the usage of John is not so much the true in contrast with the false, or the real in contrast with the fictitious. It is the absolute as contrasted with the relative, the ultimate as contrasted with the derived, the eternal as contrasted with the temporal, the permanent as contrasted with the temporary, the complete in contrast with the partial, the substantial in contrast with the shadowy. Early in the Gospel John advises us of this. 'The law was given through Moses; grace and truth came through Jesus Christ' (John 1: 17). It is to miss the thought entirely to suppose that truth is here contrasted with the false or the untrue. The law was not false or untrue. What John is contrasting here is the partial, incomplete character of the Mosaic dispensation with the completeness and fulness of the revelation of grace and truth in Jesus Christ. John had said this in the preceding context: 'We beheld his glory, glory as of the only-begotten from the Father, full of grace and truth' (John 1: 14). The Mosaic revelation was not destitute of grace or truth. But grace and truth in full plenitude came by Jesus Christ. The ultimate reality of which Moses was the shadow, the archetype of which Moses was the ectype, now appeared. The *true* light (John 1: 9), the *true* grace were now manifested.

It is in this sense that we are to understand our Lord when he said, 'I am the way, the truth, and the life'. He is enunciating the astounding fact that he belongs to the ultimate, the eternal, the absolute, the underived, the complete. The predications made with reference to him are those than which nothing is more ultimate. Jesus' own witness is not less than the profound and simple propositions with which John opens his Gospel: 'In the beginning was the Word, and the Word was with God, and the Word was God' (John 1: 1). The predications are these indubitably—the eternity of the Word, his eternal co-ordination with God, his eternal identity with God. He is distinguished from God and yet identified with him. He is all that God is and yet he is not the only one who is God.

When our Lord in his high-priestly prayer says, 'This is life eternal, that they might know thee the only true God and Jesus Christ whom thou hast sent' (John 17: 3), he is predicating of the Father the most ultimate and absolute in respect of deity that biblical language provides. No higher predication is possible than this, 'the only true God'. Jesus says and means that the Father is ultimate, self-existent, self-subsistent, eternal being, that he is such as God, and that as God he is such. The Father is 'truth' in the ultimate and highest conceivable sense. But it is an inescapable fact that John makes this same predication with reference to Jesus Christ himself. It is implied in John 1: 1, 'the Word was God'; and it is expressly affirmed by John in his first Epistle: 'And we know that the Son of God is come, and hath given to us an understanding that we may know him that is true: and we are in him that is true, in his Son Jesus Christ. This is the true God and eternal life' (I John 5: 20). That the person designated 'the true God' is Jesus Christ the exegetical considerations converge to establish. Hence all the ultimacy, reality, eternity belonging to 'the true' in terms of Johannine usage is predicable not only of the Father, as Jesus himself expressly said, but also of the Son himself; he also is 'the true God'. It is this alone that could warrant the word of Jesus to his disciples, 'Believest thou not that I am in the Father and the Father is in me: the words which I say to you I speak not of myself; but the Father dwelling in me doeth his works. Believe me that I am in the Father and the Father in me' (John 14: 10, 11).

We are thus getting to the basis and heart of the question of 'truth'. God is 'the truth', truth absolute, ultimate, eternal, in contradistinction from all that is relative, derived, partial, and temporal. And when we say this, the foregoing data show that it is of the triune God in the mystery of unity in trinity and trinity in unity that we make this predication. Only trinity in unity can explain such terms as 'the Word was with God, and the Word was God', together with the correlative teaching of Scripture respecting the Holy Spirit. The Spirit also is the truth (I John 5: 6; cf. John 14: 17; 15: 26; 16: 13). When we speak, therefore, of the sanctity of truth, we must recognize that what underlies this concept is the sanctity of the being of God as the living and true God. He is the God of truth and all truth derives its sanctity from him. This is why all untruth or falsehood is wrong; it is a contradiction of that which God is. And this is why God cannot lie (Titus 1: 2; Hebrews 6: 18; cf. Romans 3: 4).[1] To lie would contradict himself and he cannot deny himself (II Timothy 2: 13). It is his perfection to be consistent with himself, and all his ways are truth. 'The works of his hands are truth and judgment; all his precepts are sure. They stand fast for ever and ever, and are done in truth and uprightness' (Psalm 111: 7, 8; cf. Deuteronomy 32: 4; Isaiah 25: 1). This attribute of God is often expressed as his 'faithfulness' and is exemplified in the certainty and immutability of his promises and threatenings. God's covenant is one of faithfulness to such an extent that promise and fulfilment are essential features of the covenant concept (cf. Genesis 9: 16; 15: 18). And there can be little doubt that the specifically redemptive name of God, 'I am that I am', in terms of which we are to interpret the tetragram, points distinctly to the immutability of his covenant grace and promise (cf. Malachi 3: 6).[2]

In God's address to man the first express allusion to God's

[1] Cf. also Numbers 23: 19; I Samuel 15: 29.
[2] Cf. also Exodus 3: 15; 6: 5-8; 33: 17, 19; Deuteronomy 7: 9; Psalm 135: 13; Isaiah 26: 4, 8; Hosea 12: 5, 6 (Hebrew vv. 6, 7).

truthfulness and to the necessity on man's part of crediting God's word is in connection with the forbidden tree. 'In the day thou eatest thereof thou shalt surely die' (Genesis 2: 17). It was by this prohibition that man's faithfulness was to be tested; and his faithfulness would have required as an essential ingredient unrelenting trust in the faithfulness of God. It is here that the craft of the tempter appears, as also his malignity. The temptation to which Eve was subjected was directed in two stages, first by a question of fact and then by flat denial. It is this latter stage that interests us now. 'Ye shall not surely die' said the tempter. The form of the denial is to be noted. It is not that God would be unsuccessful in fulfilling his threat, that he would not be able to carry it into effect. The allegation carried with it that implication. But that is not the pivot of the denial; it is not simply a denial of God's power. It is much more diabolical. Nor is it an impeachment of God's knowledge. The serpent is not saying that God is ignorant and that he knows more than God does. Such an allegation would have been blasphemous enough, but not for the serpent. He credits God with knowledge, indeed with full knowledge of what the outcome would be, and on that assumption makes the thrust which is the genius of his attack. He directly assails God's *veracity*. 'God doth know that in the day ye eat thereof, your eyes will be opened, and ye shall be as God, knowing good and evil' (Genesis 3: 5). He accuses God of deliberate falsehood and deception. God has perpetrated a lie, he avers, because he is jealous of his own selfish and exclusive possession of the knowledge of good and evil! 'Ye shall not surely die.'

The denial is not then an attack upon God's knowledge, nor merely upon his power. The tempter openly assails the integrity and veracity of God. In a word, it is the truthfulness of God that is impugned. And this was directed to the end of securing assent on the woman's part to the monstrous allegation. In this the tempter was successful, and disobedience to the divine command was the sequel. It was the strategy of skilfully framed and designed attack upon man's integrity by eliciting distrust in the integrity of God. Man's integrity is dissolved when God's veracity is questioned. The way of integrity for man is unreserved commitment to God, totality trust in his truthfulness.

God's truth is his glory. The epitome of malignity is to assail this glory. That was the tempter's strategy, and by acquiescence our first parents fell. Sin entered into the world, and death by sin.

When we speak of the sanctity of truth in relation to ethics, we have particularly in view 'truthfulness' on our part in our dealings with God, ourselves, and our fellowmen. The necessity of truthfulness in us rests upon God's truthfulness. As we are to be holy because God is holy, so we are to be truthful because God is truthful. The glory of God is that he is the God of truth; the glory of man is that he is the image of God and therefore 'of the truth' (cf. John 18: 37). It is not without significance that the arch-enemy of God and his kingdom is the father of lies; 'he does not stand in the truth, because there is no truth in him. When he speaketh a lie, he speaketh of his own, because he is a liar and the father of it' (John 8: 44). All untruth has its affinity with that lie by which Eve was seduced, and nothing exemplifies the contradiction of God and of man's integrity more than the lie. It is the acme of reprobation when God sends upon men 'a working of error to the end that they may believe the lie' (II Thessalonians 2: 11) and gives them over to a reprobate mind (cf. Rom. 1: 28-32). The foundations of all equity are destroyed when truth has fallen. It was the lament of the prophet that 'none pleadeth in truth', that 'truth is fallen in the street, and equity cannot enter. Yea, truth faileth; and he that departeth from evil maketh himself a prey' (Isaiah 59: 4, 14, 15). And Jeremiah's lamentation is to the same effect: 'This is a nation that obeyeth not the voice of the Lord their God, nor receiveth correction: truth is perished, and is cut off from their mouth' (Jeremiah 7: 28). 'And they bend their tongue like their bow for lies: but they are not valiant for the truth upon the earth' (Jeremiah 9: 3). Hosea has the same complaint: 'Hear the word of the Lord, ye children of Israel: for the Lord hath a controversy with the inhabitants of the land, because there is no truth, nor mercy, nor knowledge of God in the land' (Hosea 4: 1). When our Lord himself was made manifest to Israel, one of his severest indictments was this: 'Ye are of your father the devil, and the lusts of your father ye will to do' (John 8: 44). And why such a charge? 'But because I say the truth, ye do not believe me' (John 8: 45). An apostle can describe the deeds of the old man and of the

manner of life by which the old man is characterized as those
of lying and falsehood (cf. Ephesians 4: 22-25; Colossians 3:
9, 10).

That untruth is the hallmark of impiety is borne out by numerous examples of Scripture. The envy of Joseph's brethren by
which they sold him into Egypt is matched by the deception
perpetrated to conceal the vile deed from their father (Genesis
37: 31-35). Joseph's piety is proven by his chastity: 'how can I
do this great wickedness and sin against God?' (Genesis 39: 9).
The lust of Potiphar's wife is paralleled by the malicious lie by
which she sought either to conceal her own wickedness or, more
probably, to wreak vengeance on Joseph for his refusal to gratify
her lewd designs (Genesis 39: 13-18). The perfidy of Pharaoh
is but an index to the hardness of his heart (cf. Exodus 9: 28).
Judas played the part of the father of lies, who had entered into
him (Luke 22: 3; John 13: 27), when he acted a lie and betrayed
the Son of man with a kiss (Matthew 26: 49; Mark 14: 45;
Luke 22: 48). Ananias and Sapphira lied by an act of pretension.
Again it is eloquent of affinity with the father of lies and with
the deception by which sin entered the world that Peter said,
'Ananias, why hath Satan filled thy heart, to lie to the Holy
Spirit, and to keep back part of the price of the land?' (Acts
5: 3). Lying is of the devil; it is the work of darkness. And when
the consummated order of righteousness is portrayed for us it
is, as we should expect, an order also of truth: 'And there shall
in no wise enter into it anything that is unclean, or he that
worketh abomination and a lie' (Revelation 21: 27). 'Without
are the dogs, and the sorcerers, and the fornicators, and the
murderers, and the idolaters, and whosoever loveth and maketh
a lie' (Revelation 22: 15). Liars, like murderers, fornicators
sorcerers, and idolaters, have their part 'in the lake that burns
with fire and brimstone, which is the second death' (Revelation
21: 8). Such a result is inevitable. The new Jerusalem is the holy
city and 'the throne of God and of the Lamb shall be in it'. His
servants 'shall see his face, and his name shall be on their fore-
heads. And there shall be no night there' (Revelation 22: 3-5).
The Lord God who 'is light and in whom is no darkness at all'

(I John 1: 5) will be their everlasting light, and the holy will be holy still.

As untruth is the hallmark of impiety, so truth is the insigne of godliness. This is true, first of all, in respect of knowledge. No words of Scripture are more relevant than those of our Lord himself. 'This is life eternal, that they might know thee the only true God and Jesus Christ whom thou hast sent' (John 17: 3). 'I am the way, the truth, and the life: no one cometh unto the Father but by me' (John 14: 6). 'If ye continue in my word, then are ye truly my disciples; and ye shall know the truth, and the truth shall make you free' (John 8: 31, 32). To know God is to know the truth; to be established in the faith and obedience of Christ is to know the truth. To know the Holy Spirit and to be indwelt by him is to be guided into all truth; the Spirit is 'the Spirit of truth' (John 16: 13). In all of this we have a rich and complex co-ordination of aspects or elements. We must not set up those false antitheses which are too frequently the coinage of dialectic scepticism. If we know God, we know the truth; but we know God only through his revelation and specifically through his Word. The Word of God is the truth; and, if we know God, we know his Word as the truth. If we abide in Christ as 'the truth', we abide in his Word, and there is no abiding in him apart from continuance in his Word (cf. John 8: 31, 32; 5: 38; 15: 7, 10). So our Lord, in like manner, could say in his address to the Father: 'Sanctify them in the truth: thy word is truth' (John 17: 17). And Paul could say of the Thessalonians that the gospel he preached came unto them 'not in word only, but also in power and in the Holy Spirit and much assurance' (I Thessalonians 1: 5), and they received the word of the message 'not as the word of men, but as it is in truth the word of God', which works effectually in them that believe (I Thessalonians 2: 13). To speak of knowing God and the truth that he is apart from the word of revelation which is incorporated for us in the Scripture is for us men an abstraction which has no meaning or relevance. When we are of the truth and know the truth we discern in the inscripturated word of truth the living voice of him who is the truth and there is no tension between our acceptance of the living God as 'the only true God' and of his Word as the truth. 'I have not written unto you because ye know not the

truth but because ye know it, and that no lie is of the truth'
(I John 2: 21). It is the certitude which is the only appropriate
response to confrontation with God himself that his Word,
the Word of Scripture, must elicit. God's Word is truth because
he is truth.

The second respect in which truth is the hallmark of godliness
is the necessity of 'truthfulness', truth in practice in thought,
word, and action. It is apparent that this second aspect depends
upon the first. In reality, truthfulness cannot guide our life unless
'the truth' is formed in us. We must know the truth if we are to
live the truth. The lie is the element of our depraved state. A
biblical ethic of truth must not ignore or discount the witness of
Scripture that every imagination of the thoughts of our hearts is
only evil (Genesis 6: 5; 8: 21), that we go astray from the womb
speaking lies (Psalm 58: 3), that we change the truth of God
into a lie (Romans 1: 25), that with our tongues we have used
deceit and the poison of asps is under our lips (Romans 3: 13),
that the god of this world, the father of lies, has blinded our
minds (II Corinthians 4: 4), that we receive not the things of the
Spirit of truth (I Corinthians 2: 14), that the mind of the flesh
is enmity against God (Romans 8: 7), and that there is no fear
of God before our eyes (Romans 3: 18). Hence the life of truth
and truthfulness can emerge only as there is the transformation
of the new creation in righteousness and holiness of the truth
and God shines in our hearts 'to give the light of the knowledge
of the glory of God in the face of Jesus Christ' (II Corinthians
4: 6). John with his usual incisiveness and decisiveness brushes
aside all camouflage when he says, 'Who is a liar but he that
denieth that Jesus is the Christ?' Where this central tenet of the
truth of the gospel is disbelieved, there the lie is enthroned. The
life of truth takes its genesis from the faith of Jesus, that the Son
of God is come in the flesh. 'He that acknowledgeth the Son hath
the Father also' (I John 2: 23), and in this confession we discern
the Spirit of God (I John 4: 2) as the Spirit of truth.

If faith is constituted by, and terminates upon, the truth of
Jesus, the life of faith continues in obedience to the truth. It was
the truth of the gospel (Galatians 2: 5) that was at stake in the
churches of Galatia when Paul penned his Epistle. His reproofs
and expostulations take many forms, and one of them is this:

'Ye were running well: who hindered you that ye should not obey the truth?' (Galatians 5: 7). In writing to Timothy, Paul makes plain that if men like Hymenaeus and Philetus were over-throwing the faith of some it was because they erred concerning the truth (II Timothy 2: 18); and that men of corrupt mind and reprobate concerning the faith were those who, though ever learning, were not able to come to the knowledge of the truth (II Timothy 3: 7, 8). Those reprobated to damnation are those who did not receive the love of the truth that they might be saved (II Thessalonians 2: 10-12; cf. Romans 2: 8). On the positive and favourable side the witness is equally explicit. Paul gives thanks that God had chosen some 'unto salvation in sanctification of the Spirit and belief of the truth' (II Thessalonians 2: 13), the brethren beloved of the Lord. The love that abides, the love that is greatest of all, without which nothing else profits, is the love that 'rejoices not in iniquity, but rejoices in the truth' (I Corinthians 13: 6). The fruit of the light in all who are the children of light is in all truth as well as in all goodness and righteousness (Ephesians 5: 9). And John has no greater joy than to hear that his children were walking in the truth (III John 4; cf. verse 3 and II John 4). In a word, it is the truth of the gospel, dwelling richly in us in all wisdom and spiritual understanding, that insures the truthfulness of our practical life; sincerity, honesty, integrity are formed in us by the truth.

What is truthfulness? It is not a simple question. Moralists have written extensively on this theme and much disagreement has perplexed the solution of the problems involved.[3] It is easy

[3] Cf. Augustine: De Mendacio and Contra Mendacium (Eng. Trans. On Lying and Against Lying, Nicene and Post-Nicene Fathers (1887), Vol. III, pp. 457-500); Thomas Aquinas: Summa Theologica (Paris, 1880), Tom. V, QQ. CIX-CXIII, pp. 107-132 (Eng. Trans., London, 1922, Vol. 12, pp. 76-117); Richard Baxter: A Christian Directory: or, A Sum of Practical Theology and Cases of Conscience, Part I, Chap. IX, Tit. 3 (Practical Works, London, 1838, Vol. I, pp. 353-361); William Paley: Moral and Political Philosophy, Chaps. XV-XVII; William Whewell: The Elements of Morality, including Polity (London, 1845), Vol. I, pp. 197-201, 242-265; Francis Wayland: The Elements of Moral Science (Boston, 1839), pp. 278-294; James Henley Thornwell: Discourses on Truth (New York, 1855), pp. 140-187 (also Collected Writings, Vol.
(continued on p. 132)

to affirm that to speak, or signify, or live a lie is wrong, that to bear false witness is to violate the core of integrity. The Bible throughout requires veracity; we may never lie. 'Thoŭ shalt not bear false witness against thy neighbour' (Exodus 20: 16). 'Thou shalt not take up a false report: put not thine hand with the wicked to be an unrighteous witness' (Exodus 23: 1). 'Keep thee far from a false matter' (Exodus 23: 7). 'Speak ye every man the truth to his neighbour; execute the judgment of truth and peace in your gates: and let none of you imagine evil in your hearts against his neighbour; and love no false oath: for all these are things that I hate, saith the Lord' (Zechariah 8: 16, 17). 'Wherefore, having put away lying, speak every man truth with his neighbour: for we are members one of another' (Ephesians 4: 25).

It needs to be borne in mind that all falsehood, error, misapprehension, every deviation from what is true in thought, feeling, word, or action is the result of sin. There would be no misunderstanding and no misrepresentation if there were no sin. We may not forget that sin began in this world with the acquiescence of the woman in the misrepresentation respecting God, averred by the tempter. In the last analysis, all misunderstanding and misrepresentation are misunderstanding and misrepresentation of God; all truth is derived from him and only in relation to him is anything true. Quite apart from sin there would have been ignorance and lack of full understanding on the part of all created rational beings. But limited knowledge is one thing, falsehood in understanding or representation is another.

It is true, of course, that misunderstanding and misrepresentation often arise when the persons involved in either or both are not directly or deliberately intending to create misunderstanding or misrepresentation. A person receives information that is erroneous, for example; he believes the report and passes it on to

II, pp. 519-542); Charles Hodge: Systematic Theology, Vol. III, pp. 437-463; H. Martensen: Christian Ethics. First Division: Individual Ethics (Eng. Trans. Edinburgh, 1888), pp. 216ff.; Newman Smyth: Christian Ethics (Edinburgh, 1893), pp. 386ff.; Theodor von Haering: The Ethics of the Christian Life (Eng. Trans., New York, 1909), pp. 227ff.; Antony Koch: A Handbook of Moral Theology (St. Louis and London, 1933, ed. Arthur Preuss), Vol. V, pp. 52ff.; Kenneth E. Kirk: Conscience and its Problems (London, 1948), pp. 121-125, 182-195, 337-354, 392-395.

another. He is acting, as we say, in good faith. And we do not call such a person a liar because, though mistaken as to the facts, he utters what he believes to be true and is not motivated by malice or any evil intent. We are all involved to some extent in such reporting. It appears to be a necessity of the credit we must accord to others and of the limitations that encompass life in this world. We should be doing grave injustice if everyone involved in erroneous representations were charged with lying and esteemed accordingly. Ordinarily, at least, the person who is to be branded as a liar is the person who affirms to be true what he knows or believes to be false or affirms to be false what he knows or believes to be true.[4]

But we think very superficially and naïvely if we suppose that no wrong is entailed in purveying misrepresentation of fact. Even when the conditions aforementioned exist and persons are, as we say, the innocent victims of misinformation, we are not to suppose that they are relieved of all wrong. What we need to appreciate is that the representation is false; it does not accord with truth. Such a representation ought not to be; it is a violation of truth and, in the final analysis, a misrepresentation of God's truth. It has its affinities with the original lie. Consequently to be the agent of passing on that misrepresentation, however noble may be our motives and designs, and however deeply unaware of its untruth, must entail for us in some way or other involvement in the intrinsic wrong of the untruth. What we ought to discern and assess more carefully than we are wont is the involvements in sin arising from our communal and corporate relationships as members of the race. The misrepresentation or untruth of which we are now speaking is a wrong that ought not to be. It is not simply an evil consequent upon sin which is not itself sinful, such as disease. It is intrinsically wrong because it is false. It does not cease to be false as it continues to be communicated. How we are to measure the wrong of the apparently innocent purveyor is beyond our power of analysis and beyond our province. But to dismiss the entail of wrong is to fail in an

---

[4] Moralists have various ways of distinguishing between the objective truth and subjective truthfulness, as, for example, the distinction between the material and formal, the physical and the moral, the speculative and the practical (cf. Augustine, Aquinas, Wayland, Thornwell in works as cited).

analysis which the nature of the misrepresentation and our involvements require us to make.

This consideration that all falsehood, as a deviation from truth, is *per se* wrong should arouse us to the gravity of our situation in relation to the prevalence of falsehood and to our responsibility in guarding, maintaining, and promoting truth. Moralists have devoted a great deal of attention to the question of what is overtly a lie and of what constitutes a person a liar. It is all-important to define and foster sincerity and honesty of heart and expression. But we must not overlook more basic questions pertinent to the sanctity of truth. This sanctity requires that we not only avoid and hate all deliberate lying, but also that thought and conviction be in accordance with truth, that not only must we refrain from uttering or signifying what we believe to be false but that belief itself be framed in accordance with truth.[5] In entertaining belief or conviction it is necessary that our minds be so informed and our judgment so disciplined that we shall not allow conviction to be induced, judgment registered, or representation made until adequate evidence is discovered and evaluated to ground conviction, judgment, and representation. No warning or plea is more germane to the question of truth than that we cultivate the reserve and exercise the caution whereby we shall be preserved from rash and precipitate judgments and from the vice of peddling reports that are not authenticated by the proper evidence. And we must also strive to be blinded by no prejudice, nor impeded by the remissness of sloth and indifference, which render us impervious to the force of the compelling evidence with which we are confronted. Jealousy for truth and for the conviction that is correspondent will make us alert to evidence when it is presented

[5] The necessity for this warning can well be illustrated by the perversity of those persons who have espoused the lie to such an extent that they actually believe the lies which they invent. Are we to say that such are not liars simply because their intellectual and moral perversity is so aggravated that they come to believe their own lies? This is a case of such aggravated perverseness that the ordinary criterion of lying no longer applies and we must therefore realize how complex the matter of lying is, and how deeply involved we may be in this vice even when we complacently consider ourselves innocent. Our prejudices and passions make us the ready victims of lies and insensitive to the claims of truth.

and to the absence of evidence when it is not sufficient. The man of truth is the man of resolute, decisive conviction; he is also the man of scrupulous reserve. 'Thou shalt not go up and down as a talebearer among thy people' (Leviticus 19: 16).

The injunctions of Scripture which bear directly on the demand for truthfulness have reference to speech or utterance. 'Speak every man truth with his neighbour' (Ephesians 4: 25). 'Thou shalt not bear false witness against thy neighbour' (Exodus 20: 16). 'Lie not one to another' (Colossians 3: 9). It will have to be understood that this covers other forms of signification as well as the spoken word. Words spoken are simply signs by which thought and meaning are conveyed, and there are numerous other means of communication by which truth can be conveyed or lying perpetrated. There are particularly the signs of gesture and action, sometimes closely associated with the spoken word and sometimes wholly intelligible without words. But as the Scripture itself deals with the question in terms of speech, and since that is the most common means of communication, we may do likewise.[6] What does the Scripture mean by 'lying' as the prohibited thing and by 'speaking truth' as that required? May we under any circumstances utter what we know to be untrue, what we believe to be false? Are we always under obligation to declare what we know or believe to be true?[7]

---

[6] 'Language is not the only vehicle of thought. A greater prominence is given to it than to any other sign, because it is the most common and important instrument of social communication. But the same rule of sincerity which is to regulate the use of it, applies to all the media by which we consciously produce impressions upon the minds of others' (Thornwell: *op. cit.*, pp. 159ff.).

[7] It is to be understood that we are to make full allowance for a variety of literary and rhetorical forms of speech. In irony, for example, the opposite of fact is formally expressed. But it is intended to be understood in that way and there is no intention to deceive. We have notable examples in Scripture (*cf.* I Kings 18: 27; 22: 15). Parables do not necessarily portray actual happenings, though they represent truth. They are understood as illustrative and not always as literally true (*cf.* II Samuel 12: 1-6). Literature and language is full of parabolic, figurative, and fictitious forms of expression, and truth only requires that they be used and understood as such.

In like manner truth is compatible with change of intention, behaviour, and action. The angels at Sodom said to Lot 'We will abide in the street all

(*continued on p. 136*)

May we affirm part of the truth and conceal the rest? These are the questions that inescapably arise, not only in the exigencies of life but in the interpretation of Scripture. We are compelled to come to terms with such questions because the biblical record supplies us with instances in which untruth was blatantly spoken and in which truth was concealed. Does the Scripture approve such conduct under certain circumstances?

In Old Testament history there are notable instances of obvious untruth. Without determining the precise category of Abraham's action both in Egypt and in the land of Abimelech in averring that Sarah was his sister, there is the indubitable untruth of Jacob and of Rebekah as his instigator when he went to Isaac his father to secure the covenant blessing. That Jacob pretended to be Esau and stated a deliberate falsehood cannot be denied. 'Who art thou, my son?' said Isaac. 'I am Esau thy firstborn,' said Jacob. And Isaac said, 'Art thou my very son Esau? and he said, I am' (Genesis 27: 18, 19, 24). It might appear utterly impossible to condemn Rebekah and Jacob for the deception and untruth of act and word since it was the very occasion upon which divine blessing was administered to Jacob. Could the Lord countenance such a stratagem if it were a lie of act and word? And, furthermore, we may discover in Rebekah's action jealousy for the fulfilment of the divine promise she had received, 'The elder shall serve the younger'. There was undoubted faith in Rebekah's action, indeed the urgent impulsion of faith. And there must have been faith in Jacob, too. If he were indifferent to the blessing he

---

night' (Genesis 19: 2), but when Lot urged them greatly they entered into his house. In response to Lot's earnest entreaty they had a right to reverse the former resolution. When new circumstances arise which we may not have foreseen we have a right to alter what may have been our expressed intent. Truth often requires such a change of act and word. To behave truthfully is to behave in consonance with the facts as they are and not as they may have previously been or as they may be in the future. We have in the case of our Lord himself examples of this change of behaviour in response to the developments which had emerged (cf. Matthew 8: 7, 13; 15: 23, 24, 26, 28; Luke 24: 28, 29). Truth demands that we act in accordance with relevant facts and conditions and when these facts and conditions change our action changes accordingly. It would be untruth to do otherwise. The same applies to words and significations (cf. Ezekiel Hopkins: An Exposition of the Ten Commandments, New York, n.d., p. 403).

would not have acted as he did. And, no doubt, much more could be said of the resolute faith which lay behind the whole episode as devised and arranged by Rebekah.

But it is poor theology and worse theodicy that will seek to derive from God's action in the bestowal of the blessing upon Jacob, or in the faith of Rebekah which lay back of her design, a vindication of the method devised by Rebekah and enacted by Jacob. We know little of biblical theology if we do not recognize that God fulfils his determinate purpose of grace and promise notwithstanding the unworthy actions of those who are the beneficiaries of that grace. He fulfils his determinate purpose in spite of the actions which are alien to the integrity of character which his will demands. And surely we have here a signal example of the sovereign grace as well as of the determinate purpose of God. He even fulfils his holy and sovereign will in connection with the unholy means adopted by Rebekah and Jacob. And if we think of Rebekah's faith we can readily discern the insistent impulsion of faith conjoined with an action that was not of faith. Are we to say that faith is never mixed with the devices of unbelief? Or, to put it otherwise, are we to say that strong faith cannot coexist with the infirmities of unbelief? There is no ground upon which we may seek to justify the deception and untruth of Rebekah and Jacob.[8] Jacob spoke and acted a lie, and this fact only enhances our astonishment at the sovereignty of God's grace and the faithfulness of his promise.

[8] Calvin: *Comm. ad* Genesis 27: 5 says: 'And surely the stratagem of Rebekah was not without fault; for although she could not guide her husband by salutary counsel, yet it was not a legitimate method of acting, to circumvent him by such deceit. For, as a lie is in itself culpable, she sinned more grievously still in this, that she desired to sport in a sacred matter with such wiles. She knew that the decree by which Jacob had been elected and adopted was immutable; why then does she not patiently wait till God shall confirm it in fact, and shall show that what he had once pronounced from heaven is certain? Therefore, she darkens the celestial oracle by her lie, and abolishes, as far as she was able, the grace promised to her son. Now, if we consider farther, whence arose this great desire to bestir herself; her extraordinary faith will on the other hand appear. For, as she did not hesitate to provoke her husband against herself, to light up implacable enmity between the brothers, to expose her beloved son Jacob to the danger of immediate death, and to disturb the whole family, this certainly flowed from no other source than her faith' (as translated by John King, C.T.S., Grand Rapids, 1948).

In this instance we find no justification of the falsehood per-petrated.

The vindication of deliberate untruth under certain circum-stances receives more plausible support from the case of Rahab the harlot. That Rahab uttered an explicit falsehood is apparent. She hid the spies upon the roof. The king of Jericho sent to Rahab and asked her to bring forth the men who had come to her. Her reply is not one of evasion; it is plain contradiction of known fact. 'Yea, the men came unto me, but I knew not whence they were: and it came to pass about the time of the shutting of the gate, when it was dark, that the men went out: whither the men went I wot not: pursue after them quickly; for ye shall overtake them' (Joshua 2: 4, 5). Rahab was a woman of faith. She is in-cluded in the great cloud of witnesses. 'By faith Rahab the harlot perished not with them that had been disobedient, having re-ceived the spies with peace' (Hebrews 11: 31). Again we read, 'Was not Rahab the harlot justified by works, in that she received the messengers and sent them out another way?' (James 2: 25). How could her conduct in reference to the spies be so com-mended, we might say, if the untruth by which she shielded them were itself wrong?

It should not go unnoticed that the New Testament Scriptures which commend Rahab for her faith and works make allusion solely to the fact that she received the spies and sent them out another way. No question can be raised as to the propriety of these actions or of hiding the spies from the emissaries of the king of Jericho. And the approval of these actions does not logi-cally, or in terms of the analogy provided by Scripture, carry with it the approval of the specific untruth spoken to the king of Jericho. It is strange theology that will insist that the approval of her faith and works in receiving the spies and helping them to escape must embrace the approval of *all* the actions associated with her praiseworthy conduct. And if it is objected that the preservation of the spies and the sequel of sending them out another way could not have been accomplished apart from the untruth uttered and that the untruth is integral to the successful outcome of her action, there are three things to be borne in mind. (1) We are presuming too much in reference to the providence of God when we say that the untruth was indispensable to the successful outcome of her believing action. (2) Granting that, in the *de facto* providence of God, the untruth was one of the means through which the spies escaped, it does not follow that Rahab was morally justified in using this method. God fulfils his holy, decretive will through our unholy acts. (3) The kind of argumentation that seeks to justify the untruth because it is so closely bound up with the total result would be akin to the justification of Jacob's lie in connection with the blessing of Isaac; Jacob's deception in deed and word is integral to the *de facto* outcome of the episode, and yet we need not and may not justify his lie.

We see, therefore, that neither Scripture itself nor the theological inferences derived from Scripture provide us with any warrant for the vindication of Rahab's untruth[9] and this instance, consequently, does not support the position that under certain circumstances we may justifiably utter an untruth.

One of the most pertinent incidents in the Scripture is the instruction received by Samuel from the Lord himself on the occasion of the anointing of David as king. 'Fill thy horn with oil, and go; I will send thee to Jesse the Beth-lehemite: for I have provided me a king among his sons' (I Samuel 16: 1). Samuel feared the consequences if Saul heard of this. 'How can I go? if Saul hear it he will kill me. And the Lord said, Take an heifer with thee, and say, I am come to sacrifice to the Lord' (I Samuel 16: 2). Without question here is divine authorization for concealment by means of a statement other than that which would have disclosed the main purpose of Samuel's visit to Jesse. We may call this evasion, if we will. But, in any case, there is sup-

[9] Calvin: *Comm. ad* Joshua 2: 4-6 takes a position similar to that quoted above respecting Rebekah: 'As to the falsehood, we must admit that though it was done for a good purpose, it was not free from fault. For those who hold what is called a dutiful lie (*mendacium officiosum*) to be altogether excusable, do not sufficiently consider how precious truth is in the sight of God. Therefore, although our purpose be to assist our brethren, to consult for their safety and relieve them, it never can be lawful to lie, because that cannot be right which is contrary to the nature of God. And God is truth. And still the act of Rahab is not devoid of the praise of virtue, although it was not spotlessly pure. For it often happens that while the saints study to hold the right path, they deviate into circuitous courses' (as translated by Henry Beveridge, C.T.S., Grand Rapids, 1949).

pression of the most important facts relevant to Samuel's mission. We do not know if direct speech to Saul himself was intended or necessary, but, if so, there was the divine sanction for the concealment. The question is: Was untruth involved? There are three considerations that must be borne in mind.

(1) Samuel carried into effect what the Lord asked him to say and do. 'And Samuel did that which the Lord spake, and came to Beth-lehem. And the elders of the city came to meet him trembling, and said, Comest thou peaceably? And he said, Peaceably: I am come to sacrifice unto the Lord: sanctify yourselves, and come with me to the sacrifice. And he sanctified Jesse and his sons, and called them to the sacrifice' (I Samuel 16: 4, 5). Hence Samuel was authorized to say nothing more than what he actually did say and perform. He did not speak what was contrary to fact. There was no untruth in what the Lord authorized. If it is objected that this is a fine-spun distinction akin to sophistry and quibbling, we must take note that these are precisely the facts which the Scripture itself is meticulously, almost repetitiously, careful to set before us. It is an indisputable fact that what Samuel was told to say was strictly in accord with the facts which followed and there is surely purpose in the explicitness of the narrative to this effect. We are compelled to take account of the agreement between statement and fact. It is looseness to ignore this consideration. (2) This incident makes clear that it is proper under certain circumstances to conceal or withhold part of the truth. Saul had no right to know the whole purpose of Samuel's mission to Jesse nor was Samuel under obligation to disclose it. Concealment was not lying. (3) This instance gives us no warrant whatsoever for maintaining that in concealing the truth we may affirm untruth. It is the eloquent lesson of this incident, borne out by the plain facts referred to above, that what was affirmed was itself strictly true. This passage is perhaps unique in the Scripture because there is the explicit authorization of the Lord as to the method of concealment. It is just for that reason that the precise conditions are to be observed; there is no untruth involved. It is necessary to guard jealously the distinction between partial truth and untruth. If we are not hospitable to this distinction it may well be that we are not sensitive to the ethic of Scripture and the demands of truth. After

all, this is not a fine distinction; it is a rather broad distinction. But if we wish to call it a fine distinction, we must remember that the biblical ethic is built upon fine distinctions. At the point of divergence the difference between right and wrong, between truth and falsehood, is not a chasm but a razor's edge. And if we do not appreciate this fact then certainly we are not sensitive to the biblical ethic.[10]

The apparent prevarication of the midwives in Egypt has been appealed to as warrant for untruth under proper conditions. 'And the midwives said unto Pharaoh, Because the Hebrew women are not as the Egyptian women; for they are lively, and are delivered ere the midwives come in unto them. And God dealt well with the midwives' (Exodus 1: 19, 20). The juxtaposition here might seem to carry the endorsement of the reply to Pharaoh.

We need not suppose that the midwives' reply to Pharaoh was altogether void of truth. There is good reason to believe that the Hebrew women often bore their children without the aid of the midwives. We may therefore have an instance of partial truth and not total untruth, and partial truth relevant to the circumstances. And since the midwives feared God and therefore disobeyed Pharaoh's command, it was not an obligation to tell Pharaoh the whole truth. Hence it is possible that the midwives' answer shows not falsehood but concealment through the means of part truth.[11] But that the reason they gave was not the whole truth is apparent—the midwives 'saved the men children alive' (Exodus 1: 17).

Let us grant, however, that the midwives did speak an untruth and that their reply was really false. There is still no warrant to conclude that the untruth is endorsed, far less that it is the untruth that is in view when we read, 'And God dealt well with the midwives' (Exodus 1: 20). The midwives feared God in disobeying the king and it is because they feared God that the Lord blessed them (cf. verses 17, 21). It is not at all strange that

[10] Jeremiah 38: 24-28 is similar to I Samuel 16: 1-5 and need not be dealt with.

[11] Cf. John Lightfoot: Works (ed. Pitman, London, 1822), Vol. II, pp. 357f.; George Bush: Notes, Critical and Practical, on the Book of Exodus (New York, 1846), p. 20; Richard Baxter: op. cit., p. 360.

their fear of God should have coexisted with moral infirmity. The case is simply that no warrant for untruth can be elicited from this instance any more than in the cases of Jacob and Rahab.[12]

The statement of Elisha the prophet of Israel to the host of the king of Syria when they encompassed the city of Dothan, evidently for the purpose of apprehending him, is one that appears untruthful. 'And Elisha said unto them, This is not the way, neither is this the city; follow me, and I will bring you to the man whom ye seek. And he led them to Samaria' (II Kings 6: 19). If we say that this is a case of untruth spoken in order to deceive the host of Syrians, it would be difficult to take the position that Elisha had done wrong. The total circumstance of signal protection on the part of God, and of both justice and mercy on Elisha's own part, especially the latter, would make it precarious to infer that Elisha had done wrong in leading the host to Samaria. And so, if untruth is involved, this instance would provide an example of untruth justifiably uttered in order to fulfil a worthy end. Perhaps more than any other incident in Scripture this would be the justification of the untruth of exigency or necessity (*mendacium officiosum*). As we study Elisha's statement, however, it is just as difficult to find untruth in what Elisha said. Let it be granted that the Syrians understood Elisha's words in a way entirely different from Elisha's intent, does it follow that Elisha spoke untruth? Elisha was under no obligation to inform them that he was the man whom they sought. The Lord had miraculously intervened to guard him from their intent, and to disclose himself to them would have been counter to the miraculous providence by which he was shielded. Furthermore, when Elisha said, 'This is not the city', how are we to know precisely what he intended? He may have meant, 'This is not the city in which you will find the man whom ye seek'. Apparently he was outside the city when he addressed them and he did not intend to re-enter the city. Of what purpose would it have been for Elisha to say, 'This is the city'? If there was deception in what Elisha said, it would have been more of deception to have said 'This is the city'. Was he to encourage them to wander aimlessly in Dothan to find their man when he would not have been there and especially since their eyes had been blinded? Again, when he

[12] *Cf.* Calvin: *Comm. ad* Exodus 1: 18; Aquinas: *op. cit.*, p. 92.

said, 'Follow me, and I will bring you to the man whom ye seek', he carried this into effect, though not with the result which the Syrians envisaged or might have envisaged. In the light of the providence by which their eyes had been blinded and of the sequel of mercy and justice meted out to these Syrians at Elisha's demand, how can we say that Elisha had spoken an untruth? Elisha did bring them to the city in which they found the man whom they sought. He did this in a way that they could not have anticipated, but he did it with such a merciful outcome for both the Syrians and for Israel that the Syrians themselves could not have accused Elisha of falsehood. If they had any capacity for intelligent reflection, they would have said, 'How true it was, "This is not the city. Follow me, and I will bring you to the man whom ye seek", though strangely and wonderfully true'. Hence when we view Elisha's statement in the light of all the facts, unseen indeed to the Syrians at the time but envisaged by Elisha, facts which Elisha had a right to take into account when he made the statement in question, we can see how true, after all, Elisha's statement was. And we have no right to insist that the understanding of the Syrians at the time of its having been made should have dictated the sense of Elisha's statement. The meaning of Elisha's words are to be understood in the light of all the facts and not in terms of the temporary blindness and bewilderment which had overtaken the Syrians. Is this not oftentimes the way of truth? We make statements or promises which are very imperfectly understood by others and have, even for them, a far more real and beneficent meaning than they could have anticipated. The meaning is dictated by the facts which come within the purview of the person making the statement or promise and not by the limited or erroneous conception of these facts entertained by others. In a word, the utterance is determined by the relevant facts which come within the horizon of the person speaking; it is dictated by what is true. If another person is temporarily deceived by inadequate understanding or foresight, this is not deception springing from untruth on the part of the speaker. And this is the question with which we are now concerned. Elisha's statement was not untrue to the facts which in due time were disclosed.

What may we infer to be the biblical ethic regarding the stratagems of war? It is understood, of course, that truthfulness is con-

cerned not only with words, but also with other forms of signification. What we are concerned with now is action intended to
deceive the enemy as to the strategy of the opposing forces.
When something is pretended, is there not untruth of action,
though not necessarily of words? We have a concrete example
in the stratagem by which Joshua conquered the city of Ai
(Joshua 8: 3-29). In this incident it is not the setting of the ambush
nor the action of the men who took part that raises the question
of untruth. The ambush was an action of concealment as such.
It is the retreat on the part of the other division of Joshua's army
that poses the question (verse 15); they fled the way of the wilder-
ness. That this was designed and feigned retreat is made plain by
the narrative (see verses 5, 6). So Joshua and Israel feigned an
action which did not itself reflect the intent but was designed to
lead the people of Ai to think that Israel was fleeing before them.
It was simulated defeat. And the question is: May we simulate
contrary to actual fact?

In this instance it would surely be futile to try to categorize
this action on Joshua's part as wrong. The Lord himself was
party to the stratagem (*cf.* verse 18), and it would be sophistry
indeed to attempt to abstract this element of the strategy from
that which the Lord himself authorized. Is there not here, therefore, the divine sanction upon untruth?

When we ask ourselves the question, Was there untruth? or,
Wherein did the untruth reside?, we find ourselves in real
difficulty, and the untruth we may have assumed is not as obvious
as it at first appeared to be. Israel did what they intended to do;
there was no action on Israel's part contrary to fact or intent.
There was indeed retreat when, in the ordinary sense, there was
no need for retreat. In other words, it was a strategic retreat.
But Israel did retreat and there was no unreality to that action
of withdrawal. Israel was under no obligation to inform the
people of Ai what the meaning or intent of this retreat was.
Joshua suspected or knew beforehand that the men of Ai would
have interpreted it in a way that was contrary to fact and to
Joshua's intent. Joshua was taking advantage of Ai's unwariness
and lack of proper reconnaissance, that is to say, of Ai's failure to
interpret the action of retreat for what it truly was. But are we to
say that Joshua was under obligation to act on the basis of their

misapprehension of the meaning of his movements rather than on the basis of his own interpretation which had been dictated by all of the facts? The men of Ai were deceived as to the meaning of the retreat of Israel, but that deception arose from their failure to discover its real purpose. So when we view the action concerned in terms of truth, that is, in terms of consonance with all the facts which the agents of that action were not only justified but obliged to take into account, we are at a loss to find wherein untruth resided. That is to say, we are at a loss to find untruth. The case is somewhat similar in the sphere of action to what we found in Elisha's case in the sphere of utterance. When Elisha spoke to the Syrians he spoke, as we found, in accordance with the facts which he knew and envisaged, and any misapprehension on their part arose from their ignorance of the facts which came within Elisha's purview and which he rightly took into account. When Joshua acted in retreating he acted in accordance with all the facts which his strategy embraced and the misapprehension on the part of the men of Ai arose from their ignorance of the facts which Joshua rightly took into account.

The allegation that Joshua acted an untruth or a lie rests upon the fallacious assumption that to be truthful we must *under all circumstances* speak and act in terms of the data which come within the purview of others who may be concerned with or affected by our speaking or acting. This is not the criterion of truthfulness. It would oftentimes be incompatible with justice, right, and truth to apply this criterion. When we speak or act we do so in terms of all the relevant facts and considerations which come within our purview, and if we are misunderstood or misrepresented we are not to be charged with falsehood. When mutual understanding is one of the relevant or requisite considerations, then we are under obligation to do our utmost to insure that we speak or act in terms of the understanding of others. But this is not the indispensable criterion of truthfulness. And it could not be imposed as the criterion of truth and truthfulness in making a moral assessment of the actions of an opposing force in time of war and in the exigencies of battle.

The sustained emphasis of Scripture is upon the condemnation of untruth and falsehood and upon the necessity of speaking the truth. [13]'Wherefore having put away lying speak truth each one with his neighbour' (Ephesians 4: 25). It is fully admitted that Scripture confronts us with difficulties. In this study an attempt has been made to deal with these difficulties as they appear at various points in the biblical record. In some instances it might appear that Scripture condones or approves untruth when untruth promotes a higher end. Hence many interpreters have taken the position that the Scripture recognizes the legitimacy of the lie of utility, exigency, necessity (*mendacium officiosum* as distinguished from *mendacium perniciosum*). It has not been difficult to show how unwarranted such an inference is in some of the instances which might appear to lend it support. Other instances give more plausible support to the inference. But the upshot of our examination has been that no instance demonstrates the propriety of untruthfulness under any exigency. We would require far more than the Scripture provides to be able to take the position that under certain exigencies we may speak untruth with our neighbour. In other words, the evidence is not available whereby we may justify deviation from the sustained requirement of the biblical witness that we put away falsehood and speak truth. We would need the most explicit evidence to warrant such deviation and it is that evidence that is wanting. How then could we justify it?

It is quite true that the Scripture warrants concealment of truth from those who have no claim upon it. We immediately recognize the justice of this. How intolerable life would be if we were under obligation to disclose all the truth. And concealment is often an

---

[13] It is scarcely necessary to show that Paul is not saying in II Corinthians 12: 16 that 'being crafty he caught them with guile'. That was the charge brought against him by his detractors which he is vigorously protesting and denying, as is apparent from the rhetorical questions of verses 17, 18. And with reference to Romans 3: 7: 'But if the truth of God hath abounded unto his glory by my lie, why am I also still judged as a sinner?', Paul is not justifying the sin which he here calls his 'lie'. He is doing the very opposite. What he is controverting is the pernicious logic that we may do evil that good may come (*cf.* verse 8), the argument that, since the grace and righteousness of God abound all the more where sin abounded, therefore we may sin in order that God may be all the more glorified. What Paul is saying is that such an inference from his doctrine of the grace of God is a slander and that the condemnation of those who use it is just. This passage is in reality one of the most pertinent to the position propounded above—we may never do evil that good may come.

obligation which truth itself requires. 'He that goeth about as a
talebearer revealeth secrets; but he that is of a faithful spirit
concealeth a matter" (Proverbs 11: 13). It is also true that men
often forfeit their right to know the truth and we are under no
obligation to convey it to them.

But these facts of the right and duty of concealment and of
forfeiture of certain rights are not to be equated with our right to
speak untruth. Forfeiture of right to know the truth and the right
of concealment in such cases do not mean that our obligation to
speak truth is ever forfeited. There is a chasm of difference between the forfeiture of right to know the truth, which belongs to
one man, and the right to speak untruth on the part of another.
The latter is not an inference to be drawn from the former. Those
who argue for the right to speak untruth on the basis that others
have forfeited their right to know or be told the truth have
committed an egregious logical error and have sought to justify
a deviation from truthfulness which the Scripture does not
support.

No claim is more basic or ultimate than that of truth. We
cannot regard any other sanction as higher on the altar of which
truth may be sacrificed. By what warrant may we plead, as many
have done,[14] that love is a higher end out of consideration for
which untruth is sometimes justifiable and dutiful? Is life itself
more sacred than truth? God is love (I John 4: 8, 16). But God
is truth also (cf. I John 1: 5; John 1: 9; 17: 3; I John 5: 20; John
14: 6; I John 5: 6). Love and truth do not conflict in him and his

[14] Cf., e.g., Newman Smyth: op. cit., pp. 395ff. Although the position taken
by H. Martensen (cf. op. cit., pp. 217ff.) is subject to the same criticism, yet
his final analysis shows sounder judgment. 'But while we thus find the ground
of manifold collisions especially in the corruption of human society, we must
with no less emphasis insist that their insolubility very often proceeds from the
weakness and frailty of individuals. For the question ever still remains, whether
the said collisions between the truth of the letter and that of the spirit could not
be solved if these individuals only stood on a higher stage of moral and religious
ripeness, possessed more faith and trust in God, more courage to leave the
consequences of their words and actions in the hand of God, and likewise
considered how much in the consequences of our actions is hidden from our
view, and cannot be reckoned by us; if these individuals possessed more
wisdom to tell the truth in the right way; in other words, whether the collision
could not be solved if we were only, in a far higher degree than is the case,
morally educated characters, Christian personalities?' (op. cit., pp. 221f.).

truth is never curtailed or prejudiced in maintaining and promoting the interests of his love. God so loved the world that he gave his only-begotten Son and sent him into this world of sin and misery and death. This was love. But nothing could be more significant than this that when the Son came and was embarking upon the climactic commitment of his mission he said: 'For this end am I born and for this purpose am I come into the world, that I might bear witness to the truth' (John 18: 37).

Truthfulness in us is derived from, and is patterned after, 'the truth', and 'no lie is of the truth' (I John 2: 21). It is because untruth is the contradiction of the nature of God that it is wrong.[15] Truth and untruth are antithetical because God is truth. And this is the reason why truthfulness and untruth do not cohere.

[15] Cf. Calvin: *Comm. ad* Exodus 1: 18; Zechariah 13: 3.

CHAPTER VII

OUR LORD'S TEACHING

No part of Scripture is more relevant to the question of the biblical ethic than the teaching of our Lord in what is called the sermon on the mount. A large section of that discourse is concerned with the relation to the law of God of the order of things which Jesus came into the world to establish. And as we focus attention upon the precise question of the relations of love and law in the kingdom of God, nothing could be more germane than the deliverances of our Lord on this occasion. That part of the discourse with which we are particularly concerned begins with these striking words: 'Do not think that I came to destroy the law or the prophets; I came not to destroy but to fulfil' (Matthew 5: 17). Jesus is not reflecting primarily on the keeping of the law or commandments of God; he does that later on. Here he is dealing with a much deeper question. The exact force of this word is to be derived from the two pivotal verbs, 'destroy' and 'fulfil'. The meaning of 'destroy'[1] is not to break or transgress but to dissolve. It is similar to our English word 'abrogate' or, as in Wiclif's translation, 'undo'. Jesus says that he did not come to abrogate the law or the prophets. The law and the prophets should be regarded as embracing the whole of the Old Testament canon. So Jesus says that he did not come to abrogate any of the existing Scriptures.

Just as the word 'destroy' does not mean simply to break or transgress, so the word 'fulfil' does not mean merely to keep or obey. And it is this word 'fulfil' that needs to be assessed if we are to appreciate Jesus' positive assertion. The substantive form of this word, often rendered 'fulness', means the full tale, the full

---

[1] The Greek word is καταλύω. In Joseph Addison Alexander's words (*Comm. ad loc.*) it means the 'dissolution or disintegration, the destruction of a whole by the complete separation of its parts, as when a house is taken down by being taken to pieces, the very act denoted by the verb in the passage just cited (Matthew 26: 61; 27: 40). In the same sense, but with a figurative application, Paul employs it to describe the dissolution of the body (2 Cor. 5, 1), and of a system of belief and practice (Gal. 2, 18), which last is precisely its use here.'

measure or complement of something.[2] Hence what Jesus means is that he came to realize the full measure of the intent and purpose of the law and the prophets. He came to complete, to consummate, to bring to full fruition and perfect fulfilment the law and the prophets. Jesus refers to the function of validating and confirming the law and the prophets and includes much more than the fulfilment of the predictions of the Old Testament regarding himself. He means that the whole process of revelation deposited in the Old Testament finds in him its completion, its fulfilment, its confirmation, its validation. Still more, it finds in him its embodiment. To use John's terms, 'grace and truth came by Jesus Christ' (John 1: 17). That is to say, grace and truth in complete manifestation and embodiment came by Jesus Christ.

The inclusiveness of Jesus' statement requires us to regard 'the law' as comprising more than those aspects of the law of Moses which have permanent application and sanction. Jesus is saying that he came not to abrogate any part of the Mosaic law. What we call the ritual or ceremonial comes within the scope of his declaration as well as the moral. We ask, of course, how can this be? Did Jesus not come to abrogate the ritual law of the Pentateuch? He did come to discontinue the observance of the rites and ceremonies of the old economy. But it is not correct to say that he came to abrogate them. The process of redemptive revelation embraces the Levitical economy of Moses and it is this process of increasing and accumulating disclosure that reaches its culmination and consummation in him who is the image of the invisible God, the effulgence of his glory and the express image of his substance. Hence the Levitical economy must never be viewed in abstraction from the sum total of God's redemptive action and revelation. This is just to say that the ritual ordinances stand in the most intimate organic connection with Christ and his work. In the circumstances of Israel's history they are ectypes of an archetype; they are adumbrations of an archetypal reality that received its historical accomplishment in the fulness of the time when God sent forth his Son. Particularly when we think of Jesus' sacrifice of himself upon the cross, and his high-priestly entrance into the holies of the heavenly sanctuary, must we think

---

[2] See J. B. Lightfoot's excursus on the meaning of πλήρωμα in his *Saint Paul's Epistles to the Colossians and to Philemon* (London, 1927), pp. 255-271.

of the Levitical sacrifices as anticipatory accomplishments of the same great redemptive facts. Jesus himself as the great high priest, in his finished work and in his continued high-priestly activity, is the permanent and final embodiment of all the truth portrayed in the Levitical ordinances. Strictly speaking the Levitical ritual did not serve as the pattern for the work of Christ; rather, the high-priestly work of Christ provided the archetype by which the prescriptions of the Levitical law were fashioned and patterned (cf. Hebrews 9: 24, 25). The Levitical were the ectypes and models drawn from the heavenly exemplar. It was for this reason that they possessed meaning and efficacy. And it is for this reason that Jesus could say, even with reference to the ritual ordinances, which as regards observance have been discontinued, 'I came not to abrogate but to fulfil'.

The next word of Jesus in this connection, whether it be considered to be causally connected with the preceding or simply co-ordinate with it, offers unmistakeable evidence of the esteem with which our Lord regarded the details of the Old Testament. If there is anything that is distasteful to the modern mind it is concern for detail, and particularly is this the case in the field of ethics. By a lamentable confusion of thought concern for detail is identified with legalism and insistence upon the authenticity of the Scriptures in detail is identified with a petrified orthodoxy. How this whole attitude of mind fares in the presence of Jesus' words here, it is for latitudinarians to judge. 'One jot or one tittle.' It is a clear assertion that the law in all its details must come to fulfilment and be accomplished. It indicates two things. First, our Lord recognized that the minutiae of the law had significance. If we do not like minutiae or insistence upon them, then we are not at home with the attitude of Jesus. We are moving in an entirely different world of thought. Second, Jesus here posits an inspiration in the sense of divine origin, authority, and character for the minutiae of the law. We are not to suppose that Jesus is speaking of these details in themselves apart from the relation they sustain to the words and clauses and sentences in which they appear. For example, when we speak of verbal inspiration we are never thinking of the inspiration of words in abstraction and independence. Such words are not inspired because such words do not exist in the Scripture. Jesus is speaking here of jot and tittle inspiration, of nothing less. But he is not speaking of jot and tittle in abstraction, because a jot or tittle in abstraction has no meaning. In fact a jot or tittle does not exist in abstraction because a jot in abstraction is not a jot but a meaningless mark, perhaps a blot, and a tittle in abstraction is not a tittle but a meaningless stroke. When Jesus speaks here of jot and tittle as indestructible, and therefore, by implication, of jot and tittle as being of divine origin, character, and authority, he is thinking of jot and tittle in construction and combination with relevant words, clauses, and sentences. It is then that they have significance; and they have such significance that inspiration extends to them, and does so precisely because it extends to the combinations of which they are component parts.

In this we are instructed regarding the direction in which we are to find Jesus' teaching. We are not to expect an undervaluation, far less disparagement, of the details of law; and we may as well expect from the outset that, if our perspective is one that looks for the wood but not the trees, then we shall not be at home in the teaching of Jesus.

As we proceed we find that Jesus' discourse is progressively pointed to the precise question of the relation of the kingdom of heaven to the law of God until his teaching becomes focused very specifically in the words of the decalogue. 'Whosoever therefore shall break one of these least commandments, and shall teach men so, he shall be called the least in the kingdom of heaven: but whosoever shall do and teach them, the same shall be called great in the kingdom of heaven. For I say unto you, that except your righteousness shall exceed the righteousness of the scribes and Pharisees, ye shall in no case enter into the kingdom of heaven' (Matthew 5: 19, 20). Broadly speaking both of these verses deal with the question of our relation to the kingdom of heaven. But this question is explicated in terms of our attitude to the law. That is to say, our relation to the kingdom of heaven is defined in terms of our relation to the law. The question arises whether the same thing is being stated in both verses, namely, the criterion by which entrance into the kingdom is determined. To express the question pointedly in terms of the respective verses: Is the clause 'he shall be called least in the kingdom of heaven' a rhetorical understate ment of the same truth expressed in verse 20 in the words 'ye shall by no means enter into the kingdom of heaven'? There does not appear to be any good reason for answering this question in the affirmative, and to equate the thought of the two verses, when the terms are different, would require good evidence. The terms of the passage would naturally indicate that in verse 19 Jesus is dealing with the criteria of gradation in the kingdom of God whereas in verse 20 he is enunciating the principle of exclusion from it. The law is the norm in both cases, in the former case the criterion by which our relative position in the kingdom of God is determined, in the latter case the criterion by which we are excluded entirely from the kingdom. Hence there can be no escape from the conclusion that the law is directly relevant to membership in and station within the kingdom of God.

When Jesus speaks of *breaking* one of these least commandments there is a patent distinction between this word 'breaking' as used here and the word 'destroy' or 'abrogate' in verse 17. Jesus is speaking now of what we may do in reference to the breach of the commandments and he contrasts it with doing or obeying. What needs to be particularly stressed is the co-ordination or conjunction of breaking and inculcating the breach of one of the least of the commandments, on the one hand, and of doing and teaching the observance on the other. The thought is that the person who entertains such a view of even one small commandment that he himself breaks it, and inculcates the belief that it may or should be broken, will be called least in the kingdom of heaven. It is not therefore the mere breach of such a commandment that establishes the criterion in this case, but the settled belief that it may or should be broken; that is to say, the belief, the practice of that belief, and the propagating of that belief and practice. Disobedience and the inculcation of disobedience in others define the grade that is called least in the kingdom of heaven just as obedience and the inculcation of obedience define the grade that is called great in the kingdom of heaven. In each case it is the classification or gradation that is in view and not the identification of any one person in distinction from all others as the least or the greatest.

These criteria of gradation in the kingdom of God warn us against the injustice of the judgment that is too widespread within the church of Christ. Too often the person imbued with meticulous concern for the ordinances of God and conscientious regard for the minutiae of God's commandments is judged as a legalist, while the person who is not bothered by details is judged to be the practical person who exemplifies the liberty of the gospel. Here Jesus is reminding us of the same great truth which he declares elsewhere: 'He that is faithful in that which is least is faithful also in much, and he that is unjust in the least is unjust also in much' (Luke 16: 10). The criterion of our standing in the kingdom of God and of reward in the age to come is nothing else than meticulous observance of the commandments of God in the minutial details of their prescription and the earnest inculcation of such observance on the part of others.

It needs to be noted, also, that what we do in this matter is not our own private concern. The least of God's commandments, if they bind us, bind others. We must resist the virulent poison of individualism which tolerates in others the indifference and disobedience which we cannot justify in ourselves, just as we must resist the tendency to tolerate in ourselves the disobedience which we condemn in others. The moment we become complacent to the sins of others then we have begun to relax our own grip of the sanctity of the commandments of God, and we are also on the way to condoning the same sin in ourselves. 'Whosoever shall do and teach, this one shall be called great in the kingdom of heaven' (verse 19).

When our Lord continues, 'For I say to you, except your righteousness shall exceed the righteousness of the scribes and Pharisees, ye shall in no wise enter into the kingdom of heaven', he is stating the principle of exclusion from the kingdom of heaven. There is, of course, a close connection between the criterion of exclusion and the criterion of gradation. The connection might be stated thus: if the criterion by which our relative position in the kingdom of God is determined is meticulous concern for the commandments of God, then the criterion of membership in the kingdom of God cannot be divorced from that righteousness of which the commandments of God are the norm and standard. Jesus is explicit to the effect that a righteousness of a certain character is indispensable if we are to be members of the kingdom of heaven. We could have inferred this from the preceding verse. For if gradation in the kingdom is apportioned in accordance with what we do and teach in reference to the commandments, it is impossible to think of the members as destitute of that conformity which the commandments require. But now Jesus is explicit. What does Jesus mean by this righteousness that is in excess of the righteousness of the scribes and Pharisees?

We might suppose that the thought is that of extension. The righteousness of the scribes and Pharisees goes a certain distance; it brings them, as it were, to the threshold of the kingdom. But we must supplement it by going further. This interpretation misses the genius of Jesus' word which is to the effect that the righteousness of the scribes and Pharisees is one that has no affinity with the kingdom of heaven. This kind of indictment is the more remarkable when we remember that the righteousness of the scribes was one characterized by great concern for detail, for the minutiae of observance. In the context it is concern for detail that Jesus is emphasizing. It is this common element that serves to set off in bold relief the contrast. What Jesus is saying is that the righteousness of the scribes, notwithstanding its meticulous adherence to the minutiae, does not begin to qualify for the kingdom of heaven; it has no affinity with the demands of the kingdom of heaven. This is so not because the kingdom of heaven does not demand righteousness, not because it is indifferent to the minutiae of divine prescription, but because the demands of the kingdom of heaven are far greater than anything that ever enters into the conception of the scribes and Pharisees. They have not begun to reckon with the demands of the kingdom of heaven. Paradoxically, it was their concern for detail that led them to miss the whole genius of kingdom righteousness; the detail was not the detail of divine prescription. They made void the law of God by their own traditions. What then is the righteousness of the kingdom of heaven?

It might be supposed that the righteousness in view here is the righteousness of imputation. What else, we might say, will fit into the evangelicalism of the gospel of pure grace? The context, however, offers no warrant for this interpretation. There is a close relationship between verses 19 and 20. In the former Jesus is speaking of human behaviour, as regards breaking the least of the commandments and teaching accordingly, of doing the commandments and teaching accordingly. It would be utterly harsh to suppose a complete break in the thought at verse 20 and a transition from the thought of doing and teaching on our part to the doing that does not in the least degree engage or include our doing in obedience to divine commandments. It must be the doing of the commandments that Jesus has in view when he speaks of the righteousness that abounds more than the righteousness of the scribes and Pharisees. Besides, Jesus speaks of 'your righteousness'. It is scarcely compatible with the doctrine of imputed righteousness to refer to it in this fashion. For although it is a righteousness that becomes ours, it is characteristic of Paul, who is the chief proponent of such a doctrine, to contrast the righteousness of imputation with our own righteousness (*cf.* Philippians 3: 9). Hence, to import the notion of imputed righteousness at this point is contrary to the direction of thought in the context, and would be an importation for which there is no warrant in the passage as a whole. The righteousness that exceeds that of the scribes and Pharisees is therefore that of character and behaviour, the righteousness of doing and teaching the commandments of God.

We are now faced with a much more difficult question. Does Jesus represent the righteousness of our own doing as that which fits us for the kingdom of heaven and gives us entrance into it? If this were the case would there not be a flat contradiction between Jesus' teaching here and that in John 3: 3, 5? And would not the teaching here be akin to legalism and not to the gospel of grace?

In reply, we must note, first of all, that the main emphasis of Jesus in this verse is the principle of exclusion. He is telling his disciples in the most emphatic terms that the righteousness of the scribes and Pharisees has no affinity with the kingdom of heaven and that a righteousness of that kind will never secure entrance into it. It is this negative emphasis that must be appreciated. If we place too much stress on the positive counterpart we disturb the burden of Jesus' message. We need not suppose that Jesus is here reflecting overtly on the way of entrance into the kingdom of heaven. Second, Jesus is not here setting forth the whole doctrine of the kingdom of heaven and certainly not the whole doctrine of the way of entrance into it. There is no allusion here to the new birth (*cf.* John 3: 3-8), nor even to what Jesus says elsewhere, 'Except ye be converted, and become as the little children, ye shall by no means enter into the kingdom of heaven' (Matthew 18: 3). It would be unjustifiable to take this text and abstract it from the other elements of Jesus' teaching which deal expressly with the question of entrance into the kingdom of heaven.

Hence, if we are to find in this verse the positive complementary truth to that of the negative, all we need to do is to recognize that, if we are to be members of the kingdom of heaven, our righteousness, that is to say, the righteousness of our attitude, character, and behaviour, will have to be of an entirely different sort; different not in respect of concern for details, but different in respect of the details for which we entertain concern, and in respect of the intensity with which the law is applied to heart, thought, and word as well as to overt action. Jesus, however, does not inform us here of the way by which we come to possess that righteousness.

The part of Jesus' discourse which follows to the end of the chapter is an application to specific commandments of the principles which had been established in verses 17-20. If we may recapitulate, there are three main lessons in verses 17-20. (1) Jesus did not come to abrogate the law. (2) The kingdom of heaven demands the most meticulous observance of the law of God, not only in its broad principles but in its minutial details. (3) There is a complete contrast between the righteousness which the kingdom of heaven requires and that exemplified in the scribes and Pharisees. These principles are applied in six specific instances directly related to Old Testament commandments. It is the third principle particularly that needs to be borne in mind in the interpretation of the sustained contrast between rabbinic and pharisaic perversion, on the one hand, and the righteousness characteristic of the kingdom of heaven, on the other.

The contrast instituted in this discourse and expressed in the repeated formula 'Ye have heard that it was said . . . but I say to you' is not a contrast between the teaching of the Old Testament and the teaching of Jesus himself.[3] It is too readily interpreted in

[3] On the antitheses in the sermon on the mount *cf.* Ned Bernard Stonehouse: *The Witness of Matthew and Mark to Christ* (Philadelphia, 1944), pp. 198ff.

this way, but there are several reasons for the rejection of this interpretation. (1) Jesus has just said, 'Do not think that I came to destroy the law or the prophets: I came not to destroy but to fulfil', and then confirmed this by the series of endorsements which we have just considered. How could he have made all these endorsements of the Old Testament and then forthwith proceed to set up his own teaching in antithesis to the law which he had established as the norm of the righteousness of the kingdom of heaven? (2) Not only would this interpretation contradict the principles which he had established in the introduction, but the teaching which follows in direct connection with these contrasts is teaching that rests upon the validity and sanctity of the Old Testament commandments. This is apparent, for example, in connection with the seventh commandment. How could Jesus have brought the indictment that 'whosoever looketh on a woman to lust after her hath committed adultery with her already in his heart' if he had in any way interfered with the permanent sanctity of the commandment, 'Thou shalt not commit adultery'? (3) If Jesus were contrasting his own teaching and the law of the Old Testament, then the formula 'Ye heard that it was said' would refer to the Old Testament Scripture. But Jesus elsewhere does not use such a formula when he refers to the Old Testament. He uses, rather, such a formula as 'it is written'. (4) In some of the most significant instances our Lord's statement as to what was spoken 'to them of old time' is not a reproduction of Old Testament Scripture, but contains additions which have no counterpart in the Old Testament. To say the least, this would lead us to suspect that what Jesus is quoting as having been said to the ancients is not Scripture precisely but Scripture plus some interpretative and applicatory comment. Hence the contrast cannot be between Scripture itself and his own teaching; that construction would not fit into the quotation which Jesus makes.

We must conclude, therefore, that the antithesis Jesus institutes repeatedly in this discourse is that between his own interpretation and application of the law of the Old Testament and the externalistic interpretation of rabbinic tradition.

When Jesus says, 'it was said to them of old time'[4] he is

---

[4] Usage would indicate that ἐρρέθη τοῖς ἀρχαίοις should be rendered thus

(continued on p. 159)

alluding to the rabbinic practice of appealing for authority to what was said of old. We have abundant evidence of this practice. The Talmud witnesses to this on almost every page in the ever-recurring formula, 'Our Rabbis taught'. There are the numerous variations of this type of appeal, such as, 'Rabbi Eleazar said', 'Rabbi Judah says in the name of Rabbi Eleazar', 'This is the view of Rabbi Meir; and the Sages say'—an endless citation and quotation of authority. Hence we cannot mistake the identity of this formula used by our Lord, 'Ye heard that it was said'.

We shall deal with a few of the instances to discover what the intent and effect of the antithesis instituted really are. The first instance, that concerned with the sixth commandment, offers us, perhaps, more assistance in discovering the direction of thought to be followed than any other. Jesus says: 'Ye heard that it was said to them of old time, Thou shalt not kill, and whosoever shall kill shall be in danger of the judgment' (Matt. 5: 21). The question would arise: How much of this is included in what was said to the ancients, the quotation from the sixth commandment together with the addition, or simply the addition? This is not an important question because on either alternative the interpretation must be the same. It is probable that the sixth commandment was quoted by the Rabbis and then interpreted in the way Jesus indicates by his quotation. The important consideration is that the Rabbis interpreted the commandment, at least its penal sanction, in these terms, 'whosoever shall kill shall be liable to the judgment'. And the question for us is: How is this interpretive comment to be understood so as to provide a contrast between the teaching of the Rabbis and the teaching of Jesus?

In view of the fact that Jesus in his own interpretation and

---

rather than 'it was said by them of old time'. Elsewhere ἐρρέθη (aor. pass. of ῥέω) when used with the simple dative means 'it was spoken to' (Romans 9: 12, 26; Galatians 3: 16; Revelation 6: 11; 9: 4). In like manner τὸ ῥηθέν (Aor. Pass. Part.) with the dative has this force (Matthew 22: 31). τὸ ῥηθέν or ὁ ῥηθείς frequently occurs in the sense of that which was 'spoken by' but in such cases it is followed by ὑπό or διά with the genitive. ἐρῶ (fut.) with the dative frequently occurs and means to 'speak to'. τὸ εἰρημένον (perf. pass. part. of εἴρω) occurs with διά (Acts 2: 16) and with ἐν (Luke 2: 24; Acts 13: 40). Usage, therefore, points to the conclusion that ἐρρέθη τοῖς ἀρχαίοις means 'it was spoken to the ancients'.

application lays the emphasis upon the inward feeling and upon the words of abusive contempt, we are forced to conclude that the addition supplied in the rabbinic tradition had the intent and effect of saying, 'Only he who commits the overt act of murder shall be liable to the judgment'. That is to say, rabbinical tradition had concentrated attention both in thought and instruction upon the external act, with the effect, if not also the intent, of restricting the prohibition of murder to the overt act. It is this externalism that Jesus proceeds to correct; he focuses attention upon the emotions of the heart and the words of the lips. 'But I say to you': in contrast with such a cabined and restricted conception of the sixth commandment, and in elucidation of its true and full intent, he teaches that the sixth commandment condemns the murder of heart and lips as well as the overt act of lawless killing. 'Everyone who is angry with his brother shall be liable to the judgment: and whosoever shall say to his brother, Raka, shall be liable to the sanhedrin: and whosoever shall say, Fool, shall be liable to the gehenna of fire' (Matthew 5: 22).

The anger which Jesus indicts as a transgression of the sixth commandment is obviously malicious, causeless anger, the unholy anger that is in line with the words of abuse and unholy resentment of which Jesus gives examples in the following clauses.

Much discussion has turned on the question: What is the force of the progression from 'the judgment' to 'the gehenna of fire'? 'The judgment' is, no doubt, the local council,[5] 'the sanhedrin'[6]

[5] Cf. Deuteronomy 1: 16-18; 16: 18-20; 25: 1-3; I Chronicles 23: 4; 26: 29; II Chronicles 19: 5-11. I am more disposed to this view of the import of κρίσις in verse 21 because of the contrast in verse 22 between κρίσις and συνέδριον. J. A. Alexander, on the contrary, thinks that 'far more obvious and suited to the context is the usual and wide sense of judicial process, without specification of the time, place, or form, in which it is conducted' (op. cit., ad loc.). The specificity of κρίσις in verse 22 makes it difficult to adopt this view.

[6] Cf. The Babylonian Talmud, tractate Sanhedrin (Soncino Press translation, London, 1935, in two volumes); Emil Schürer: A History of the Jewish People in the Time of Jesus Christ, Eng. Trans. (Edinburgh, 1890), Div. II, Vol. I, pp. 163-195; W. Bacher: art. 'Sanhedrin' in A Dictionary of the Bible, ed. James Hastings (New York, 1902), Vol. IV, pp. 397-402; Sidney B. Hoenig: The Great Sanhedrin (Philadelphia, 1953). There was the distinction between the lower Jewish courts and the Sanhedrin as the highest court of Jewish religious jurisdiction. For New Testament references to the Sanhedrin see Matthew 26: 59; Mark 14: 55; 15: 1; Luke 22: 66; John 11: 47; Acts 4: 15; 5: 21, 27, 34, 41; 6: 12, 15; 22: 30; 23: 1, 6, 15, 20; 24: 20.

is the supreme Jewish tribunal, and 'the gehenna of fire' is the place of final woe. Did Jesus then mean that 'unholy anger' was worthy only of the judgment to be executed by the local council, the contempt expressed in 'Raka' worthy of the severer judgment to be executed by the supreme tribunal, whereas the disdain expressed in the invective 'Fool' is of such gravity that the appropriate judgment is nothing less than eternal torment? It is hard to believe that this was Jesus' intent. For one thing it would be hard to find such a difference between Raka and Fool, as far as gravity of offence is concerned, that the latter makes liable to hell while the former only to the judgment of the Sanhedrin. It will hardly satisfy to find here an intentional graduation of offence with the corresponding graduation of judgment or penalty. Surely what we have here is a rhetorical device; and we can easily suppose that the purpose of this device of language is to expose the fallacy of the interpretive comment of rabbinical tradition. In regard to the sixth commandment this tradition had done two things: it confined the breach of the commandment to the overt act and in respect of the penal sanction went no further than that imposed by the local council.[7] The underestimations in both particulars are complementary. Jesus' rhetorical statement is his way of bringing forcefully to the attention of the disciples the complete contrast between his own evaluation of the gravity of murder and of its just retribution, on the one hand, and traditional evaluation, on the other. And he does this by affirming that the sin which the Rabbis had ignored as a violation of the commandment was worthy of the most ultimate judgment of all, the punishment of hell fire. He

---

[7] It is not being suggested that rabbinical tradition did not recognize capital punishment as the penalty to be exacted for murder. In the Talmud there is abundance of reference to this provision of the Old Testament as well as to the other offences which were punished by death in terms of the Mosaic law. Cf. The Babylonian Talmud (as cited above), tractate Sanhedrin, pp. 74, 224f., 355, 391, 493, 503, 518ff.; tractate Baba Kamma, p. 474. On the distinction between judgment in the first clause of verse 22 and the judgment of the Sanhedrin in the second clause cf. the interesting remarks of John Lightfoot: Horae Hebraicae et Talmudicae (Works, ed. Pitman, London, 1823, Vol. XI), pp. 107f. On the rabbinical tendency to lighten the penalties prescribed by the law of Moses, especially the death penalty, see Alfred Edersheim: History of the Jewish Nation (Grand Rapids, 1954), pp. 373ff.

thus evinced the depth and breadth of the application of the sixth commandment. Rabbinic tradition had focused attention upon the external act and assigned the judgment upon it to the local council. Jesus did not underestimate the gravity of the overt act. He enhanced our conception of its gravity by showing that the emotion of causeless and unholy anger was worthy of the judgment which the Rabbis predicated of the overt act and assigned to the words of abusive disdain and contempt a punishment which the Rabbis had left out of their reckoning entirely. The effect, in summary, of what Jesus says is that, if a contemptuous word is worthy of hell fire, how much more must the actual murder be. And the total effect of Jesus' emphasis is that murder has its fountain in the malice of the heart and has its judicial issue in the blackness of darkness for ever.

The logical connection between verses 23-26 and the two preceding verses is apparent from the terms with which verse 23 is introduced, 'if therefore'. We might think that, since Jesus is dealing in verses 21 and 22 with what falls strictly into the realm of ethical behaviour and in verses 23-26 with what principally concerns an act of worship, there is at verse 23 a transition from teaching respecting ethics to teaching respecting religion in the most specific sense of that term. It is quite true that there is transition. The two preceding verses deal specifically with ethical evaluation and verses 23-26 deal specifically with an act of specific worship; and these two subjects must be distinguished, just as the aspects of human life with which they are concerned must be. But it is precisely because there is transition, and because the aspects of human life with which they deal must be distinguished, that the logical correlation is all the more significant. The correlation advises us that, in the esteem of our Lord, ethics and worship cannot be divorced, that worship can never be made a cloak for ethical delinquency nor a method of escape from the demands of ethical integrity. Verses 23-26 are an application, within what is strictly the sphere of worship, of the demands of the sixth commandment which Jesus had distinctly enunciated in the two preceding verses. So we must ask: What relation can the demands of the sixth commandment sustain to the specific acts of worship? The answer can be stated very simply and briefly. Acceptable worship and ethical integrity are inseparable. Worship, however proper it may be in itself, however closely conformed it may be to the regulative prescriptions of divine revelation, is, nevertheless, not acceptable to God nor edifying to ourselves if it is not complemented by the strictest regard for the demands of ethical equity.

Jesus is not here declaring anything essentially new in the progress of divine revelation. He is reiterating and reinforcing the requirements of the sixth commandment in the preceding verses. Here he is reiterating and enforcing what had been emphasized again and again in the Old Testament.[8] The condemnation of hypocritical formalism in worship in the Old Testament prophets has been interpreted as a contrast between the ethical teaching of the prophets and the priestly emphasis upon the ritual code. And these passages are too readily interpreted as involving an undervaluation of the ritual of worship in favour of the requirements of ethical integrity. This is a totally false antithesis. The proper interpretation is surely the line of thought which we discover here in the teaching of our Lord.

Jesus here deals with a hypothetical case in order to illustrate the interpretation which he had just given of the sixth commandment, and to show its application to human relationships, and its bearing upon the acceptable worship of God. The features of this hypothetical case are such that they set off sharply the requirements arising from the law of conduct which must be complied with if our worship is to be preserved from mockery and hypocrisy. These features should be noted.

1. There is not the least suggestion that the formal act of worship in which the person was engaged was a wrong act or that there was anything out of place in the ritual details of his action. The action was intrinsically proper because, when certain other provisions are envisaged as having been fulfilled, Jesus does not prescribe any modification in the act of worship but says, 'Then come and offer thy gift'.

What is to be observed, then, is that the interruption of the act of worship was not for the purpose of correcting any detail of the ritual of worship but only for the purpose of remedying another circumstance of the total situation, a circumstance which

[8] *Cf.* Isaiah 1: 10-17; Amos 5: 21-24; Micah 6: 6-8.

falls into the category of the ethical, and specifically into the category of the ethic required by the sixth commandment.

2. The act of worship was to be interrupted. The charge is particularly abrupt: 'go thy way' in the sense of 'be gone'. Discontinue your act of worship. Why? The reason is that a brother has something against the worshipper. It is the *relationship* to this other person that is weighted with relevance in this case.

It is not assumed nor is it suggested that the worshipper entertains any malice against the brother. It might be or it might not be as far as the description of the case goes. But there is no intrusion of such a factor into the situation. The factor that is given as the reason for the interruption is simply and solely that there is something which the brother considers to be a culpable breach of brotherly relations on the part of the worshipper. And let it be noted still further that it is not necessary to suppose that the brother is justified in entertaining this grievance against the worshipper. The brother may have just cause of grievance or he may not. But the justice of his charge is not the reason for the interruption of the act of worship. What the worshipper is commanded to do he is commanded to do irrespective of the justice or injustice of the brother's judgment in this case.

3. What the worshipper is commanded to do is to go his way and be reconciled to the brother. This reconciliation as act consists in the removal of the grounds of disharmony; as result it consists in the resumption of relations of harmony, understanding, and peace. In a word, the worshipper is required to do what is necessary so that the brother will no longer have any grievance against him.

What is the lesson of principle, relevant to the sixth commandment, that is set forth in this hypothetical instance? It is the jealousy which we must entertain for the state of mind of other people as well as for our own, concretely the state of mind of other people as that state of mind is directed towards our persons. The worshipper may have had no fault in this case. He may well have argued with himself: 'I have no grudge against that man; I have done him no wrong; the fault lies entirely with him'. And all of this may have been true but of no avail as an argument for continuing his act of worship. Even then he must desist, be

gone, and be reconciled to his brother. He is not relieved of the
necessity of being reconciled to his offended brother. And the
reason for this is not difficult to find when we study it in the light
of the context. The grievance entertained by the brother is
something that disturbs the relationship between brethren; it
causes disharmony and estrangement. And such estrangement is
the fountain of the sin with which Jesus is here dealing, the sin
of murder. This rupture of relations the worshipper cannot
ignore even though he be faultless. This grievance on the part of
the brother may be but the rudimentary movement of estrangement. Yet, if it is not remedied, it will fester and will develop
into the antithesis of 'Thou shalt love thy neighbour as thyself'.
Here we have illustrated what our Lord considers the sixth
commandment to involve. We would not have thought that the
ramifications of the commandment were so far-reaching. It is
just the thought of the psalmist, 'I have seen an end of all perfection: but thy commandment is exceeding broad'. It extends
to the deepest recesses and most rudimentary motions of the
human spirit.

Though verses 25, 26 are not a continuation of the procedure
enjoined in reference to an offended brother, Jesus is still dealing
with the interpretation and application of the sixth commandment. The main point of these verses is that our adversaries, no
less than our brethren, come within the scope of those whose
enmity and anger we must do our utmost to placate. We must
take all reasonable measures amicably to settle litigious disputes before we become involved in those judicial judgments
from which we cannot extricate ourselves, and which place us
outside the opportunity of amicable settlement. And the reason
for this is that the animosities provoked and fostered by such
litigious disputes are the animosities which constitute a violation
of the sixth commandment. Nothing could demonstrate more
pointedly the far-reaching practical implications of the commandment. It is the counterpart in our Lord's teaching to the
teaching of the apostle, 'If possible, as much as lieth in you, be at
peace with all men. Avenge not yourselves, beloved, but give
place unto the wrath, for it is written, Vengeance is mine, I will
recompense, saith the Lord' (Romans 12: 18, 19). Again in the

Epistle to the Hebrews we have the same kind of injunction: 'Follow peace with all men, and holiness, without which no man shall see the Lord, looking diligently lest any one fail of the grace of God, lest any root of bitterness springing up trouble you, and thereby the many be defiled' (Hebrews 12: 14, 15; *cf.* James 3: 18; Matthew 5: 9).

The sixth commandment is but one concrete way of expressing the principle that human life, in all its aspects and in all its relationships, must be guarded and promoted. Have we sufficiently appreciated the fact that, in a sinless world, there would have been no 'against'? The essence of sin is comprehended in the word 'against'. Sin is first of all against God and because we are against God we are against our fellowman. It is an eloquent witness to this fact that, after the first sin of our first parents, the first overt sin in the realm of ethics that is brought to our attention in the Scripture is the sin of Cain in slaying his brother Abel. 'Cain rose up against Abel his brother, and slew him' (Genesis 4: 8). The first sin of our first parents was against God; the sin of Cain was 'against' his brother. It is this 'against' that the sixth commandment condemns and its positive counterpart is that we 'take all lawful endeavours to preserve our own life and the life of others'. The opposite of 'against' is concord, harmony, peace, and love. And the demand of love is no less than that we love our enemies (*cf.* Matthew 5: 44). We are to love those who are 'against' us. The 'against' on one side does not abrogate the requirement of love on the other; one 'against' does not justify another. It is nothing less than this that Jesus' interpretation and application of the sixth commandment exemplify. Could our Lord's ethic of human relations, summed up in the words, 'Thou shalt love thy neighbour as thyself', have come to more concrete and relevant expression than in his teaching here respecting the sixth commandment? The principle that undergirds the sixth commandment is the sanctity of life. Our Lord shows the endless ramifications of that principle and pushes his analysis to the source and fountain of its preservation and violation. The spring of its preservation is the agreement of love; the root of its violation is the rudimentary feeling of unholy enmity, the disruptive imagination of the thought of the heart whereby the concord of human relations is desecrated. The teaching of our Lord is to the effect that the sixth commandment brings within its purview the enmity of the heart and all unnecessary and unholy dispute which fans the embers of animosity.[9]

It is not necessary to regard verses 29, 30 as a parenthesis. They can well be regarded as enunciating a principle of life illustrated concretely in that with which Jesus had dealt in verse 28. The eye is the instrument of the lustful desire referred to. What could more pointedly illustrate the stumbling of verse 29 than the looking upon a woman to lust after her of verse 28? And what could more pointedly illustrate the necessity of plucking out the eye and casting it from us than that it should be the occasion of leading us into the sin with which Jesus is dealing in the preceding verses?

It does not follow, however, that the truth set forth in verses 29, 30 is to be restricted to the particular commandment which served as the convenient occasion for its expression. Obviously the lesson of verses 29, 30 has relevance to every sin. The thought is that, however precious an asset may be in itself, if this asset becomes the occasion of our falling into sin, we must be prepared to renounce it rather than be the victim of the sin of which it is the occasion. Jesus is not here teaching self-mutilation as in itself sanctifying. We must sense the rhetoric of his hyperbole. But we must not allow the simple truth here expressed to escape us. If the alternatives are the retention of something that is itself good and sin, then we must on all accounts sacrifice that good thing rather than fall into sin. Nothing of earthly possession is too precious to dispense with if sin is for us the inevitable cost of retention. This is the principle that alone explains and warrants martyrdom. The martyr sacrifices life itself and therefore *all* of temporal possession rather than commit the sin of betrayal. We cannot tone down the full literalness of this principle that there is absolutely nothing of earthly possession, including life itself, that must not be surrendered rather than fall into sin. And when we appreciate this lesson, then we do not demur at the stringency and severity of Jesus' teaching; it is tremendously real and literal. The strength of the terms used here by Matthew is to be distinctly marked: ἔξελε, βάλε, βληθῇ, ἔκκοψον, ἀπέλθῃ. The peremptori-

[9] Verses 27 and 28 have been dealt with in Chapter III. On Matthew 5: 31 32 see my book *Divorce*, pp. 17-28.

ness of the demand lies on the face of the passage, and analysis
will show that nothing less is the condition of discipleship. 'If
any man will come after me, let him deny himself' (Matthew
16: 24).

Scarcely any part of the sermon on the mount has given
occasion for more difference of interpretation and application
than that which deals with oaths and vows. 'Again ye heard that
it was said to them of old time, Thou shalt not forswear thyself,
but shalt perform unto the Lord thine oaths: but I say to you,
Swear not at all; neither by heaven, for it is God's throne; nor by
the earth, for it is the footstool of his feet; nor by Jerusalem, for
it is the city of the great King. Neither shalt thou swear by thy
head, for thou canst not make one hair white or black. But let
your speech be, Yea, yea; Nay, nay; and what is more than
these is of the evil one' (Matthew 5: 33-37). While verse 33 is
not an exact quotation from the Old Testament, yet its component parts are found there and it is probably a conflate quotation
drawn from Leviticus 19: 12; Numbers 30: 2; Deuteronomy
23: 21. The question that arises is: What was the abuse, sanctioned
and encouraged by tradition, against which our Lord directed
his reproof and correction? It is quite apparent that there must
have been some looseness in the thinking and practice of the
Jews which violated the sanctity of the oath. Otherwise there
would be no relevance in Jesus' word, 'But I say to you, Swear
not at all'. It is difficult to ascertain what this looseness in thought
and practice was. But by inference from Jesus' own words, and
from some evidence which we possess regarding rabbinical
tradition, we are able to gain some knowledge of that which
provides the background of our Lord's teaching in this passage.
The Babylonian Talmud is of later date but it does reflect
tradition which in many particulars must have been current in
the days of our Lord. The tractate on this subject of oaths does
show that, while there was considerable difference of opinion in
rabbinical tradition on various questions, yet there was a good
deal of sentiment to the effect that when substitutes for the
divine name were used in adjuration then the person thus ad-
juring was exempt from the obligation and sanction attaching to

adjuration by God's name.[10] A reading of this tractate will make obvious the sophistry by which reasoning had been degraded and the loopholes of abuse that had been given the sanction of antiquity. The teaching of our Lord becomes not only intelligible but luminous on the background of this rabbinical tradition. When he says, 'Swear not at all; neither by heaven, for it is God's throne; nor by the earth, for it is the footstool of his feet', he was striking directly at that profanity which enlisted substitutes for the name of God in order to secure the virtual emphasis of adjuration and yet at the same time sought escape from the obligations and sanctions that the use of the divine name itself would have involved. It is the evil of surreptitiously securing for oneself the advantages of adjuration while attempting to escape from its obligations and, in the event of falsehood, from the penalties attaching to perjury. We readily sense the iniquity and hypocrisy of the practice. And its iniquity is peculiarly aggravated because, in reality, it is the name of God that is being

---

[10] A few quotations will illustrate the difference of opinion and yet the prevalence of the sentiment concerned. *The Babylonian Talmud* (as cited), tractate *Shebu'oth*: '[If he said,] "I adjure you"; "I command you;" "I bind you": they are liable. "By heaven and earth!": they are exempt. "By Alef Daleth"; "by Yod He"; "by Shaddai"; "by Zebaoth"; "by the Merciful and Gracious One"; "by the Long Suffering One"; "by the One Abounding in Kindness"; or by any of the substitutes [for the name]: they are liable. He who blasphemes by any of them is liable: this is the opinion of R. Meir; but the Sages exempt him. He who curses his father or mother by any of them is liable: this is the opinion of R. Meir; but the Sages exempt him. He who curses himself or his neighbour by any of them transgresses a negative precept. [If he said,] "the Lord smite you"; or "God smite you": these are the curses written in the Torah. "May [the Lord] not smite you"; or "may he bless you"; or "may he do good unto you [if you bear testimony for me]": R. Meir makes [them] liable, but the Sages exempt [them]' (pp. 202f.). With reference to substitutes for the divine name: 'He who blasphemes by any of them is liable: this is the opinion of R. Meir; but the Sages exempt him. Our Rabbis taught: *Whosoever curseth his God shall bear his sin.* Why is it written? Is it not already said: *And he that blasphemeth the name of the Lord shall surely be put to death?*— I might think he should be liable only for the actual Name; whence do we know to include the substitutes? Therefore it is said: *Whosoever curseth his God*—in any manner; this is the opinion of R. Meir; but the Sages say: for the actual Name, [the penalty is] death; for the substitutes, there is a warning' (p. 211).

Cf. on this subject John Lightfoot: *op. cit.*, pp. 120-124.

enlisted in the service of this hypocrisy. Jesus is saying in effect: You are not relieved in the least degree from the obligations and sanctions of an oath by using the word 'heaven' as a substitute, because in adjuration the Godward reference of the word 'heaven' is inescapable. This is so for the reason that the only purpose for the use of the word in such a connection is that heaven is God's throne; it is this Godward reference that supplies the force deemed necessary, and without it the asseverative strength desired and intended would disappear.

In the same way the Godward reference of the word 'earth' is apparent; it is the Godward reference implicit in the fact that the earth is God's creation and the footstool of his feet that affords to the asseverative use of the word adjurative force. And Jerusalem would only be used for adjurative purposes because it was uniquely associated with God's presence. What Jesus is exposing therefore is the profanity involved in this surreptitious use of substitutes for the name of God; the reason for the use of the substitutes consisted in the Godward reference, and yet it was supposed that the substitutions relieved of the sanctions which adjuratory appeal to God entailed.

We can also see the implications for perjury of this kind of sophistry. If substitutes such as heaven, earth, and Jerusalem are not to be regarded as implying the obligations and sanctions of the use of the actual name of God, then even falsehoods enforced by the aid of these substitutes would not be in the category of perjury. They would be falsehoods, indeed, and falsehoods enforced by this kind of asseveration. But they would not be wrongs of such an aggravated character simply because they fell short of perjury; the persons would not be guilty of a false *oath*. By implication, at least, Jesus was exposing the fallacy of this subterfuge, and he is saying in effect that we are not relieved of the sin of perjury if we asseverate falsely by such terms as heaven, earth, and Jerusalem.

The next question which our Lord's teaching here poses for us is: Does Jesus condemn all oath-taking?[11] The injunction 'swear not at all' appears to many to bear this import. For it can be pleaded plausibly that this is an absolute statement, and how can we qualify it? It should be borne in mind in this connection

[11] *Cf.* Stonehouse: *op. cit.*, pp. 206f.

what an oath is. It is a solemn protestation in which we call upon the name of God to bear witness to the truth of what we are affirming. It is therefore a strictly religious exercise. A promissory oath is of the same religious character and is distinguished from the oath proper only in this that it is a *promise* in which we appeal to God to witness our sincerity of heart and faithfulness of purpose. And so the question is: Does Jesus here proscribe all such swearing? If this were the case we should encounter insuperable difficulty. Our Lord's teaching would be in conflict with Scripture analogy. There are the following considerations.

(1) The oath is sanctioned and even commanded in Scripture under certain conditions (*cf.* Deuteronomy 6: 13; 10: 20; Romans 1: 9; II Corinthians 1: 23; Philippians 1: 8; I Thessalonians 2: 5, 10). (2) If Jesus condemned all oath-taking, we should have to regard these New Testament instances as wrong and the Old Testament instances as concessions without any intrinsic sanction or legitimation. It would be difficult to the point of impossibility to think of Paul as violating expressly a prohibition of the Lord in those cases cited. And the Old Testament instances can hardly be placed in the category of concessions. (3) God himself is represented as having sworn (Genesis 22: 16; Psalm 110: 4; Hebrews 6: 17, 18). It is true that God may do what we may not do. But in the context of Scripture injunction and example, what God has done in this particular suggests, at least, that this is one of those things in which God's action is a pattern for us. (4) The most reasonable, if not necessary, interpretation of Matthew 26: 63, 64 is that Jesus consented to the oath form of asseveration. If Jesus consented to an oath, how could we regard him as violating his own canon? (5) We are not violating good and necessary principles of interpretation if we regard the word of Jesus, 'swear not at all', though absolute in its terms, as having reference simply to the kind of profanity with which he was expressly dealing, the disguised swearing of which Jesus proceeds forthwith to give examples. In other words, if we infer that what Jesus *unreservedly* prohibits is the subterfuge with which he is expressly dealing, namely, the surreptitious use of terms which have a Godward reference on the supposition that thereby we get away from profane and false *swearing*, then we have not only an acceptable but a sufficient interpretation of the prohibition,

'swear not at all'. If this is a tenable view of Jesus' reference, and if it is a view that is consonant with the analogy of Scripture, then it is the interpretation which we are compelled to adopt. (6) This interpretation explains the terms of verse 37. If we were to take verse 37 with the literalness with which some contend we must take the words 'swear not at all' in verse 34, then we should have the sharpest conflict between Jesus' injunction in verse 37 and his own practice, an impossible supposition. If we recognize, as we must, that verse 37 is to be interpreted as directed against and proscribing the profanity with which Jesus is concerned in verses 34-36, then the same kind of restrictive reference which we must find in verse 37 should be applied to the injunction of verse 34, to wit, 'swear not at all'.

For these various reasons we are compelled to the conclusion that Jesus does not prohibit all oath-taking, but only such oath-taking as violates the conditions under which the oath, as an act of religious worship, must be undertaken.

Assuming that Jesus does not condemn all swearing, are we to interpret verses 34-36 as implying that in taking an oath, whether it be in the form of protestation or promise, we should use only the name of God and not any of the substitutes of which Jesus here gives examples? A negative answer to this question appears to be required. (1) There are instances in Scripture where sacred oaths were taken in terms of expressions other than that of God's name expressly (cf. Genesis 42: 15; I Samuel 1: 26; 17: 55; II Kings 2: 2, 4, 6). (2) In Matthew 23: 17-22 Jesus deals with a situation similar to that with which he deals in the sermon on the mount and with one closely pertinent to our question. In this case he does not condemn the practice of swearing by the temple, or by the altar, or by heaven. But he is emphasizing that which is the main thought of Matthew 5: 34-36, namely, that if we swear by the temple we swear by it and 'by him that dwelleth therein', and if we swear by heaven we swear 'by the throne of God, and by him that sitteth thereon'. There is no suggestion that the use of such terms is improper so long as we realize the Godward reference and understand that the adjuratory use carries all the implications of the direct and express use of the name of God. (3) It would be difficult to understand the principle that Jesus is enunciating in both passages, namely, that the adjuratory use of the symbols of God's glory carries all the weight of the direct use of God's name, if the use of substitutes were in itself illegitimate. If, when we use the word 'heaven', we refer to God's throne and to him who sits on it (Matthew 23: 22), surely no impiety can attach to this solemn and religious use of the word 'heaven' any more than the use of such a substitute in prayer or praise would involve impiety.

The final question that may be asked is: Does Scripture or Jesus here by implication, condemn all voluntary swearing, even if it is religious and serious? The question would be unnecessary were it not the case that some have maintained that the only kind of swearing which is permissible is that which is imposed upon us by legitimate authority.[12] This position is not tenable if we are to be guided by biblical examples. In both Testaments there are examples of the use of the oath which cannot be regarded as oaths required or imposed by some constituted authority. Examples already given will illustrate. These are oaths declared in all seriousness and with reverence because the occasion was recognized by the oath-taker as one properly calling for the use of such appeal to the divine witness and yet there was no requirement arising from any human institution.

What our Lord is condemning in this passage (Matthew 5: 33-37) is all irreverent, needless, disguised, and surreptitious swearing. He was dealing with an abuse current not only then but now, the practice of reinforcing affirmations or denials or promises by expressions which have the force of adjuration, but which we may think for one reason or another do not carry such weight, and so we suppose that we are not guilty of profane or false swearing. And Jesus is striking not only at irreverence but also at the untruthfulness and falsehood which, in reality, lie back of this practice and give rise to it. The irony of the practice is this, that resort to these means of asseveration presupposes the assumption that this kind of reinforcement is necessary in order to secure credit. And this means that our simple word is not enough; our word is suspect. What our Lord is pleading for is simplicity, honesty, forthrightness of expression in the interest of truth and truthfulness. A simple 'yes' or 'no' should be enough for credit. Our Lord came to bear witness to the truth, and his

[12] *Cf.* Joseph Addison Alexander: *op. cit. ad* Matthew 5: 37.

kingdom is one in which the sanctity of truth is paramount. The mark of truth is chastity of speech. If we are truthful and if our tongues are mellowed by the love of truth, we shall not need to embellish and reinforce our affirmations, denials, and promises by expressions which are the coinage of profanity and ultimately of untruthfulness. It is when we assess our Lord's teaching in this context that his word is full of meaning: 'But let your speech be, Yea, yea; Nay, nay; and whatsoever is more than these is of the evil one' (Matthew 5: 37).

The next paragraph in the sermon on the mount deals with what is known as the *lex talionis*. When Jesus refers to that which had been said, namely, 'an eye for an eye, and a tooth for a tooth', he is quoting literally from the Mosaic law (Exodus 21: 24; Leviticus 24: 20; Deuteronomy 19: 21). While it would not be contrary to the analogy of our Lord's teaching elsewhere to regard him as here abrogating the regulatory penal provisions of the Mosaic economy (which could not be regulatory in the New Testament age) and in that respect doing in this case what he had done in reference to divorce in Matthew 5: 31, 32, yet it would appear to be more in accord with the thrust of this discourse as a whole to find here also some abuse to which the Old Testament provision had been subjected, an abuse which Jesus proceeds to correct.

The *lex talionis* was part of the Mosaic jurisprudence; it was one of the measures instituted for the penalizing of injury inflicted. It was part of the order of public justice and not of private revenge. It is easy to see how this distinction could be overlooked or discarded and two distortions would readily result: (1) the transfer to private life of a rule which applied only in the sphere of public justice; (2) the misappropriation of the provision to justify personal vindictiveness. The latter distortion would be more heinous than the first because it proceeds from a misconstruction of the motive in criminal punishment. Retribution is never for the purpose of placating vindictive revenge but for the purpose of satisfying justice. Justice is not vindictive though it is vindicatory.

We can reasonably infer that this is the evil Jesus has in view— vindictiveness which seeks personal revenge and wreaks it if possible. The series of injunctions takes on meaning in that context. How totally different is the attitude of mind reflected in the conduct which Jesus enjoins from that which is vengeful and calculating in terms of repayment.

When Jesus says, 'Resist not him that is evil', we are not to suppose that he is inculcating passive non-resistance under all circumstances of attack upon our persons or property, and that when injured or insulted we are to invite more. We must make allowance for the rhetorical hyperbole which we find elsewhere in Jesus' teaching. The form of statement is dictated by the necessity of showing the complete contrast in personal relations between the attitudes and reactions of the disciple of Christ and the attitudes and reactions of the person controlled by vengeful passion. It is the same contrast that must obtain even in legal and judicial proceedings. 'And if any man would go to law with thee, and take away thy coat, let him have thy cloak also' (Matthew 5: 40). The lesson is surely not that we are to avoid all appeal to public justice as administered by magisterial authority. But, in line with what we have found in verses 25, 26, our Lord is inculcating the virtue of forbearance, even with reference to those who do us injustice, and the necessity of resigning ourselves to privations which spring from the miscarriage of justice.

The sum of the passage (Matthew 5: 38-42) can be stated negatively and positively. Negatively, when subjected to wrongs of various kinds, when our rights are infringed upon and our liberties invaded, let us not be animated and our conduct dictated by vindictive resentment.[13] Positively, let us be generous and forbearing even to those who inflict wrong. Is this not the royal law from which we are never released? It is that propounded by an apostle in plain didactic terms. 'Render to no man evil for evil. Take thought for things honourable in the sight of all men. If it be possible, as much as lieth in you, be at peace with all men. Avenge not yourselves, beloved, but give place to the wrath: for it is written, Vengeance is mine, I will recompense, saith the Lord. But if thine enemy hunger, feed him; if he thirst, give him drink: for in so doing thou shalt heap coals of fire upon his head. Be not overcome of the evil, but overcome the evil with the good' (Romans 12: 17-21; cf. Proverbs 25: 21, 22; Hebrews 10: 30; 12: 14, 15).

[18] Cf. Stonehouse: op. cit., p. 208.

No part of our Lord's teaching bears upon the Christian ethic with greater effect than that which we find in Matthew 5: 43-48. When he says, 'Ye heard that it was said, Thou shalt love thy neighbour and hate thine enemy', he undoubtedly has in mind some distortion of Old Testament teaching. By what reasoning tradition had come to append to the Old Testament injunction 'Thou shalt love thy neighbour' (Leviticus 19: 18) the addition 'Thou shalt hate thine enemy' it is difficult to determine.[14] But that this addition or inference is without warrant is apparent, and Jesus proceeds to correct the perversion. 'But I say to you, Love your enemies and pray for those who persecute you.' There are lessons of far-reaching significance to be derived from our Lord's words.

The reason Jesus gives why the disciples should love their enemies is that, by so doing, they might be sons of their Father who is in heaven. As sons of the Father they must reflect the character of him who has adopted and begotten them; they must resemble him in attitude, disposition, and conduct. This blunt assertion may seem to be irreverent. Who among the sons of men can be like unto the Lord? It is indeed true that, in one sense, to aspire to be like God would be the essence of iniquity. Was this not the pivot of the tempter's appeal to Eve in the garden, 'Ye shall be as God, knowing good and evil'? It was because Eve gave sympathetic entertainment to such an averment and coveted such a prerogative that she fell. Yes, to seek to be as God and to place ourselves on a parity with God is the deadliest sin. It is the contradiction of all the virtue that originally characterized man and of the virtue unto which man is redeemed.

But to be like God in the sense of reflecting his image in knowledge, righteousness, and holiness is the essence of divine obligation and the glory of human virtue. This shows us how fine

---

[14] It might be that the process of thought was approximately as follows. The Old Testament said, 'Thou shalt love thy neighbour as thyself' (Leviticus 19: 18). Since this referred expressly only to one's neighbour, it might have been inferred that the requirement did not apply to those who were outside this category, and therefore not to an enemy. And since there was no requirement to love one's enemy the opposite emotion might properly be entertained toward him. At least, such a frame of mind would be compatible with the self-complacent and self-righteous isolationism which we find among the Pharisees of Jesus' day. Cf. J. A. Alexander: op. cit., ad Matthew 5: 43.

is the line between virtue and sin, right and wrong, life and death. To aspire to be like God in one sense is the essence of virtue, to aspire to be like him in another sense is iniquity. To preserve this line of distinction is indispensable to all right thinking on truth and right.

The disciples must love their enemies. The reason is that they, the disciples, are sons of God, and therefore they must be like God in attitude and behaviour. This is the basic truth connected with ethical demand. In the last analysis, why must we behave in one way and not in another? Is it because experience has proved the one to be better than the other, that the one leads to happiness and contentment and the other to misery and ruin? Our Lord in this passage sets forth the only proper criterion. The ultimate standard of right is the character or nature of God. The basis of ethics is that God is what he is, and we must be conformed to what he is in holiness, righteousness, truth, goodness, and love. Any doctrine of God's transcendence which, in effect, removes the character and action of God from all relevance to our obligation destroys the foundation of ethical demand. God made man in his own image and after his likeness. Man must, therefore, be like God.

It needs to be noted, however, that when Jesus says, 'in order that ye may be sons of your Father who is in heaven', he is not making a general statement to the effect that God is the Father of all men, good and evil, just and unjust. He does not say that it is because God is the Father of all men that he sends rain upon the just and the unjust and makes his sun to shine upon the evil and the good. Jesus does say that those whom he is addressing, and who will reflect the attitude and beneficence of the Father, are sons of the Father. But he does not say, nor does he imply, that all those who are the recipients of God's favours are sons of the Father who is in heaven. It is true that it is the Father in heaven who sends the favours of his beneficent providence upon all without discrimination; it is the heavenly Father who is the God of providence. But it is not said that he is Father in heaven to all. Our Lord refrains from the use of terms which would carry that implication.

The appeal to the beneficence of God in making his sun to rise upon evil and good and in sending rain upon just and unjust is for the purpose of commending to his disciples the necessity of loving their enemies. The implication is that it is because there is lovingkindness in God that he sends rain and sunshine upon unjust as well as just. It is not simply that the gifts of rain and sunshine are bestowed, not simply that just and unjust receive and enjoy these blessings; it is implied that these gifts bestowed are expressions of the goodness and lovingkindness of God to them. If any doubt should be entertained as to the presence of this sequence in Matthew 5: 44, 45, it is placed beyond all doubt by a parallel passage in Luke. 'But I say to you who hear, Love your enemies, do good to those who hate you, bless those who curse you, pray for those who despitefully use you . . . But love your enemies and do good and lend, hoping for nothing again. And your reward will be great, and ye shall be sons of the Most High, because he is kind to the unthankful and to the evil' (Luke 6: 27, 28, 35, 36). The reason why God bestows these gifts is that he is kind even to the evil. There is in God a disposition of lovingkindness, and gifts bestowed and enjoyed are the expressions of that lovingkindness. Jesus is commending this sequence to his disciples *because* it is the sequence in their heavenly Father. They must emulate their Father in heaven. *Love* your enemies and *do them good*; this reflects the heavenly exemplar.

From another angle of thought this expresses the same principle as we found earlier in another connection. The disciples are not to render evil for evil (verses 38-42). Their ethic is not to be that of *quid pro quo*; it is not to be one of reciprocation. So now, in the matter of love and well-doing, they are not to calculate in the commercial terms of receipt and indebtedness and compensation. 'For if ye love them that love you, what reward have ye? do not even the publicans the same? And if ye salute your brethren only, what do ye more than others? do not even the Gentiles the same?' (verses 46, 47). It is the divine example that is to be the pattern. If God's dealings with men were after the fashion of *quid pro quo*, of reciprocation and compensation, what of good should we sinners receive? God's kindness to the evil and all the favours bestowed are of pure grace. So must our conduct be patterned.

These passages have been a source of difficulty to many in connection with military warfare. How can we engage in war if Christ's ethic is that we should love our enemies, bless them who curse us, do good to them who hate us, and pray for them who despitefully use us? Is not non-resistance the only ethic for a believer?

It must be admitted that much actual warfare and a great deal of the atrocity perpetrated in the conduct of war are utterly contrary to the requirements of our Lord's teaching and are to be unsparingly denounced. It is also true that war arises from failure to conform to the attitudes and principles inculcated by the Lord. If there were no sin there would be no war.

But the interpretation and application of these passages, which would brand all war as sinful and participation in war as wrong, proceed from failure to make necessary distinctions. The demand of love, unrelenting and all-pervasive as it is, does not abrogate the demand of justice. Love is not inconsistent with the infliction of punishment for wrong. Love is first of all love to God, and therefore love of justice. Hence, when we view the demand of love in its broader proportions, the demand of love and the demand of justice are really one. A just war is simply war undertaken and conducted in the defence and promotion of the dictates of justice; there can be no incompatibility between the demands of love and the conduct of such a war. The wounding and killing involved are the use of the sword which God has put into the hand of the civil magistrate as the instrument of maintaining justice and punishing evil-doers. The sword is never intrinsically, and should never be in practice, the instrument of vindictive and malicious hate. Whenever a nation, or even a soldier on the field of battle, uses the weapons of war as the instruments of vindictive revenge rather than as the instruments of retributive justice, then the dictates of both justice and love are desecrated. This is to say that war is never just when it is the instrument of hate. It is hate that contradicts love, and it always does. But war in the protection and vindication of justice is not prompted by hate but by the love of justice, and such love never contradicts the love of our enemies which the Lord himself always and unequivocally demands.

All that Jesus has been saying in these verses (43-47) is brought to summary expression in his concluding word, 'Ye therefore shall be perfect as your heavenly Father is perfect' (verse 48). No doubt the thought is focused in the aspect of the Father's perfection exemplified in lovingkindness manifested to the ungodly. And, in like manner, the demand of God's perfection is focused in loving our enemies and doing them good. But we cannot suppress the generic character of this statement, 'Ye therefore shall be perfect as your heavenly Father is perfect'. It covers the whole range of divine perfection as it bears upon human behaviour, and it utters the most ultimate consideration regulative of human disposition and conduct. The reason of the biblical ethic is God's perfection; the basic criterion of ethical behaviour is God's perfection; the ultimate goal of the ethical life is conformity to God's perfection. Surely nothing less is implicit in Jesus' word.

How inadequate is any interpretation of the sermon on the mount that relegates its ethic to another dispensation and excludes its relevance from life here and now! One wonders what kind of ethical standard or what conception of God's perfection can underlie such a construction. The ethical requirements of the sermon on the mount reach their climax in the word of Jesus, 'Ye therefore shall be perfect as your heavenly Father is perfect'. And shall we say that this standard can ever cease to be relevant? It is to trifle with the sanctities which ever bind us as creatures of God, made in his image, to think that anything less than perfection conformable to the Father's own could be the norm and the goal of the believer's ethic. It is precisely this that underlies the sermon on the mount; it is this that it inculcates; in this it finds its epitome. And that, in summary, is the ethic which our Lord's teaching exhibits.

CHAPTER VIII

LAW AND GRACE

No subject is more intimately bound up with the nature of the gospel than that of law and grace. In the degree to which error is entertained at this point, in the same degree is our conception of the gospel perverted. An erroneous conception of the function of law can be of such a character that it completely vitiates our view of the gospel; and an erroneous conception of the antithesis between law and grace can be of such a character that it demolishes both the substructure and the superstructure of grace. Nothing could advertise this more than the fact that two of the major Epistles of the New Testament, and the two most polemic, have this subject as their theme. Our attention is irresistibly drawn to the gravity of the issue with which the apostle is concerned in his Epistle to the Galatians when we read at the outset, 'But even if we or an angel from heaven preach to you any gospel other than that which we have preached to you, let him be anathema. As we have said before, so now again I say, if anyone preach any gospel to you other than that which ye received, let him be anathema' (Galatians 1: 8, 9). And we are no less startled when we read in the same apostle's Epistle to the Romans, 'I say the truth in Christ, I lie not, my conscience bearing witness with me in the Holy Spirit, that I have great sorrow and unceasing pain in my heart. For I could wish that I myself were anathema from Christ on behalf of my brethren, my kinsmen according to the flesh' (Romans 9: 1-3). What was the question that aroused the apostle to such passionate zeal and holy indignation, indignation that has its kinship with the imprecatory utterances of the Old Testament? In a word it was the relation of law and gospel. 'I do not make void the grace of God: for if righteousness is through the law, then Christ died in vain' (Galatians 2: 21). 'For if a law had been given which could make alive, verily from the law righteousness would have been' (Galatians 3: 21). 'By the works of the law shall no flesh be justified in his sight' (Romans 3: 20).

The simple truth is that if law is conceived of as contributing in the least degree towards our acceptance with God and our justification by him, then the gospel of grace is a nullity. And the issue is so sharply and incisively drawn that, if we rely in any respect upon compliance with law for our acceptance with God, then Christ will profit us nothing. 'Ye have been discharged from Christ whosoever of you are justified by law; ye have fallen away from grace' (Galatians 5: 4). But lest we should think that the whole question of the relation of law and grace is thereby resolved, we must be reminded that Paul says also in this polemic, 'Do we then make void the law through faith? God forbid, yea we establish the law' (Romans 3: 31). We are compelled therefore to recognize that the subject of law and grace is not simply concerned with the antithesis that there is between law and grace, but also with law as that which makes grace necessary and with grace as establishing and confirming law. It is not only the doctrine of grace that must be jealously guarded against distortion by the works of law, but it is also the doctrine of law that must be preserved against the distortions of a spurious concept of grace. This is just saying that we are but echoing the total witness of the apostle of the Gentiles as the champion of the gospel of grace when we say that we must guard grace from the adulteration of legalism and we must guard law from the depredations of antinomianism.[1]

In relation to the topic with which we are concerned now it is the latter that must claim our attention. What is the place of law in the economy of grace?

It is symptomatic of a pattern of thought current in many evangelical circles that the idea of keeping the commandments of God is not consonant with the liberty and spontaneity of the Christian man, that *keeping* the law has its affinities with legalism and with the principle of works rather than with the principle of grace. It is strange indeed that this kind of antipathy to the notion of keeping commandments should be entertained by any believer who is a serious student of the New Testament. Did not our Lord say, 'If ye love me, ye will keep my commandments' (John 14: 15)? And did he not say, 'If ye keep my commandments, ye shall abide in my love, even as I have kept my Father's

[1] See Appendix E, pp. 263ff.

commandments and abide in his love' (John 15: 10)? It was John who recorded these sayings of our Lord and it was he, of all the disciples, who was mindful of the Lord's teaching and example regarding love, and reproduces that teaching so conspicuously in his first Epistle. We catch something of the tenderness of his entreaty when he writes, 'Little children, let us not love in word, neither in tongue, but in deed and truth' (I John 3: 18), 'Beloved, let us love one another, for love is of God" (I John 4: 7). But the message of John has escaped us if we have failed to note John's emphasis upon the keeping of the commandments of God. 'And by this we know that we know him, if we keep his commandments. He that says, I know him, and does not keep his commandments, is a liar, and the truth is not in him. But whoso keeps his word, in him verily the love of God is made perfect' (I John 2: 3-5). 'Beloved, if our heart does not condemn, we have confidence toward God, and whatsoever we ask we receive from him, because we keep his commandments and do those things that are well-pleasing in his sight . . . And he who keeps his commandments abides in him and he in him' (I John 3: 21, 22, 24). 'For this is the love of God, that we keep his commandments' (I John 5: 3). If we are surprised to find this virtual identification of love to God and the keeping of his commandments, it is because we have overlooked the words of our Lord himself which John had remembered and learned well: 'If ye keep my commandments, ye shall abide in my love' (John 15: 10) and 'He that hath my commandments and keepeth them, he it is that loveth me' (John 14: 21). To say the very least, the witness of our Lord and the testimony of John are to the effect that there is indispensable complementation; love will be operative in the *keeping* of God's commandments. It is only myopia that prevents us from seeing this, and when there is a persistent animosity to the notion of keeping commandments the only conclusion is that there is either gross ignorance or malignant opposition to the testimony of Jesus.

A great deal of the antipathy to the idea of obligation to keep the commandments of God has arisen from misconception regarding the word of the apostle Paul, 'Ye are not under law but under grace' (Romans 6: 14). And much apparent support may be derived from this text to justify and reinforce this antipathy. It is easy to see how an insistence that believers are under obligation to keep the law of God would seem to contradict the express statement of the apostle that believers are not under law. In like manner, when Paul says that 'before faith came we were kept in ward under law, shut up to the faith about to be revealed' (Galatians 3: 23), it is obvious that the bondage implied in being kept in ward under law is terminated with the revelation of faith. Hence to speak of the believer as bound to the obedience of God's law is to bring the believer again into that bondage which it is the great burden of Paul in both Romans and Galatians to resist and controvert! 'For freedom has Christ made us free: let us stand fast therefore and not be entangled again in the yoke of bondage' (Galatians 5: 1).

It must be appreciated that when Paul says in Romans 6: 14, 'Ye are not under law but under grace', there is the sharpest possible antithesis between 'under law' and 'under grace', and that in terms of Paul's intent in this passage these are mutually exclusive. To be 'under law' is to be under the dominion of sin; to be 'under grace' is to be liberated from that dominion. What then is the antithesis and how does it bear upon our question? To answer this question it is necessary to establish what law as law can do and what law as law cannot do.

What law can do is in some respects quite obvious, in other respects frequently overlooked. (1) Law commands and demands; it propounds what the will of God is. The law of God is the holiness of God coming to expression for the regulation of thought and conduct consonant with his holiness. We must be perfect as God is perfect; the law is that which the perfection of God dictates in order to bring about conformity with his perfection. (2) Law pronounces approval and blessing upon conformity to its demands. The commandment was ordained to life (Romans 7: 10), and the man that does the things of the law will live in them (Galatians 3: 12). Law not only enunciates justice; it guards justice. It ensures that where there is righteousness to the full extent of its demand there will be the corresponding justification and life. Only when there is deviation from its demands does any adverse judgment proceed from the law. (3) Law pronounces the judgment of condemnation upon every infraction of its precept. The law has nought but curse for any person who has once broken its sanctity; he who is guilty at one point is guilty of all. 'Cursed is every one that continueth not in all things written in the book of the law to do them' (Galatians 3 : 10). (4) Law exposes and convicts of sin. It exposes the sin that may lie hid in the deepest recesses of the heart. The law is Spiritual and as the word of God it is living and powerful, searching the thoughts and intents of the heart (*cf.* Romans 7: 14; Hebrews 4: 12). It is this discriminating and searching function of the law that Paul describes when he says. 'I had not known lust except the law had said, Thou shalt not covet' (Romans 7: 7); the law lays bare the self-complacency that blinds us to the depravity of our hearts. (5) Law excites and incites sin to more virulent and violent transgression. Law, of itself, so far from renewing and reforming the depraved heart, only occasions more intensified and confirmed expression of its depravity. 'But sin taking occasion through the commandment wrought in me all manner of lust' (Romans 7: 8; *cf.* verses 9, 11, 13). The law, therefore, instead of relieving or relaxing our bondage to sin, intensifies and confirms that bondage. The more the light of the law shines upon and in our depraved hearts, the more the enmity of our minds is roused to opposition, and the more it is made manifest that the mind of the flesh is not subject to the law of God, neither can be.

What law as law cannot do is implicit in what we have found to be the utmost of its potency. (1) Law can do nothing to justify the person who in any particular has violated its sanctity and come under its curse. Law, as law, has no expiatory provision; it exercises no forgiving grace; and it has no power of enablement to the fulfilment of its own demand. It knows no clemency for the remission of guilt; it provides no righteousness to meet our iniquity; it exerts no constraining power to reclaim our waywardness; it knows no mercy to melt our hearts in penitence and new obedience. (2) It can do nothing to relieve the bondage of sin; it accentuates and confirms that bondage. It is this impossibility to alleviate the bondage of sin that is particularly in view in Romans 6: 14. The person who is 'under law', the person upon whom only law has been brought to bear, the person whose life has been determined exclusively by the resources and potencies of law, is the bondservant of sin. And the more intelligently and resolutely a person commits himself to law the more abandoned becomes his slavery to sin. Hence deliverance from the bondage of sin must come from an entirely different source.

It is in this light that the apostle's antithetical expression 'under grace' becomes significant. The word 'grace' sums up everything that by way of contrast with law is embraced in the provisions of redemption. In terms of Paul's teaching in this context the redemptive provision consists in our having become dead to the law by the body of Christ (Romans 7: 4). Believers died with Christ and they lived again with him in his resurrection (*cf.* Romans 6: 8). They have, therefore, come *under* all the resources of redeeming and renewing grace which find their epitome in the death and resurrection of Christ and find their permanent embodiment in him who was dead and is alive again. The virtue which ever continues to emanate from the death and resurrection of Christ is operative in them through union with Christ in the efficacy of his death and the power of his resurrection life. All of this Paul's brief expression 'under grace' implies. And in respect of the subject with which Paul is dealing there is an absolute antithesis between the potency of law and the potency of grace, between the provisions of law and the provisions of grace. Grace is the sovereign will and power of God coming to expression, not for the regulation of thought and conduct consonant with God's holiness, but for the deliverance of men from thought and conduct that bind them to the servitude of unholiness. Grace is deliverance from the dominion of sin and therefore deliverance from that which consists in transgression of the law.

The purity and integrity of the gospel stand or fall with the absoluteness of the antithesis between the function and potency of law, on the one hand, and the function and potency of grace, on the other. But while all this is true it does not by any means follow that the antithesis eliminates all relevance of the law to the believer as a believer. The facile slogan of many a professed evangelical, when confronted with the claims of the law of God, to the effect that he is not under law but under grace, should at least be somewhat disturbed when it is remembered that the same apostle upon whose formula he relies said also that he was not without law to God but under law to Christ (I Corinthians 9: 21). This statement of the apostle demands careful examination because it bears the implication that Paul was under law to God and he expressly states that he was under law to Christ. It would seem as if he said the opposite of what he says in Romans 6: 14. But in any case what Paul says to the Corinthians prohibits us from taking the formula 'not under law' as the complete account of the relation of the believer to the law of God.

Paul is affirming that he was all things to all men—to Jews as a Jew, to those under law as under law, to those without law as without law. There is an anomalous contrast here; his conduct at one time would seem to be the moral opposite of what it was at another time. In relation to some he was 'as under law' (ὡς ὑπὸ νόμον), in relation to others he was 'as without law' (ὡς ἄνομος). And it is not only the apparent contradictoriness of the modes of conduct that strikes us as strange; the expressions in themselves are anomalous. How can Paul speak of himself as acting at any time as one 'under law'? And how can he speak of himself as acting 'without law'? It is not only we, his readers, who sense the anomaly; Paul himself anticipates the question and the implicit objection. Hence he is well aware of the necessity of guarding both expressions from misunderstanding. He adds in reference to the first, 'not being myself under law', and in reference to the second, 'not being without law to God but under law to Christ'.

Examination of this passage will disclose something very important respecting Paul's use of the expression 'under law'. When he says that for those under law he behaved as one 'under law', he cannot mean that he behaved as one 'under law' in the sense in which he uses that expression in Romans 6: 14. In that passage 'under law' bears the sense, or at least the implication, of being in bondage to sin. But Paul in I Corinthians 9: 20, 21 cannot in the least be suggesting that he behaved as one under bondage to sin. Such a thought is inconceivable and therefore completely removed from the universe of discourse. So he must be using the expression 'under law' in some sense other than that of Romans 6: 14. And the precise meaning is not obscure. He means 'under law' in the sense in which Jews who had not yet understood the significance of the death and resurrection of Christ for the discontinuance of the Mosaic rites and ceremonies considered themselves to be under law, and therefore obliged to keep the rites and customs of the Mosaic economy. When Paul characterizes the people in question as those under law, he is not reflecting upon their moral and spiritual state as one of bondage to sin. All unbelievers are in that category of being in bondage to sin and therefore 'under law' in the sense of Romans 6: 14; consequently the characterization, 'under law' of Romans 6: 14 would not differentiate between the diverse sorts of people whom Paul has in view in I Corinthians 9. It must be therefore that 'under law' in this latter instance carries the import of being under the rites and ceremonies of the Mosaic economy. We are not to suppose that Paul is admitting that any at that stage of redemptive revelation were in reality bound to the observance of the Mosaic rites; he is reflecting simply upon what a certain group of people considered to be their obligation. And when he says that he was for such as one under law, he means that he accommodated himself to the customs and rites which these people observed and to which they considered themselves obligated.

This force of the expression 'under law' throws a great deal of light upon the same expression in Galatians 3: 23: 'Before faith came we were kept in ward under law'. The context makes it abundantly clear that what Paul means by the law in this context is the Mosaic economy. In the preceding verses he asks the question, 'What then is the law?' and he answers, 'It was added on account of the transgressions' (Galatians 3: 19). He is thinking of that economy which was instituted four hundred and thirty years after the giving of the promise to Abraham (cf. verse 17), that economy which, he says, was 'ordained through angels in the hand of a mediator' (verse 19). When, in verse 23, he says that 'before faith came we were kept in ward under law' he is contrasting the pedagogical nonage and tutelage of the Mosaic economy with the mature sonship and liberty enjoyed by the New Testament believer. He is not here equating the 'under law' of which he speaks with the same expression in Romans 6: 14; he is not suggesting, far less is he intimating, that the people of Israel who were kept in ward 'under law' were under the bondage of sin which is the obvious import of the 'under law' of Romans 6: 14.

In like manner when Paul says in I Corinthians 9: 20 that he became to those under law as under law, he is referring to those who had not yet recognized the epochal change that had been signalized by the New Testament redemptive events, and to his own behaviour in conforming by way of concession to the prejudices and customs of those who considered themselves bound by what were in reality only the temporary provisions of the older economy. And when he appends the qualifying clause, 'not being myself under law', he means that, though accommodating himself by way of expediency to these customs, he did not consider himself under any divine obligation to observe such rites and practices; he was not himself under that law. Again we see how impossible it is to apply the same sense of 'not under law' in Romans 6: 14 to the 'not under law' of I Corinthians 9: 20. For if we were to do this then we should have to understand Paul as adjusting his behaviour to the practices of those who were under the dominion of sin, an utterly impossible and unthinkable supposition.

The second qualification which Paul felt constrained to make in I Corinthians 9: 20, 21 is the one that is more directly germane to our topic: 'not being without law to God but under law to Christ'. He is guarding himself against the inference that, in becoming to those without law as without law, he recognized himself as free from obligation to the law of God and of Christ. What he means when he says that to those without law he became as without law is that, in his relations with such people, he did not conform to Mosaic customs and ordinances. 'Without law' in this case is the contrary of 'under law' in the same context. And since 'under law' means conformity to Mosaic rites, 'without law' means the opposite, namely, nonconformity with such rites. But lest this assertion of nonconformity should be misunderstood as implying release from all conformity to law he immediately adds that he is bound in and to the law of God and of Christ. Paul is not lawless in respect to God; he is law-bound in respect to Christ.

The expression Paul uses, 'under law to Christ', is a particularly impressive one. It is as if he had said 'inlawed to Christ', 'bound in law to Christ', 'under the obligation of the law of Christ'. The intent of Paul's terms is not to contrast the law of God and the law of Christ, as if he had said, 'not under law to God but rather under law to Christ'. The negative clause is not at all, 'not under law to God', but 'not without law to God'. The implication is that he is under law to God and this 'under law to God' finds its validation and explanation in his being under law to Christ. Paul asserts most unequivocally, therefore, that he is bound by the law of Christ and of God.

The conclusions to which we must come are as follows. (1) In one sense the believer is not under law. To be 'under law' in this sense is correlative with the dominion and bondservice of sin. The believer has been discharged from the law (Romans 7: 6), he has been put to death to the law through the body of Christ (Romans 7: 4), and therefore he has died to the law (Romans 7: 6). Having died to the law he died to sin (Romans 6: 2), and sin will not have dominion over him (Romans 6: 14). (2) In still another sense the believer is not under law; he is not under the ritual law of the Mosaic economy. This pedagogical tutelary bondage has been terminated by the epochal events of Calvary, the resurrection, and Pentecost. Christ redeemed them that were once under this law so that all without distinction may enjoy the mature and unrestrained privilege of sons. Freedom from the law in this specific sense is just as absolute as freedom from law in the preceding sense. (3) There is another sense in which the believer *is* 'under law'; he is bound in law to God and to Christ. The law of God and of Christ binds him precisely because of his relation to Christ.

This third conclusion is not only derived from I Corinthians 9: 21. There are several other considerations which demand the same conclusion. The fallacy of the interpretation that Paul conceives of the believer as in no sense under law and seeks to derive this from Romans 6: 14; 7: 1-6 should have been corrected by a more careful study of the context in which these same passages occur.

(1) Romans 6: 14 cannot be dissociated from Romans 6: 15: 'What then? shall we sin, because we are not under law but under grace? God forbid.' The apostle repudiates in the most emphatic way any insinuation to the effect that grace gives licence to sin or provides an inducement to sin. Grace intervenes and rules over us to deliver from the dominion of sin, and therefore establishes and promotes the opposite of sin, namely, righteousness. Deliverance from the dominion of sin does not leave the person in a vacuum

or in a state of neutrality; it is deliverance *to* if it is deliverance *from*. And it is deliverance to holiness and righteousness. It is this thought that Paul develops in the succeeding verses. He speaks not only of deliverance from sin but of its positive counterpart. 'Being then made free from sin ye were made bondservants to righteousness' (Romans 6: 18; *cf.* verse 22). Here he is saying not simply that believers became the servants of righteousness; he is saying that they were the subjects of the action of God's grace so that they were bound over to righteousness. How can we understand righteousness as the positive opposite of sin unless we construe it as the opposite of what sin is? And if sin is the transgression of the law, righteousness must be conformity to the law. The law of God which Paul characterizes in this Epistle as Spiritual, that is to say, divine in its origin and nature, and holy and just and good after the pattern of him who is its author (Romans 7: 12, 14), must be regarded as the criterion of righteousness no less than it is the criterion of sin.

(2) If Paul thought of himself as released from obligation to the law of God, how could he ever have confessed as a believer, 'I consent unto the law that it is good . . . I delight in the law of God after the inward man . . . Consequently then I myself with the mind serve the law of God' (Romans 7: 16, 22, 25)? It is fully admitted that the inner conflict and tension delineated in Romans 7: 14-25 pose acute exegetical difficulties; but there is surely little room for question that when Paul describes his most characteristic self, the self that he most centrally and fundamentally is as one united to Christ in the virtue of his death and the power of his resurrection (*cf.* Romans 6: 2-6), he describes himself as delighting in the law of God and serving that law with his mind. This service is one of bondservice, of commanded commitment; and yet it is not the bondservice of enforced and unwilling servitude. It is service constrained by delight and consent in the deepest recesses of heart and mind and will. It is total commitment, but it is the commitment also of spontaneous delight. The restraint which Paul deplores in this context and which compels him to exclaim 'O wretched man that I am' (Romans 7: 24) is not the restraint which the law of God imposes, but the restraint arising from the lack of conformity to it, that he wills the good but does not carry it into effect. The burden he bemoans is not the law but

that which is its contradiction, the other law in his members warring against the law of his mind (Romans 7: 23).

(3) It is eloquent of what Paul had in view in these protestations regarding his delight in, and service of, the law of God that in this same Epistle Paul furnishes us with concrete illustrations of the law to which he refers and of the ways in which conformity to the law is expressed. He does this in the more immediate context of Romans 6: 14 when he says, 'I had not known lust except the law had said, Thou shalt not covet' (Romans 7: 7). But in that part of his Epistle which deals directly with the details of Christian conduct his reference to at least four of the commandments is even more illuminating. 'Owe no man anything, but to love one another. For this, Thou shalt not commit adultery, Thou shalt not kill, Thou shalt not steal, Thou shalt not covet, and if there is any other commandment, it is summed up in this word, in this, Thou shalt love thy neighbour as thyself' (Romans 13: 8, 9). What is of particular interest to us at present is to note that Paul regards these precepts of the decalogue, four of which he quotes, as relevant to the behaviour which exemplifies the Christian vocation. The emphasis falls upon the fact that love fulfils them and that they are summed up, or summarized, in the word, 'Thou shalt love thy neighbour as thyself'. But, if love fulfils them, we must still bear in mind that they are fulfilled; and if they are fulfilled they exist as precepts which call for fulfilment: and if they are summarized in one word, the summary does not obliterate or abrogate the expansion of which it is a summary. It is futile to try to escape the underlying assumption of Paul's thought, that the concrete precepts of the decalogue have relevance to the believer as the criteria of that behaviour which love dictates. And it is all the more significant that these criteria should have been enunciated by the apostle in a context where the accent falls upon love itself: 'Owe no man anything, but to love one another' (verse 8).

Other passages in Paul's Epistles yield the same lesson respecting his conception of the place of law in the realm of grace. The situation in the church at Corinth made it necessary for Paul in his first Epistle to devote a considerable part of it to questions which fall within the realm of ethics and in several particulars he was called upon to administer reproof and correction for the misconduct of believers. He takes the occasion to remind them that the unrighteous shall not inherit the kingdom of God. He lists for us a catalogue of sins, thereby illustrating the unrighteousness which excludes from the kingdom of God—fornication, idolatry, adultery, effeminacy, sodomy, thievery, covetousness, drunkenness, reviling, extortion (I Corinthians 6: 9, 10). His intent is to illustrate the character and conduct which identify those who have no inheritance in the kingdom of Christ and of God (cf. verse 10), and he is saying in effect: 'You believers have been washed and sanctified and justified, and you cannot play fast and loose with any wrongdoing; as heirs of the kingdom of God you must behave accordingly; you must appreciate the antithesis between the kingdom of God and the world'. The point of particular interest for our present study is the criterion, presupposed in Paul's teaching here, by which this antithesis is to be judged. We need but scan the sins which Paul mentions to discover what this criterion is; the precepts of the decalogue underlie the whole catalogue. Idolatry—the first and second commandments; adultery—the seventh commandment; theft and extortion—the eighth; reviling—the ninth and possibly the third; covetousness—the tenth. Hence it is only too apparent that the criteria of the equity which characterizes the kingdom of God and the criteria of the iniquity which marks off those who are without God and without hope in the world are those norms of thought and behaviour which are epitomized in the ten commandments. And it is Paul's plea that the operations of grace (cf. verse 11) make mandatory the integrity of which these precepts are the canons. It is not grace relieving us of the demands signalized in these precepts, but grace establishing the character and status which will bring these demands to effective fruition.

If it should be objected that Paul in this same Epistle provides us with an example of love as exercised in abstraction from law when he commends abstinence from meat offered to idols lest the eating of such meat should be a stumblingblock to the weak, we have not read the passage with sufficient care (I Corinthians 8). It is true that there is no law against the eating of meat offered to idols; the apostle contends in this matter for the liberty of the strong and intelligent believer. No idol is anything in the world,

and there is no other God but one. The earth is the Lord's and
the fulness thereof. For the man who entertains this faith, meat
is not contaminated by the fact that it was offered by another,
who is an idolater, to an idol; he may freely eat and give the
Lord thanks. Yet there are certain circumstances under which
considerations of love to another will constrain the strong believer
to abstain. It might be argued that here love operates in complete
abstraction from law and therefore we have an illustration of
love acting on the highest level apart from the direction or
dictation of law.

Examination of the passage in question will expose the fallacy
of such an interpretation. The law of God in its sanctity and
authority underlies the whole situation. Why is the intelligent
believer enjoined in the circumstances to abstain? Simply and
solely because there is the danger of the sin of idolatry on the part
of the weak brother, the danger of wounding his weak conscience in the eating of meat as offered to an idol. In other words,
it is the danger of transgression, on the part of the weak believer,
of the first commandment, 'Thou shalt have no other gods before
me'. Remove that fact from the situation and the whole argument
of the apostle is nullified. The law requires that we ourselves
abstain from idolatry; but it also requires that we love our neighbour as ourselves. Therefore when our doing what, so far as we
ourselves are concerned, is a perfectly innocent act, becomes,
and that to our knowledge, the occasion for the commission of
sin on the part of another believer, love to our neighbour as ourselves will impel us to abstain from so unloving and unworthy
conduct. It is not, however, love abstracted from law but love
operating under the authority and sanctity of that commandment,
'Thou shalt have no other gods before me'.

We have therefore abundant evidence from Paul's Epistles to
elucidate what he means when he says: 'Do we then make void
the law through faith? God forbid: nay, we establish the law'
(Romans 3: 31). This is the protestation with which Paul brings
to a conclusion one of the most eloquent statements of the contrast between the function of law and the operation of grace:
'But now without the law the righteousness of God is made
manifest'; 'Where then is boasting? it is excluded. Through

what law? of works? Nay, but through the law of faith. For we reckon that a man is justified by faith without the deeds of the law' (Romans 3: 21, 27, 28). It is a protestation that Paul fully establishes and verifies in the later portions of this Epistle. But, in manner characteristic of the apostle, he interjects at this early point, at the conclusion of his peroration respecting the impotence of law and the efficacy of grace, the most emphatic warning to the effect that this total impotence of law to justify the ungodly does not carry with it the inference that the law is thereby discarded or abrogated. The inferences so frequently drawn from Romans 6: 14 should have been obviated by the reminder which Paul announces in Romans 3: 31, and the context of Romans 6: 14 advises us of the reasons why grace does not make the law of none effect. 'The law is holy, and the commandment holy and just and good' (Romans 7: 12). 'The law is Spiritual' (Romans 7: 14). It is unqualifiedly and unreservedly good (Romans 7: 13, 16, 19, 21). And how could the unreservedly good be relieved of its relevance or deprived of its sanctity?

A good deal of the misconception pertaining to the relation of the law to the believer springs from a biblico-theological error of much broader proportions than a misinterpretation of Paul's statement in Romans 6: 14. It is the misinterpretation of the Mosaic economy and covenant in relation to the new covenant. It has been thought that in the Mosaic covenant there is a sharp antithesis to the principle of promise embodied in the Abrahamic covenant and also to the principle of grace which comes to its efflorescence in the new covenant, and that this antithetical principle which governs the Mosaic covenant and dispensation is that of law in contradistinction from both promise and grace.[2]

---

[2] See Appendix E in reference to Lewis Sperry Chafer and cf. also *The Scofield Reference Bible*, pp. 1115, 1244f.; Charles A. Feinberg: *Premillennialism or Amillennialism* (Grand Rapids, 1936), pp. 126, 190. The question is not whether modern dispensationalists actually maintain that, during the dispensation of law, any were actually saved by works of obedience to law. Dispensationalists will acknowledge that in all ages men were saved by the blood of Christ through the grace of God. In Feinberg's words, 'All the blessing in the world in all ages is directly traceable to the death of Christ' (*op. cit.*, p. 210). 'Paul's argument in the fourth chapter of the Romans seeks to make clear that God has always justified guilty sinners by faith' (p. 202; cf. pp. 217f. and Roy L.

(*continued on p. 196*)

It is thought, therefore, that the Mosaic covenant is the outstanding example of works of law as opposed to the provisions
of promise and grace. It is easy to see how such an interpretation
of the Mosaic economy would radically affect our construction
not only of the Mosaic economy itself but also of the Abrahamic
covenant, on the one hand, and of the new covenant, on the
other; the Mosaic would stand in sharp antithesis to both in
respect of constitutive and governing principle. And the contrast
between law and grace which we find in the New Testament
would naturally be interpreted as a contrast between the Mosaic
economy and the gospel dispensation of grace. In other words,
the real contrast between 'under law' and 'under grace', as it
appears in Romans 6: 14 and Romans 7: 1-4, would be exemplified in the realm of the historical unfolding of covenant revelation
in the contrast between the Mosaic covenant and the new
covenant. This interpretation has exercised a profound influence
upon the history of interpretation and it has cast its shadow over
the exegesis of particular passages. It is necessary for us to consider this question: What is the governing principle of the Mosaic
covenant? Is this principle one of law as contrasted with grace
and therefore antithetical to that of the new covenant?

There is a plausible case that could be made out for this construction of the Mosaic covenant. The first express reference to
the covenant made with Israel at Sinai is framed in terms of
obedience to the commandments of God and of keeping the
covenant. 'Now therefore if ye will obey my voice indeed, and
keep my covenant, then ye shall be a peculiar treasure unto me
above all people: for all the earth is mine. And ye shall be unto
me a kingdom of priests and a holy nation' (Exodus 19: 5, 6).

Aldrich in *Bibliotheca Sacra*, January, 1955, pp. 49ff.). The question is whether
the dispensationalist construction of the Mosaic dispensation is correct and
whether the concession that people had been even then saved by grace through
the blood of Christ is consistent with this construction. Obviously, if the
construction is erroneous, the error involved is of such a character that it must
radically affect not only the view entertained of the Mosaic dispensation but
of the whole history of revelation, particularly of the revelation embodied in
the three pivotal covenants, the Abrahamic, the Mosaic, and the New. For
criticism of modern dispensationalism in general *cf.* Oswald T. Allis: *Prophecy
and the Church* (Philadelphia, 1945). On the place of law in Scripture *cf.*
Patrick Fairbairn: *The Revelation of Law in Scripture* (New York, 1869).

And the engagement of the people is in similar terms: 'All that the Lord hath spoken will we do and be obedient' (Exodus 24: 7). Surely, we might say, these are not the terms of a covenant of grace but the terms of a covenant of legal and contractual stipulations.[3] How, we might ask, does the condition of obedience comport with the provisions of an administration of grace? If grace is contingent upon the fulfilment of certain conditions by us, then surely it is no more grace. Hence, it may well be argued, this conditional feature of the Mosaic covenant requires that it be placed in a different category. In dealing with this question we must take several considerations into account.

1. The Mosaic covenant in respect of this condition of obedience is not in a different category from the Abrahamic. 'And God said unto Abraham, Thou shalt keep my covenant therefore, thou, and thy seed after thee in their generations' (Genesis 17: 9). Of Abraham God said, 'For I know him, that he will command his children and his household after him, and they shall keep the way of the Lord, to do justice and judgment; that the Lord may bring upon Abraham that which he hath spoken of him' (Genesis 18: 19). There is nothing principially different in the necessity of keeping the covenant and of obeying God's voice, characteristic of the Mosaic covenant, from what is involved in the keeping of the covenant required in the Abrahamic.

2. The Mosaic covenant, no less than the Abrahamic, contemplates a relation of intimacy and fellowship with God epitomized in the promise 'I will be your God and ye shall be my people' (cf. Exodus 6: 7; 18: 1; 19: 5, 6; 20: 2; Deuteronomy 29: 13). Religious relationship on the highest level is in view. If the covenant contemplates religious relationship of such a character, it is inconceivable that the demands of God's holiness should not come to expression as governing and regulating that fellowship and as conditioning the continued enjoyment of its blessings. This note is frequent in the Pentateuch (cf. Leviticus 11: 44, 45; 19: 2; 20: 7, 26; 21: 8; Deuteronomy 6: 4-15). It is summed up in two words: 'Ye shall be holy, for I the Lord your God am holy' (Leviticus 19: 2); 'Thou shalt love the Lord thy

[3] Cf. my booklet, The Covenant of Grace (London, 1953), for a more detailed study of the concept of covenant and of the Mosaic covenant as one of grace.

God with all thy heart and with all thy soul and with all thy
might' (Deuteronomy 6: 5). And the import is that the holiness
of God demands holiness on the part of those who enter into
such a covenant relation with him. It is the same principle as that
expressed in the New Testament, 'Without holiness no man
shall see the Lord' (Hebrews 12: 14), and is reiterated in Old
Testament terms by Peter when he says, 'As he who hath called
you is holy, so be ye holy in all manner of conversation, because
it is written, Be ye holy, for I am holy' (I Peter 1: 15; *cf.* Leviticus
11: 44; 19: 2; 20: 7). The holiness which is demanded by the
covenant fellowship is expressed concretely in obedience to the
divine commandments. This is really all that needs to be said
to demonstrate not only the *consonance* of the demand for obedience with the covenant as one of religious relationship on the
highest level of spirituality but also the *necessity* of such a demand.
It is because the covenant is one of union and communion with
God that the condition of obedience is demanded.

3. Not only is holiness, as expressed concretely and practically
in obedience, demanded by the covenant fellowship; we must
also bear in mind that holiness was itself an integral element of
the covenant blessing. Israel had been redeemed and called to be
a holy people and holiness might be regarded as the essence of
the covenant blessing. For holiness consisted in this, that Israel
was a people separated unto the Lord. Their election is meaningless apart from that to which they were elected. And this holiness
again is exemplified in obedience to the commandments of God
(*cf.* Psalm 19: 7ff.).

4. Holiness, concretely and practically illustrated in obedience,
is the means through which the fellowship entailed in the covenant
relationship proceeds to its fruition and consummation. This is the
burden, for example, of Leviticus 26. It is stated both positively
and negatively, by way of promise and by way of threatening.
'If ye walk in my statutes, and keep my commandments, and do
them . . . I will set my tabernacle among you: and my soul shall
not abhor you. And I will walk among you, and will be your
God, and ye shall be my people' (Leviticus 26: 3, 11, 12).

We may therefore sum up the matter by saying that the holiness
of God demanded conformity to his holiness, that holiness was of
the essence of the covenant privilege, that holiness was the con-

dition of continuance in the enjoyment of the covenant blessings and the medium through which the covenant privilege realized its fruition. Holiness is exemplified in obedience to the commandments of God. Obedience is therefore entirely congruous with, and disobedience entirely contradictory of, the nature of God's covenant with Israel as one of union and communion with God.

In all of this the demand of obedience in the Mosaic covenant is principially identical with the same demand in the new covenant of the gospel economy. The new covenant also finds its centre in the promise, 'I will be your God and ye shall be my people'. The new covenant as an everlasting covenant reaches the zenith of its realization in this: 'Behold, the tabernacle of God is with men, and he will dwell with them, and they shall be his people' (Revelation 21: 3). But we must ask: Do believers continue in this relationship and in the enjoyment of its blessing irrespective of persevering obedience to God's commands? It is one of the most perilous distortions of the doctrine of grace, and one that has carried with it the saddest records of moral and spiritual disaster, to assume that past privileges, however high they may be, guarantee the security of men irrespective of perseverance in faith and holiness. Believers under the gospel continue in the covenant and in the enjoyment of its privileges because they continue in the fulfilment of the conditions; they continue in faith, love, hope, and obedience. True believers are kept unto the end, unto the eschatological salvation; but they are kept by the power of God *through faith* (*cf.* I Peter 1: 5). 'We are made partakers of Christ, if we hold fast the beginning of confidence stedfast unto the end' (Hebrews 3: 14). It is through faith and patience we inherit the promises (*cf.* Hebrews 6: 11, 12). We shall be presented holy and unblameable and unreproveable before God if we 'continue in the faith grounded and settled and not moved away from the hope of the gospel' (Colossians 1: 22, 23). Paul the apostle could exult in the assurance that his citizenship was in heaven and that one day Christ would change the body of his humiliation and transform it into the likeness of the body of his glory (Philippians 3: 20, 21). But co-ordinate with this assurance and as the condition of its entertainment is the protestation, 'Brethren, I do not yet reckon myself to have apprehended;

but this one thing I do, forgetting those things which are behind and reaching forth unto those things which are before, I press on toward the goal, unto the prize of the high calling of God in Christ Jesus' (Philippians 3: 13, 14). Paul knew well that if he were to attain to the resurrection of the dead all the resources of Christ's resurrection power must be operative in him and all the energies of his personality enlisted in the exercise of those means through which he would apprehend that for which he was apprehended by Christ Jesus (cf. Philippians 3: 10-12). This is just to say that the goal is not reached, the consummation of covenant blessing is not achieved in some automatic fashion but through a process that engages to the utmost the concentrated devotion of the apostle himself. It is not reached irrespective of perseverance, but through perseverance. And this means nothing if it does not mean concentrated obedience to the will of Christ as expressed in his commandments. We readily see, however, that the attainment of the goal is not on the meritorious ground of perseverance and obedience, but through the divinely appointed means of perseverance. Obedience as the appropriate and necessary expression of devotion to Christ does not find its place in a covenant of works or of merit but in a covenant that has its inception and end in pure grace.

The disposition to construe the demand for obedience in the Mosaic economy as having affinity with works rather than grace arises from failure to recognize that the demand for obedience in the Mosaic covenant is principially identical with the same demand under the gospel. When we re-examine the demand for obedience in the Mosaic covenant (cf. Exodus 19: 5, 6; 24: 7) in the light of the relations of law and grace in the gospel, we shall discover that the complex of ideas is totally alien to a construction in terms of works as opposed to grace. Obedience belongs here no more 'to the legal sphere of merit'[4] than in the new covenant.

---

[4] Geerhardus Vos: *Biblical Theology. Old and New Testaments* (Grand Rapids, 1954), p. 143. The context is worthy of quotation. 'It is plain, then, that law-keeping did not figure at that juncture as the meritorious ground of life-inheritance. The latter is based on grace alone, no less emphatically than Paul himself places salvation on that ground. But, while this is so, it might still be objected that law-observance, if not the ground for receiving, is yet made the

(continued on p. 201)

The New Testament believer is not without law to God but under law to Christ. He delights in the law of God after the inward man and he therefore reiterates the exclamation of the Old Testament saint, 'O how love I thy law! it is my meditation all the day' (Psalm 119: 97). And he also is not forgetful that he who was the incarnation and embodiment of virtue, he who is the supreme and perfect example, said, 'I delight to do thy will, O my God: yea, thy law is within my heart' (Psalm 40: 8).

---

ground for retention of the privileges inherited. Here it can not, of course, be denied that a real connection exists. But the Judaizers went wrong in inferring that the connection must be *meritorious*, that, if Israel keeps the cherished gifts of Jehovah through observance of His law, this must be so, because in strict justice they had earned them. The connection is of a totally different kind. It belongs not to the legal sphere of merit, but to the symbolico-typical sphere of *appropriateness of expression*.'

CHAPTER IX

THE DYNAMIC OF THE BIBLICAL ETHIC

IT is impossible to segregate the biblical ethic from the teaching of Scripture on other subjects. The ethic of the Bible reflects the character of the God of the Bible. Remove from Scripture the transcendent holiness, righteousness, and truth of God and its ethic disintegrates. 'Ye shall be holy; for I the Lord your God am holy' (Leviticus 19: 2; *cf.* Leviticus 11: 44, 45; 20: 7, 26; 21: 6-8; Deuteronomy 7: 6-9; I Corinthians 3: 17; I Peter 1: 15, 16). 'I am holy'; therefore 'ye shall fear every man his mother, and his father' (Leviticus 19: 3). 'Ye shall be perfect, therefore, as your heavenly Father is perfect' (Matthew 5: 48). This is such a patent fact that only the unreflecting would deny it. And this is no more than to say that the teaching of Scripture involves a system of truth. One aspect of truth dovetails into another. Those who have an antipathy to system are either hostile to the biblical ethic or fail to take account of the most salient facts.

One feature of the witness of Scripture that bears directly upon the biblical ethic is its teaching on the depravity of human nature. 'There is none righteous, no, not one . . . There is none that doeth good, no, not even one' (Romans 3: 10, 12). According to the Bible human depravity is such that the fulfilment of the demands of the biblical ethic is an impossibility. The mind of the flesh, the mind of the natural man, 'is not subject to the law of God, neither indeed can it be' (Romans 8: 7). It is this impossibility that makes necessary the provisions of redemptive grace. In relation to the ethic of Scripture the question then becomes: How are the provisions of redemptive grace brought to bear upon the fulfilment of ethical demand?

The answer is that we men must be brought within the orbit of the forces of redemption. In its broader implications the redemptive process, both as objective accomplishment and as effectual application, is the only answer to the impossibility inherent in our depravity. Certain elements of that redemptive process, however, stand in more intimate relation to the realization of ethical demand. It is easy to see, for example, that justification lays the foundation upon which alone we may do that which is well-pleasing to God. For justification removes our guilt and gives us acceptance with God. Again, regeneration is the only way whereby there may begin to be formed in us that disposition and character which have affinity with the demands of holiness.

There is, however, one aspect of the biblical witness that is particularly relevant and yet one that is not always sufficiently appreciated. This truth may be stated broadly as union and communion with Christ. More specifically it is the truth of union with Christ in the virtue of his death and the power of his resurrection.

If we accept the biblical witness to human depravity and iniquity, then there must be a radical breach with sin in its power and defilement if the demands of the biblical ethic are even to begin to be realized in us. This radical breach with sin is indicated in other phases of the application of redemption. That act of God by which we are translated into the kingdom of God as the kingdom of righteousness, power, life, and peace is nothing less radical than a new birth, a birth from above, and therefore supernatural in character. But at no point is the emphasis of Scripture upon the radical breach with sin more patent and pointed than in connection with the relation which the believer sustains to the death and resurrection of Christ.

From apostolic times the doctrine of the free grace of God, especially as exemplified in a full and free justification, has been loaded with the charge that it promotes licentiousness. And how plausible the inference appears to be! If grace superabounds where sin abounded, if the very grace of God abounds unto his glory through our sin (cf. Romans 3: 5-8; 5: 20, 21), shall we not sin all the more in order that the grace and righteousness and truth of God may be all the more glorified in the superabundance of their manifestations? Let us continue in sin that grace may abound! It is with this objection that Paul deals, and its logic he controverts with a decisiveness and severity second to none in the polemics of his Roman Epistle. What Paul pleads as the decisive argument is that, if we are the partakers of God's free grace, it is in union with Christ that we have been thus blessed. And if in union with Christ, then it is in union with him in his death, burial, and resurrection (Romans 6: 1-4). If we have been united with Christ, we have been united with him in his death. And what did the death of Christ mean? 'For in that he died he died to sin once for all' (Romans 6: 10). Hence, if we died with him, we also died to sin once for all. And 'we who died to sin, how shall we any longer live therein?' (Romans 6: 2). It is this concept of having died to sin that expresses, perhaps more eloquently than any other in Scripture, the definitive cleavage with sin which takes place when in the work of God's grace a person is united to Christ. Just as the expression 'dead in trespasses and sins' (Ephesians 2: 1) intimates our helpless enslavement in the service of sin, so death to sin expresses our emancipation from this servitude.

We must fully appreciate the strength of Paul's statement, 'we died to sin'. The simple and apodictic directness must not be allowed to obscure the far-reaching implications. Our understanding of the force of this description must be derived from the obvious meaning of the phenomenal, psychico-physical death with which we are so well acquainted. When a person dies we know from bitter experience that the bond which united that person to life and activity in this world has been severed. He is no longer active in the sphere, realm, or relationship in reference to which he has died; he is no longer *en rapport* with life here. The Scripture graphically portrays this obvious fact. 'But he passed away, and, lo, he was not: yea, I sought him, but he could not be found' (Psalm 37: 36). 'As for man, his days are as grass: as a flower of the field, so he flourisheth. For the wind passeth over it, and it is gone; and the place thereof shall know it no more' (Psalm 103: 15, 16). It is this analogy that must be applied to death to sin. The person who has died to sin no longer lives and acts in the sphere or realm of sin. In the moral and spiritual realm there is a translation as real and decisive as in the realm of the psychico-physical on the event of ordinary death. Those who still live in the realm of sin and whose life is constituted by sin may say with reference to the person translated from it, 'he passed away, and, lo, he was not: yea, I sought him, but he could not be found'. The place that knew him knows him no more.

There is a kingdom of sin, of darkness, and of death. The

forces of iniquity rule there. It is the kingdom of this world and it lies in the wicked one (cf. II Corinthians 4: 3, 4; Ephesians 2: 1-3; I John 5: 19). The person who has died to sin no longer lives there; it is no more the world of his thought, affection, will, life, and action. His well-springs are now in the kingdom which is totally antithetical, the kingdom of God and of his righteousness. It is of this translation that Paul speaks elsewhere when he gives thanks to the Father 'who hath delivered us from the power of darkness, and hath translated us into the kingdom of the Son of his love' and 'made us meet to be partakers of the inheritance of the saints in light' (Colossians 1: 12, 13; cf. Galatians 1: 4). And Peter reflects on the consternation of those who are left behind in the world of iniquity: 'they think it strange that ye run not with them into the same excess of riot, speaking evil of you' (I Peter 4: 4; cf. verses 1-3).

We are too ready to give heed to what we deem to be the hard, empirical facts of Christian profession, and we have erased the clear line of demarcation which Scripture defines. As a result we have lost our vision of the high calling of God in Christ Jesus. Our ethic has lost its dynamic and we have become conformed to this world. We know not the power of death to sin in the death of Christ, and we are not able to bear the rigour of the liberty of redemptive emancipation. 'We died to sin': the glory of Christ's accomplishment and the guarantee of the Christian ethic are bound up with that doctrine. If we live in sin we have not died to it, and if we have not died to it we are not Christ's. If we died to sin we no longer live in it, for 'we who are such as have died to sin, how shall we still live in it?' (Romans 6: 2).

Paul's 'death to sin' has also its more positive counterpart. The ethic which springs from the relation of the believer to Christ is not merely antithetical to and destructive of sin; it is an ethic of life as well as of death. It is indeed death to that which is the negation of life; it is death to death in trespasses and sins. But it is also life to righteousness. Grace reigns here also through righteousness unto eternal life. And it is the ethic of life because Christ rose again from the dead. 'For in that he died, he died to sin once for all: but in that he lives, he lives to God' (Romans 6: 10). The believer died to sin because he died with Christ, and he lives in newness of life because he rose with Christ. 'Therefore we were buried with him through baptism into death, in order that as Christ was raised from the dead through the glory of the Father, even so we should walk in newness of life' (Romans 6: 4). 'But if we died with Christ, we believe that we shall also live together with him, knowing that Christ being raised from the dead dieth no more, death hath no more dominion over him' (Romans 6: 8, 9). It is Jesus' resurrection that guarantees for believers life in the power of that resurrection, and they present themselves to God as those alive from the dead and their members as instruments of righteousness to God (*cf.* Romans 6: 13). In a word, it is the relation of the believer to both the death and resurrection of Christ that insures the newness of life which the redemptive ethic entails. Or we may invert the terms and say it is the relation of the death and resurrection of Christ to the believer that insures this newness of life. What, more precisely, is this relation?

It might appear to be the proper account of this relation to say that the relation of the death and resurrection of Christ to the life of holiness and new obedience is simply the relation that justification sustains to sanctification, or, more particularly, the relation which the death and resurrection of Christ as the ground of justification sustains to sanctification. The relation would then be as follows: The death and resurrection of Christ are the ground of justification; justification is the basis of sanctification, for it lays the foundation upon which a life of holiness can rest and develop; hence the death and resurrection of Christ underlie sanctification. This same thought might be stated in different terms by saying that Christ has secured by his death and resurrection every saving gift and therefore the death and resurrection of Christ are the meritorious and procuring cause of sanctification and the new life of ethical integrity.

Doctrinally all of this is true. Paul in the Epistle to the Romans makes quite clear the relation which the death and resurrection of Christ sustain to justification (*cf.* Romans 3: 21ff.; 4: 25; 5: 12-21). And it is also clear that justification is the indispensable basis for acceptable service to God (*cf.* Romans 5: 1-5; 12: 1). But we are missing the central element of Paul's thought in Romans 6 and of Paul's teaching elsewhere, as well as of other

New Testament writers, if we are content with this account of
the relation of Christ's death and resurrection to the newness of
life which characterizes the believer's ethic. For when Paul is
dealing with the newness of life which identifies the believer what
is thrust into the foreground is not the fact that Christ died and
rose again *for* believers (though this aspect is not by any means
suppressed or overlooked), but rather the fact that *believers died
and rose again with Christ*. It is that aspect from which the death
and resurrection of Christ may be viewed that is particularly
brought to bear upon the ethical demands of the faith of the
gospel (in addition to Romans 6 *cf*. II Corinthians 5: 14, 15;
Ephesians 2: 1-7; Colossians 3: 1-4; I Peter 4: 1-4). It is this abiding relationship to the death and resurrection of Christ, particularly, of course, to the latter, that constitutes the power, the
dynamic, in virtue of which believers live the life of death to sin
and of the newness of obedience. It is what we may call the virtue
emanating from the death and resurrection of Christ, viewed as
their death and resurrection also, that is the constant force in
the sanctification of believers. More properly, it is the virtue
resident in, and emanating from, the resurrected Lord by reason
of his death and resurrection that is the sanctifying agency in
the life of believers.[1] And the nexus which binds them to this
virtue is the fact that they were planted together in the likeness
of his death and resurrection. Christ's death and resurrection
were events; they are definitive and finished events. Christ,
being raised from the dead, dies no more. But his resurrection
life is an abiding fact and in that resurrection life believers share.

Hence the relation which the new life of the believer sustains
to Christ, specifically to his death and resurrection, is not simply
that Christ has by his once-for-all accomplishment secured and

[1] *The Westminster Confession of Faith* refers aptly to this aspect of New
Testament teaching when it says: 'They, who are once effectually called, and
regenerated, having a new heart, and a new spirit created in them, are further
sanctified, really and personally, through the virtue of Christ's death and
resurrection, by His Word and Spirit dwelling in them' (Chap. XIII, Sect. I).
It is the expression 'through the virtue of Christ's death and resurrection' that
needs to be noted. The expression is not 'by virtue of Christ's death and
resurrection' which would not have enunciated the precise thought intended.
The proof text cited in support of this proposition is Romans 6: 5, 6 and this
indicates what was intended.

procured for believers sanctifying grace; it is also and most relevantly the relation of abiding communion with Christ and communication from him in the definitive efficacy of his death and the power of his resurrection. We gain perhaps new insight into the significance of Paul's determination to count all things but loss that he might know Christ and 'the power of his resurrection and the fellowship of his sufferings, being made conformable to his death' (Philippians 3: 10).

A question naturally emerges: When did believers die with Christ and rise with him to newness of life? It might appear that the answer is determined by the historic once-for-allness of the death and resurrection of Christ, that since Christ died and rose again once, in the historic past, and since believers are represented as dying and rising again *with* Christ, their dying to sin and rising to newness of life can have no other date than that of the historic events of Calvary and the first Lord's day. It must be admitted that the question is not as simple as it first appears to be.

Paul is dealing with the believer's death to sin. 'We died to sin'—this is Paul's thesis. He is dealing with death to sin as an actual and practical fact, shall we not say existential fact? He brings within the scope of this statement not merely the guarantee or the promise of death to sin, but its realization in the life-history of the believer. That he has the practical life of the believer in view is made perhaps more apparent by his allusion to the newness of life in which believers walk (Romans 6: 4, 5). And when he says, 'he who died is justified from sin', he must have in view a justified person whether the verb 'justify' is used here in the sense of forensic justification or in the more inclusive sense of deliverance from the power of sin as well as its guilt. In addition, when we examine other Pauline passages in which the same doctrine is found, we cannot eliminate the actual and practical and experiential implications of that to which he refers (Ephesians 2: 1-7; Colossians 2: 20—3: 4; II Corinthians 5: 14-17; *cf.* I Peter 4: 1-4). Finally, Paul alludes in Romans 6 to baptism and therefore to the kind of union with Christ which is represented and sealed by the ordinance of baptism: 'Or are ye ignorant that as many as were baptized into Christ Jesus were baptized into his death?'

(Romans 6: 3). Hence several considerations converge to show beyond question that when Paul speaks of our dying and rising with Christ he has in view that transformation which occurs when we are actually united with Christ in the effectual operations of grace. It is the translation from the kingdom of darkness into the kingdom of the Son of God's love that Paul has in mind. In a word, it is the death to sin and life in righteousness true only of a believer.

The question is before us, however, with even greater urgency: How can this be construed as death and resurrection *with* Christ? For it is still true that the death and resurrection of Christ are once-for-all historic events, and are not repeated each time a person is effectually called into actual union with him. We have the tension between two equally relevant and important facts, the one that death and resurrection *with* Christ are brought within the realm of the actual and practical, the other that the death and resurrection *of* Christ cannot be conceived of as other than past and unrepeatable events. It is the tension between the demands of the past historical in reference to Christ and the demands of the moral and practical in reference to the believer. How are we to relieve this tension? We cannot relieve it by toning down either.

The solution we shall have to offer is that believers were in a true sense in Christ when he died and rose again, that in a true sense they died with him and rose again with him in the once-for-all events of Calvary and the resurrection on the third day. It is, of course, true that believers did not die and rise again with Christ as believers nor did this dying and rising again constitute them actual believers. But there are other respects in which we may and must conceive of believers as united to Christ prior to the operations of efficacious grace. There are various ways in which this kind of union with Christ may be expressed. But however it may be designated it is quite impossible to deny or discount it. Who, with any biblical consciousness, will deny that when Christ died upon the accursed tree he died for his people, that he was delivered up for their offences and was raised again for their justification? There was indubitably a relationship between Christ and his people when he died and rose again. But the dying of believers with Christ is but an alternative and correlative way of expressing this relationship. More accurately, it is a way of expressing the correlative implications of the relationship involved in Christ's dying for his people. And so if Christ died on the accursed tree for his people they also died with him in that death. Furthermore, it is impossible for us to exclude the people of God from union with Christ in his death and resurrection if we bear in mind that they were chosen in Christ before the foundation of the world. There is no severance of this union, and that it should not have the most fruitful relevance at the point of the climactic events of Calvary and the resurrection is totally inconceivable. And how more relevantly could this undissolved union come to expression in these climactic events than in the dying of believers with Christ in his death and their rising with him in his resurrection? That believers died with Christ and rose with him in virtue of the mysterious relationship constituted from eternal ages is a necessary datum of our Christian faith. It is no stumblingblock; it is integral to the mystery of Christ and his church.

If this is all true how are we to relate this once-for-all historic fact to the moral and the practical? When Paul says, 'we died to sin', he is thinking of actual and practical translation from the world of sin to the kingdom of God's own Son. And this did not take place once for all at Calvary. How are we to relieve the discrepancy? It will surely not be gainsaid that the virtue of Christ's death and the power of his resurrection are not efficiently operative in the hearts and lives of God's elect until they are effectually applied. It cannot be said that the virtue and power of Christ's redemption are operative in those who are dead through their trespasses and sins and are children of wrath even as others. The distinction between redemptive accomplishment and application lies on the face of the New Testament and is verified by observation and experience. And just as there is the distinction between the accomplishment of redemption and its application, so there is the distinction between the once-for-all dying and rising with Christ and the actual and practical realization of the implications of these once-for-all events. We shall have to conclude that, when the New Testament speaks of the people of God as dying and rising again with Christ, both facts, the once-for-all historical and the practical, are intentionally brought into the forefront of attention as mutually conditioning each other. If we are thinking of the past event we must also have in view the practical sequel apart from which the finished event has no meaning. If we are thinking of that which is progressively realized in the onward course of history as the people of God are actually translated from the power of darkness we may never dissociate this from the efficacy inherent in the finished events of Calvary and the resurrection on the third day.

When we appreciate the co-ordination and the correlativity of the historical events of Jesus' death and resurrection, on the one hand, and of actual death to sin and resurrection to newness of life in the life-history of believers, on the other, we are in a better position to understand the emphasis which Paul, in particular, places upon the definitive once-for-allness of the breach with sin and its power which occurs when a person is united to Christ in the effectual call of the gospel. That which occurs in the life-history of the person concerned is analogous to that which occurred when Jesus died and rose again. Jesus died once and he rose again once. In like manner, when, in the sphere of actual realization, one dies with Christ and rises again with him, the dying and rising in this case are just as decisive and definitive as in the case of the prototype. And nothing must be allowed to obscure this parallelism. 'For in that he died, he died to sin once: but in that he lives, he lives to God. Even so ye reckon yourselves to be dead indeed to sin but alive to God in Christ Jesus' (Romans 6: 10, 11).

There are several features of the New Testament teaching which are to be interpreted in the light of this decisive breach with the world of sin and which also, in turn, confirm the actuality and necessity of such a definitive transformation. Two features of Paul's teaching are particularly relevant. The first is that which bears upon the crucifixion of the old man and the second that which is concerned with freedom from the dominion of sin—'our old man has been crucified' (Romans 6: 6); 'sin shall not have dominion over you' (Romans 6: 14).

The contrast between the old man and the new man has frequently been interpreted as the contrast between that which is new in the believer and that which is old, the contrast between that which the believer is as recreated after the image of God and that which he is as not yet perfect. Hence the antithesis which exists in the believer between holiness and sin, between the Holy Spirit and the flesh is the antithesis between the new man and the old man in him.[2] The believer is both old man and new man; when he does well he is acting in terms of the new man which he is; when he sins he is acting in terms of the old man which he also still is. This interpretation does not find support in Paul's teaching; Paul points to something different. And the concept which his teaching supports is of basic significance for the biblical ethic.

When Paul says, 'our old man has been crucified', we have to take into account the terms, the background, and the context of this statement. The term 'crucified' is that of being crucified with Christ, and therefore indicates that the old man has been put to death just as decisively as Christ died upon the accursed tree. To suppose that the old man has been crucified and still

[2] *Cf.* John Calvin: *Comm. ad* Romans 6: 6: "The old man, as the Old Testament is called with reference to the New; for he begins to be old, when he is by degrees destroyed by a commencing regeneration. But what he means is the whole nature which we bring from the womb, and which is so incapable of the kingdom of God, that it must die to the extent to which we are renewed in true life' (ut interire eatenus oporteat, quatenus in veram vitam instauramur); see also *Comm. ad* Ephesians 4: 22: 'As we are first born of Adam, the depravity of nature which we derive from him is called the *Old* man; and as we are born again in Christ, the amendment of this sinful nature is called the *New* man' (as translated by William Pringle, C.T.S., Grand Rapids, 1948, pp. 294f.); James Fraser: *A Treatise on Sanctification* (London, 1898), pp. 55f.: 'What are we indeed to understand by the *old man*? That certainly signifies the corruption of nature . . . the principle of sin, with all its various lusts, which possess and influence a man's faculties and powers; and that, so far as it remains in the true Christian, who is renewed by grace, and in whom is the new man, by virtue of, and in comparison with which in him, and in him only, the former is the old man. In persons unregenerate, this evil principle is not the old man, but continues young, in full strength and vigour. It is the old man only in persons regenerate—in true Christians'; Charles Hodge: *Comm. ad* Romans 6: 6; Ephesians 4: 22; Moses Stuart: *Comm. ad* Romans 6: 6; Albert Barnes: *Notes, Explanatory and Practical, on the New Testament ad* Romans 6: 6.

On the other side of the question *cf.* Heinrich Meyer: *Comm. ad* Romans 6: 6; Ephesians 4: 22-24; Henry Alford: *Comm. ad* Romans 6: 6; W. Sanday and A. C. Headlam: *Comm. ad* Romans 6: 6; John MacPherson: *Comm. ad* Ephesians 4: 22, 24; Anders Nygren: *Commentary on Romans* (trans. by Carl C. Rasmussen, Philadelphia, 1949), pp. 234ff.; apparently also John Eadie: *Comm. ad* Ephesians 4: 22.

lives or has been raised again from this death is to contradict the obvious force of the import of crucifixion. And to interject the idea that crucifixion is a slow death and therefore to be conceived of as a process by which the old man is progressively mortified until he is finally put to death is to go flatly counter to Paul's terms.[3] He says 'our old man has been crucified', and not 'our old man is in the process of being crucified'. The context, likewise, does not admit of any interpretation other than that which is indicated by the express terms of the passage in question. The statement 'our old man has been crucified' is parallel to and epexegetical of other expressions, such as, 'we died to sin', 'we have been planted together in the likeness of his death', 'we died with Christ' (Romans 6: 2, 5, 8), and is therefore intended to denote what is as definitive and decisive as these other expressions. Finally, the complementary truth of the resurrection of Christ and that of believers in him rules out any supposition to the effect that the old man is conceived of as still living. 'Christ being raised from the dead dies no more, death no longer rules over him' (Romans 6: 9). Exegetically speaking it is no easier to think of the old man as in process of crucifixion or mortification than it is to think of the resurrected Lord as being still in process of crucifixion. The completed fact of Jesus' crucifixion and the abiding reality of his resurrection life must govern our conception of the crucifixion of the old man. And when we are thinking of the resurrection sequel as it applies to our crucifixion it is not the old man who is raised up but the new man. Paul does not use the designation 'new man' in this context. He uses it elsewhere, as we shall see. But nothing else than 'the new man', as the subject of the resurrection contemplated, will suit the complex of Paul's thought. It is the 'newness' of the resurrection life that he emphasizes throughout. 'As Christ was raised from the dead through the glory of the Father, even so we should walk in newness of life' (Romans 6: 4). And in terms of the contrast between 'the old man' and 'the new man' the only concept that will correspond to the newness following upon resurrection is 'the new man'. That inevitably is in the background, even though Paul does not overtly use the designation.

[3] Cf. Moses Stuart: op. cit., ad Romans 6: 6; Albert Barnes: op. cit., ad Romans 6: 6.

As we study other passages in Paul's Epistles this view of the contrast between the old man and the new man, so far from being negated, is confirmed. We may first refer to Colossians 3: 9, 10: 'Lie not one to another, since ye have put off the old man with his deeds, and have put on the new man who is being renewed unto knowledge after the image of him who created him'. The *prima facie* sense of this passage corroborates the interpretation propounded above. Paul is not exhorting believers to put off the old man and to put on the new. He is urging them to desist from certain sins, sins which are indeed characteristic of the old man, and the reason he adduces for such abstinence is that they have put off the old man and have put on the new man. Since this is the case, Paul is saying in effect, do not practise those sins which are after the pattern of the old man but behave as new men, as indeed you are. Besides, the figure which Paul is using, namely, that of having put off and of having put on, does not agree with the idea of being both an old man and a new man at the same time. For in that event the figure would require that we are *clothed* with both at the same time. The notion that putting off the old man is a process would involve this incoherent figure of speech. There need be no question but that Paul here regards believers as those who have put off the old man and have put on the new and therefore, in terms of his figure, as those who are clothed with the new man and not with the old.

The closely parallel passage in Paul, Ephesians 4: 22-24, would appear to offer more difficulty. It would seem as if Paul is there exhorting believers 'to put off according to the former manner of life the old man' and 'to put on the new man'. And it is true that considerations of grammar would not necessarily be violated if this interpretation were adopted.[4] But exegetical considerations

---

[4] ἀποθέσθαι and ἐνδύσασθαι are Aorist Infinitives. In New Testament Greek there is the Imperatival Infinitive. *Cf.* F. Blass: *Grammar of New Testament Greek* (London, 1898), p. 242; E. DeWitt Burton: *Syntax of the Moods and Tenses in New Testament Greek* (Chicago, 1906), p. 146; J. H. Moulton: *A Grammar of New Testament Greek*, Vol. I, *Prolegomena* (Edinburgh, 1930), pp. 179f.; A. T. Robertson: *A Grammar of the Greek New Testament* (New York, 1914), pp. 943f.; G. B. Winer: *A Grammar of the Idiom of the New Testament* (Andover, 1892), pp. 316f. Burton says that 'the New Testament furnishes but one certain instance of this usage', namely, Philippians 3: 16 and (continued on p. 215)

and the analogy of Paul's teaching elsewhere point to the entirely different conclusion, namely, that when Paul speaks of putting off the old man and putting on the new man he is thinking in terms of result rather than in terms of exhortation.[5] The passage should therefore be rendered as follows: 'But ye have not so learned Christ, if so be ye have heard him and have been taught by him as the truth is in Jesus, so that ye have put off, according to the former manner of life, the old man who is corrupted according to the lusts of deceit, and are being renewed in the spirit of your mind, and have put on the new man who after God has been

[5] On the Infinitive of Result cf. Blass: op. cit., pp. 223-225; Burton: op. cit., pp. 147-151; Moulton: op. cit., pp. 209f.; A. T. Robertson: op. cit., pp. 1089-1091. Though ὥστε is frequently used with this kind of infinitive, it also occurs without ὥστε. See Acts 5: 3; Hebrews 6: 10; Revelation 5: 5; 16: 9 (cf. Blass: op. cit., p. 224; Burton: op. cit., p. 149).

The infinitives ἀποθέσθαι and ἐνδύσασθαι could possibly be what Burton calls 'the Infinitive used to define more closely the content of the action denoted by a previous verb or noun' (op. cit., p. 150). In this case the infinitives would express what believers had learned of Christ or had been taught by him. The important consideration is not to define precisely the character of the infinitives here other than to show that to regard them as imperatival is without any good reason.

It is to be admitted that, if we take these infinitives as infinitives of result or as definitive of content, this does not per se establish the thesis that putting off the old man and putting on the new are once-for-all definitive actions. Even if believers are conceived of as progressively putting off the old man and putting on the new, the infinitives of result would still be appropriate. It would not be, however, in accord with the general (if not constant) characteristic of the aorist to interpret these aorist infinitives in this way (cf. Burton: op. cit., pp. 16-31; A. T. Robertson: op. cit., pp. 856ff.; Winer: op. cit., pp. 330ff.). But the arguments which are of greatest weight in this connection are the exegetical considerations given above. In the judgment of the writer they are conclusive.

---

that Romans 12: 15 is another probable instance. Blass shows similar reserve. Moulton says: 'The imperatival Infinitive has been needlessly objected to. It is unquestionable in Phil. 3: 16; Rom. 12: 15, and highly probable in Tit. 2: 2-10 . . . The epistolary Χαίρειν, Ac. 15: 23; 23: 26; Jas. 1: 1, is the same in origin.' A. T. Robertson finds more instances than any of the others cited above. Winer is perhaps the most reserved. 'Expositors', he says, 'have often been over-ready to discover this usage in the N.T.'

Though there is no reasonable question that the infinitive occurs with imperative force in the New Testament, Ephesians 4: 22, 24 could scarcely be an instance. It is not cited as such by any of the above authorities.

created in righteousness and holiness of the truth' (Ephesians 4: 20-24). It is apparent that this rendering, or the construction which it represents, carries with it no implication to the effect that the believer is regarded as both old man and new man, that he is exhorted to put off the former and put on the latter, and that progressive renewal consists in this process of divestiture and investiture.

In support of the construction adopted the following arguments may be advanced. (1) The close parallel in Colossians 3: 9, 10 would suggest that the same viewpoint with reference to the question at issue obtains in both passages. The import of Colossians 3: 9, 10 is quite clear and has been set forth. We should expect the Ephesians passage to reflect the same thought. (2) In this passage (Ephesians 4: 20-24) Paul provides us with a description, at least characterization, of the old man. He says that the old man 'is corrupt according to the lusts of deceit' (verse 22). He also tells us that the old man has his pattern in 'the former manner of life' (*idem*) and this manner of life is described in the preceding verses as one of vanity of mind, darkness of understanding, alienation from the life of God, ignorance, hardness of heart, abandonment to lasciviousness and all uncleanness (verses 17-19). We need but reflect on such a description; the old man is corrupt according to the lusts of deceit and his pattern is in terms of this catalogue of vices. Can we possibly think of a believer as answering to this description? To that characterization he must answer if he is still an old man as well as a new man. However keenly aware Paul is of his own sinfulness and that of believers by reason of indwelling, remaining sin, he never approaches to such a characterization of a believer. (3) The contrast which Paul institutes when he says 'But ye have not so learned Christ' indicates that he conceives of his believing readers as answering to an entirely different identification. This former manner of life which is the old man's pattern is no longer theirs; 'ye have not so learned Christ'. To use another New Testament expression, 'We are persuaded better things of you' (Hebrews 6: 9). But if the pattern of the believer's life is so different it would be strange indeed for Paul to characterize him as an old man when the pattern of the old man is precisely that of the former manner of life. The antithesis between the past and the present, which is the burden of Paul's message here, will not permit the incongruity of this construction. (4) It is altogether consonant with the contrast introduced in verse 20—'ye have not so learned Christ'—to regard verse 22 as the consequence flowing from this 'learning' of Christ.[6] Ye have learned Christ in such a way that ye have put off the old man. This is not only suitable to the sequence of thought; it is that which most fitly bears out the governing thought of the apostle. (5) The putting on of the new man, referred to in verse 24, is most suitably taken as the result. The new man is defined here as 'created after God in righteousness and holiness of the truth'. It is certain that the new man is contrasted with the old man. If the old man has been put off, as the considerations adduced above indicate, then the positive counterpart is the putting on of the new man which, in like manner, is the effect of having learned Christ. Besides, the definition of the new man 'as created after God in righteousness and holiness of the truth' is to be understood in terms of Paul's assertions elsewhere that 'if any man is in Christ, he is a new creation' (II Corinthians 5: 17), and that 'we are his workmanship, created in Christ Jesus unto good works' (Ephesians 2: 10; cf. Galatians 6: 15). The new man created after God (Ephesians 4: 24) is surely the new creation (Ephesians 2: 10). It is scarcely compatible with the concept of a new creation to think of it as that which we progressively become.[7]

[6] It is a question upon what the infinitives ἀποθέσθαι and ἐνδύσασθαι depend. Winer (op. cit., pp. 321f.) thinks that ἀποθέσθαι ὑμᾶς depends on ἐδιδάχθητε. It does not make a great deal of difference, it seems to me, to the exegesis of the passage whether these infinitives depend upon ἐμάθετέ or ἐδιδάχθητε. In the exegesis presented above I have taken them as depending upon ἐμάθετε and the thought then would be, 'Ye have not so learned Christ as to walk as other Gentiles walk (a description of which is given in verses 17-19), but ye have learned Christ so as to put off the old man and put on the new man'. If these infinitives depend on ἐδιδάχθητε, then the thought would be, 'Ye have been taught by Christ to put off the old man and to put on the new man', and the infinitives would express either the end contemplated in the teaching, or the content of the teaching, or the result actually following upon the teaching. But the governing thought is not affected, and the exegesis of the passage as a whole remains the same. At least these alternatives do not materially affect the main question at issue.

[7] It is conceivable that in Romans 6: 6; Colossians 3: 9, 10 Paul is dealing

(continued on p. 218)

For these reasons we are constrained to regard Ephesians 4: 22-24 as furnishing no other conception of the new man or of the old man than that provided by Romans 6: 6; Colossians 3: 9, 10. The case is rather, that Ephesians 4: 17-24 is corroboratory of the explicit emphasis of Romans 6: 6 to the effect that the old man has been crucified and that this is one of the ways in which Paul announces the definitive cleavage with the world of sin, which union with Christ insures. The old man is the unregenerate man; the new man is the regenerate man created in Christ Jesus unto good works. It is no more feasible to call the believer a new man and an old man, than it is to call him a regenerate man and an unregenerate. And neither is it warranted to speak of the believer as having in him the old man and the new man. This kind of terminology is without warrant and it is but another method of doing prejudice to the doctrine which Paul was so jealous to establish when he said, 'our old man has been crucified'.

This definitive transformation, summed up in the putting off of the old man and the putting on of the new, does not remove the necessity or the fact of progressive renewal. It is eloquent of this necessity and of the responsibility which is entailed for the believer

---

with the definitive crucifixion of the old man and yet in Ephesians 4: 22-24 regards the old man as still alive and needing to be mortified. This construction could plead the analogy of Paul's usage in connection with other terms. In Paul's thought believers died to sin once for all (Romans 6: 2) and yet sin lives in the believer (Romans 7: 14-25). 'They who are Christ's have crucified the flesh with the passions and the lusts' (Galatians 5: 24) and yet the flesh is still in the believer and he is still fleshly (Romans 7: 14, 18; 25). In these instances Paul in the one case is dealing with the definitive breach with sin and the flesh, in the other case with the fact that the believer is not yet perfect. Hence *pari passu* we might think of him as applying the same kind of distinction to the old man, in the one case his definitive crucifixion, in the other his continuing life and activity. The objection to this reasoning is that it finds no support in the usage of the apostle. Ephesians 4: 17-24 no more than Romans 6: 6; Colossians 3: 9, 10 betrays this viewpoint. Besides, the term 'old man' does not lend itself to the same kind of usage which we have in the case of 'sin' and 'the flesh'. 'Old man' is a designation of the person in his unity as dominated by the flesh and sin. Though Paul, indeed, identifies himself, his ego, with sin (Romans 7: 14, 20a, 25b) and then also with righteousness (Romans 7: 17a, 20b, 25a), yet he does not call the former his 'old ego' and the latter his 'new ego'. In like manner he does not call the 'sin' and 'the flesh' in him 'the old man'.

that in both passages where Paul contrasts the new man with the old there should be express notification of this progressive renovation. One of the results emanating from our 'learning Christ' is that we are 'being renewed in the spirit of our mind' (Ephesians 4: 23). And the new man who has been put on is 'being renewed unto knowledge after the image of him who created him' (Colossians 3: 10). The believer is a new man, a new creation, but he is a new man not yet made perfect. Sin dwells in him still, and he still commits sin. He is necessarily the subject of progressive renewal; he needs to be transfigured into the image of the Lord from glory to glory (cf. II Corinthians 3: 18). And this necessity enlists not only the continuously operative grace of God by which he is being renewed but also draws within its scope the responsible activity of the believer himself, so that Paul can write, 'Be not conformed to this world, but be ye transformed by the renewing of your mind, so that ye may prove what is the good and acceptable and perfect will of God' (Romans 12: 2). But this *progressive* renewal is not represented as the putting off of the old man and the putting on of the new, nor is it to be conceived of as the progressive crucifixion of the old man. It does mean the mortification of the deeds of the flesh and of all sin in heart and life. But it is the renewal of the 'new man' unto the attainment of that glory for which he is destined, conformity to the image of God's Son.

The second feature of Paul's teaching which bears upon the decisive cleavage with the world of sin is that which is epitomized in Romans 6: 14, 'Sin shall not have dominion over you'. This is not exhortation. It is categorical assurance and means that the person who is under grace is not and cannot be the bondservant of sin. Paul gives exhortation in practically identical terms in the same context. 'Therefore let not sin reign in your mortal body to the end that ye may obey its lusts' (Romans 6: 12). If we feel any incompatibility between the exhortation, 'let not sin reign', and the assurance, 'sin will not have dominion over you', it is because we are not sensitive to the logic of the gospel and to Paul's impeccable account of it.

In the matter of sin's dominion it only accentuates our servitude to be exhorted, 'let not sin reign', unless it is also true, and

antecedently so, 'sin shall not reign'. That is patently the logic of
Paul's teaching. 'Even so ye reckon yourselves to be dead indeed
to sin' (Romans 6: 11). They could not properly reckon to be a
fact what they were not persuaded was a fact. It is this assurance
and its corresponding estimation that give ground for the exhortation which follows and explains the 'therefore'; 'let not sin therefore reign'. And as we proceed to verse 14 we have the same
sequence. 'Let not sin reign . . . neither present your members
instruments of unrighteousness to sin, but present yourselves to
God as those alive from the dead . . . *for sin shall not have dominion
over you*' (Romans 6: 12-14). It is all summed up in the simple
proposition that the indicative underlies the imperative, and the
assurance of the indicative is the urge and incentive to the fulfilment of the imperative.

Sin does not have the dominion over the person who is united
to Christ and is under the governance of redeeming grace. This
is but an implication of Paul's basic premiss, 'we died to sin'.
And it is but another facet of the radical and decisive breach with
sin which is the consequence of union with Christ. It is the facet,
however, which brings to the forefront the aspect of *power*. Sin
is viewed from the angle of the power it wields and the breach
with sin from the angle of deliverance from its power. When we
die to sin we die to its power. We must not dilute the force of this
proposition any more than the others with which we have dealt.
There is the same decisiveness and finality. Sin does not rule in
the believer. To think so is to deny the lordship which belongs
to Christ by reason of his death and resurrection. And just as the
deliverance from the power of sin is decisive, so it is inclusive.
If the believer were under the dominion of any sin, then the
truth of the proposition 'sin shall not have dominion over you'
would be abrogated. The deliverance in view must therefore
apply to all sin, and the inescapable inference is that the sin which
still inheres in the believer and the sin he commits does not have
dominion over him. Sin as indwelling and committed is a
reality; it does not lose its character as sin. It is the contradiction
of God and of that which a believer most characteristically is.
It creates the gravest liabilities. But by the grace of God there is
this radical change that it does not exercise the dominion. The
self-condemnations which it evokes are the index to this fact.

It is this destruction of the power of sin that makes possible a realized biblical ethic.

Our theme in this chapter is the dynamic of the biblical ethic, the dynamic in its actualization and fruition. We have found the pivot to be the death and resurrection of Christ. Union with Christ in his death and resurrection is that which achieves the radical breach with the world of sin. Believers died to sin. The old man has been crucified. Sin will not have the dominion. The body of sin has been destroyed that henceforth they should not serve sin. But the death and resurrection of Christ mean more than the definitive breach with sin and its power. The death and resurrection of Christ are the abiding sources of sanctifying grace and therefore of ethical renewal. Christ rose from the dead through the glory of the Father and by the exceeding greatness of his power. And it is that same power exemplified in the resurrection of our Lord from the dead that is operative in believers (cf. Ephesians 1: 19, 20). Christ lives as the resurrected Lord and is the permanent embodiment of the efficacy, virtue, and grace accruing from his death and resurrection. He is invested with and is the embodiment of resurrection power. And since believers have been raised with him, they live in the abiding power, virtue, and grace of Jesus' resurrection life; they walk in newness of life (Romans 6: 4). The power and grace with which Christ is invested are operative in them, and continuously so. This is the dynamic of ethical living. We are thus brought to the threshold of another phase of New Testament teaching.

The resurrection of Christ was through the glory of the Father and by the exceeding greatness of the Father's power (Romans 6: 4; Ephesians 1: 19). The resurrection is also related to the action and work of the Holy Spirit. The New Testament does not frequently refer to the action of the Holy Spirit in the raising of Christ from the dead (cf. Romans 8: 11). But there is much emphasis upon the relation of the resurrected Lord to the Spirit and of the Spirit to the resurrected Lord. It is by reason of the resurrection that Christ is given the promise of the Spirit and it is the resurrected Lord who sends forth the Holy Spirit. On the occasion of Pentecost Peter said: 'This Jesus God raised up, of which we all are witnesses. Therefore having been exalted to the right hand of God and having received the promise of the Holy Spirit from the Father, he hath shed forth this which ye both see and hear' (Acts 2: 32, 33). Pentecost is the sequel to the exaltation of Christ. These two epochal events in the process of redemption are organically related.[8] It is undoubtedly of this correlation that our Lord spoke when he said to the disciples, 'But I tell you the truth, it is expedient for you that I go away. For if I go not away, the Comforter will not come unto you: but if I depart I will send him unto you' (John 16: 7; *cf.* 15: 26). In the same connection he also spoke of the Father as sending the Spirit (John 14: 26; *cf.* 14: 16, 17). Without question this action of Christ in sending the Spirit is one of the reasons why the Holy Spirit is called the Spirit of Christ (Romans 8: 9; I Peter 1: 11; *cf.* Acts 16: 17; Philippians 1: 19; Galatians 4: 6).

The intimacy of the relation that obtains between the exalted Lord and the Holy Spirit is even more strikingly expressed when we read in Paul, 'Now the Lord is the Spirit'. That Paul has in view the Holy Spirit is apparent. He proceeds, 'And where the Spirit of the Lord is there is liberty' (II Corinthians 3: 17). Then he speaks of the Lord, undoubtedly the Lord Christ, as the 'Lord of the Spirit' (3: 18). That Christ's identity as 'the Spirit' and his relationship to the Spirit as the 'Lord of the Spirit' emanate from a status and activity constituted by the resurrection is shown by Paul's own statement elsewhere. When he says that 'the last Adam became a life-giving Spirit' (I Corinthians 15: 45), the context makes it plain that he is thinking of the resurrection as that event by which Christ was made or became life-giving Spirit. Paul says explicitly that Christ became 'Spirit', and it is quite impossible to dissociate the assertion that 'the Lord is the Spirit' from that event by which the Lord became 'life-giving Spirit'. The apostle is not merging the person of Christ in the person of the Spirit nor obliterating the hypostatical individuality and distinctness of the two persons. But by these stupendous

[8] On the relation of the Holy Spirit to the resurrection of Christ and to the exalted Lord *cf.* Geerhardus Vos: 'The Eschatological Aspect of the Pauline Conception of the Spirit' in *Biblical and Theological Studies* by members of the faculty of Princeton Theological Seminary (New York, 1912), pp. 210-259. For an able and stimulating study of Pentecost and closely related questions *cf.* the recent contribution by Harry R. Boer: *Pentecost and the Missionary Witness of the Church*, Franeker, 1955 (?).

correlations he is intimating how the resurrection life and activity
of the Lord Christ are conditioned and how the sphere and realm
of *the resurrection* are permeated, controlled, and directed by the
Holy Spirit.[9] And yet we may not place the accent to such an
extent on the all-pervasive power and activity of the Spirit that
we make the exalted Lord subordinate, as it were, to the Spirit.
In the realm of the resurrection Christ is the life-giving Spirit
and the exalted Lord is 'the Lord of the Spirit'. The Holy Spirit
is the Spirit of the Lord. The conjunction and correlation are
expressive of the perfect unity and communion which the
trinitarian economy of redemption involves.

At best we are but touching the periphery of this great truth.
But we do gain perhaps a glimpse of the meaning of that emphasis which the New Testament places upon the pneumatical
conditioning of our Lord's resurrection life, the pneumatic endowment which is his, and the pneumatic power which he
exercises as a result of this endowment—he 'has been declared to
be the Son of God in power according to the Spirit of holiness
from the resurrection of the dead' (Romans 1: 4; *cf.* I Timothy
3: 16; I Peter 3: 18).[10] And we are in a better position to understand the bearing of Christ's resurrection upon the achievement
of the demand of the biblical ethic. It is in virtue of union with
Christ in his resurrection that the believer is able to walk in newness of life (Romans 6: 4). But if this is union with Christ in his
resurrection, it is union with the resurrected Lord in that pneumatic conditioning, endowment, and power which are his. This
is why the resurrection of Christ is the dynamic of the biblical
ethic; the resurrected Lord is *life-giving* Spirit and therefore

[9] Geerhardus Vos's terms are that 'the Spirit is both the instrumental cause
of the resurrection-act and the permanent substratum of the resurrection-
life' (*op. cit.*, p. 234; *cf.* p. 226).

[10] Vos's remarks probably reflect the proper exegesis of Romans 1: 4. 'The
reference is not to two existing sides in the constitution of the Saviour, but to
two successive stages in his life . . . The resurrection is to Paul the beginning
of a new status of sonship: hence, as Jesus derived his sonship κατὰ σάρκα
from the seed of David, he can be said to have derived his divine-sonship-in-
power from the resurrection' (*ibid.*, p. 229). It is questionable, however, if it
is proper to speak of Jesus as deriving 'his sonship κατὰ σάρκα from the seed
of David'. That thought is not overt in the text and it is doubtful if it is implied.
But otherwise Vos's exegesis is very illuminating.

communicates life to those who are in him. If we keep in view the correlation which we have found, this is but another way of saying that the dynamic of the biblical ethic is the Holy Spirit as the Spirit of Christ, sent forth in accordance with the promise of the Father. In the New Testament usage to be in Christ and to be in the Spirit, to have Christ in us and to have the Holy Spirit in us, to have the Spirit of Christ and to be Christ's have all the same effect (cf. Romans 8: 9-11). 'No one can say Jesus is Lord but in the Holy Spirit' (I Corinthians 12: 3). 'He that is joined to the Lord is one Spirit' and his body is the temple of the Holy Spirit (I Corinthians 6: 17, 19). 'In one Spirit were we all baptized into one body . . . and were all made to drink of one Spirit' (I Corinthians 12: 13).

It is scarcely necessary to draw attention to the relation which the Holy Spirit sustains to ethical life—it is only they who are after the Spirit, who have the mind of the Spirit, who are in the Spirit, who are indwelt by the Spirit of God and have the Spirit of Christ, who are able to do that which is well-pleasing to God (Romans 8: 5-13). The newness of life which is after the pattern of Jesus' resurrection is the 'newness of the Spirit' (Romans 7: 6); for it is the Spirit who makes alive (II Corinthians 3: 6). The sons of God are led of the Spirit (Romans 8: 14) and those who are led of the Spirit have been freed from the works of the flesh (Galatians 5: 17). It is by the Spirit that the called of Jesus Christ walk (Galatians 5: 16, 25). The virtues which exemplify and adorn the new life in Christ are the fruit of the Spirit (Galatians 5: 22-24). The love which is the fulfilling of the law is the love of the Spirit (Romans 15: 30; Galatians 5: 22; cf. Colossians 1: 8; Galatians 5: 14-16; Romans 13: 8-14). No more needs to be said. It is in the renewing of the Holy Ghost (Titus 3: 5) that newness of life has its inception and it is in the Holy Spirit alone that the ambit of life well-pleasing to God is defined. And this is to say, in New Testament terms, that the man of God is 'Spiritual', indwelt, governed, and directed by the Holy Spirit.

The fact that the Holy Spirit is the leading and directing agent in the believer's life brings into focus some considerations of paramount importance for the attainment of the biblical ethic. We shall reflect on but two.

First, the Holy Spirit is the Spirit of truth (John 14: 17; 15: 26;

16: 13; *cf.* I Corinthians 2: 9-15; I John 2: 26, 27). John even says that 'the Spirit is the truth' (I John 5: 6). Sin began with acceding to the lie of the father of lies. Integrity begins with the implantation of truth in our inward parts and the reception of the love of the truth and of the truth in love. The onward course of ethical integrity is not an automatic process; it is one of progressive conformation realized through the understanding and approval of the good and acceptable and perfect will of God (*cf.* Ephesians 5: 17; Romans 12: 2). It is the function of the Spirit to lead us into all the truth (John 16: 13) so that we may stand perfect and complete in all the will of God. This points us to what is central in connection with the efficient instrumentality of the truth. Our Lord, in speaking of the Holy Spirit as the Spirit of truth and as the person who would guide the disciples into all the truth, said also, 'He shall glorify me: for he shall take of mine and shall declare it to you' (John 16: 14). Christ is the truth, the embodiment of the truth, truth incarnate. He is the image of the invisible God, and the knowledge of the glory of God is resplendent in his face. In him are hid all the treasures of wisdom and knowledge. What could be more congruous than that the Holy Spirit, as the Spirit of truth, in recreating men after the image of God in righteousness and holiness of the truth, in leading them and guiding them into the truth, in refashioning them in the pattern of the truth, should place in the centre of understanding and interest him who is himself the truth, and cause them to be transformed into the same image from glory to glory (*cf.* II Corinthians 3: 18). Thus the glory of Christ is reflected in the people of God. It is not the artificial and sentimental mimicry to which the 'imitation' of Christ can be degraded. It is the efficacious and transforming enlightenment of the Holy Spirit by which the people of God attain 'unto a perfect man, unto the measure of the stature of the fulness of Christ' (Ephesians 4: 13). Christ is the great exemplar and the Holy Spirit who glorifies Christ insures that those who are indwelt and led by him count all things but loss for the excellency of the knowledge of Christ Jesus the Lord and press on 'unto the prize of the high calling of God in Christ Jesus' (Philippians 3: 14).

Second, the Holy Spirit is the Spirit of love (*cf.* Romans 15: 30;

Galatians 5: 22; Colossians 1: 8). When we thus think of the Holy Spirit we properly think of him as the one who generates love towards God in our hearts. No doubt this is the thought of Paul when he says, 'The fruit of the Spirit is love'. But the Holy Spirit is, first of all, the agent in shedding abroad in the hearts of believers the love of God towards them. This is the love spoken of when we read, 'And hope doth not put to shame, because the love of God is shed abroad in our hearts through the Holy Spirit who hath been given to us' (Romans 5: 5). We must not forget that the fountain from which our love to God flows is the love of God to us (*cf.* I John 4: 19), and love to our fellowmen proceeds from the same source (*cf.* I John 4: 11). When we are thinking of the biblical ethic as motivated by and fulfilled in love to God and our neighbour, it is a caricature and travesty of this love that we entertain unless it is a love generated in us by the apprehension of the love that passes knowledge, the love of God in Christ. 'Herein is love, not that we loved God, but that he loved us, and sent his Son to be a propitiation for our sins' (I John 4: 10). How vacuous and hypocritical are the pretensions of those whose religion and ethic consist in the maxim, 'As ye would that men should do to you, do ye even so to them' (Luke 6: 31), but who know nothing of the constraint of the love of Christ. The Holy Spirit is the Spirit of truth and therefore as the Spirit of love he captivates our hearts by the love of God and of Christ to us. In the diffusion of that love there flows also love to one another. 'Beloved, if God so loved us, we ought also to love one another' (I John 4: 11). The biblical ethic knows no fulfilment of its demands other than that produced by the constraint and claim of Christ's redeeming love (*cf.* II Corinthians 5: 14, 15; Galatians 2: 20). Our love is always ignited by the flame of Christ's love. And it is the Holy Spirit who sheds abroad in our hearts the igniting flame of the love of God in Christ Jesus. The love that is ignited is the fruit of the Spirit.

We are now brought back to the two commandments on which hang all the law and the prophets—'Thou shalt love the Lord thy God' and 'Thou shalt love thy neighbour as thyself'. It is easy to lisp this summation of the biblical ethic. It is just about as easy to brandish these commandments, especially the second, as the ethic to remedy our ills. How often have they been used (we should rather say abused) as vague generalizations to conceal antipathy to the particularities of divine demand which these commandments require us to fulfil. These are indeed the two great commandments. Our Lord himself is our authority. But at no point in the wide range of the biblical ethic are we more faced with the majesty of God's law, the sanctity of its claim, the all-pervasive relevance of its obligation, and the un-relenting demands of its perfection than when we read, 'Thou shalt love the Lord thy God with all thy heart, and with all thy soul, and with all thy mind, and with all thy strength' and 'Thou shalt love thy neighbour as thyself' (Mark 12: 30, 31). And nowhere is the impotency of fallen human nature more con-clusively registered than at the point of these commandments. It is not simply the impotency of fallen human nature, it is also the contradiction. 'The mind of the flesh is *enmity* against God' (Romans 8: 7), and enmity is the antithesis of love. How indis-pensable is the gospel thesis! It is of the Holy Spirit that love is the fruit and 'the fruit of the Spirit is love'. It is of the Spirit of the Father and of Christ that Paul here speaks, the Spirit of Pentecost, the Spirit given by the Father and sent by the exalted Lord, the Spirit with whose power the risen Christ is endowed and who conditions the world of the resurrection. It is the Spirit who generates love in the hearts of those whose delight is in the law of the Lord and who meditate thereon day and night (Psalm 1: 2; *cf.* Romans 7: 22, 25). Hence the love that fulfils the law, the love on which the law and the prophets hang, the love that blesses them who curse us and prays for them who despitefully use us, the love patterned after the perfection of the Father in heaven, is the love that is generated, fostered, maintained, and perfected in the realm of the Spirit. The powers of this realm are regnant in believers because they have been made alive together with Christ and raised up together and made to sit together in the heavenlies in Christ Jesus (*cf.* Ephesians 2: 5, 6), and these powers are regnant because the Spirit of the Lord is regnant. 'Where the Spirit of the Lord is, there is liberty' (II Corinthians 3: 17), the liberty which is complementary to the perfect law of liberty (James 1: 25; 2: 11, 12). There is liberty because love is regnant and love casts out the torment of fear (I John 4: 18). It is not liberty from law but liberty in law, for we 'fulfil the royal law according to the Scripture' (James 2: 8). This is the answer to the impossibility of our depravity—the Holy Spirit is dynamic in the realization of the biblical ethic. It is God who works in the saints 'both to will and to do for his good pleasure' (Philippians 2: 13). This is the guarantee of fulfilment, and it is the urge and incentive to the engagement of our whole being in the out-working of the eschatological salvation (cf. Philippians 2: 12).

CHAPTER X

THE FEAR OF GOD

THE fear of God is the soul of godliness. The emphasis of Scripture in both the Old Testament and the New requires no less significant a proposition. Whether it be in the form, 'The fear of the Lord is the beginning of wisdom' (Proverbs 9: 10; Psalm 111: 10) or 'The fear of the Lord is the beginning of knowledge' (Proverbs 1: 7), we are advised that what the Scripture regards as knowledge or wisdom takes its inception from the apprehension and emotion which the fear of God connotes. If we are thinking of the notes of biblical piety none is more characteristic than the fear of the Lord. 'Hast thou considered my servant Job? for there is none like him in the earth, a perfect and upright man, one that feareth God, and escheweth evil' (Job 1: 8). It is this same protestation that is repeated when our attention is particularly drawn to his persevering faithfulness and integrity (Job 2: 3)—'he still holdeth fast his integrity'. It is unnecessary to cite the scores of occasions throughout the Old Testament in which the fear of the Lord appears as the mark of God's people and enjoined as the sum of piety. Lest we should think that the religion of the Old Testament is *in this respect* on a lower level, and that the New Testament rises above that which is represented by the fear of the Lord, we need but scan the New Testament to be relieved of any such misapprehension. We are soon given to see that the notion of God's fear is not irrelevant in that piety which is the efflorescence of Old Testament faith. In the Magnificat of Mary we read: 'And his mercy is unto generations and generations for those who fear him' (Luke 1: 50). Could anything be more decisive than the words of the apostles: 'Having therefore these promises, beloved, let us cleanse ourselves from all filthiness of the flesh and spirit, perfecting holiness in the fear of God' (II Corinthians 7: 1); 'And ye servants, be subject in all things to those who are your masters according to the flesh, not with eyeservice as menpleasers, but in singleness of heart, fearing the Lord' (Colossians 3: 22); 'Honour all men, love the brotherhood, fear God, honour the king' (I Peter 2: 17)? And nothing could be more significant than that the fear of the Lord should be coupled with the comfort of the Holy Spirit as the characteristics of the New Testament church: 'So the church ... walking in the fear of the Lord and in the comfort of the Holy Spirit was multiplied' (Acts 9: 31). We may not forget that of him who is the shoot out of the stock of Jesse and the branch out of his roots, who judges the poor with righteousness and decides with equity for the meek of the earth, the girdle of whose waist is righteousness and of whose loins the girdle is faithfulness, of him it is said, 'And the Spirit of the Lord shall rest upon him, the Spirit of wisdom and understanding, the Spirit of counsel and might, the Spirit of knowledge and of the fear of the Lord; and his delight shall be in the fear of the Lord' (Isaiah 11: 2, 3). If he who was holy, harmless, undefiled, and separate from sinners was endued with the Spirit of the fear of the Lord, how can thought or feeling that is not conditioned by God's fear have any kinship with him who is the captain of our salvation and who has given us an example that we should follow his steps? The church walks in the fear of the Lord because the Spirit of Christ indwells, fills, directs, and rests upon the church and the Spirit of Christ is the Spirit of the fear of the Lord.

That ethical integrity is grounded in and is the fruit of the fear of God scarcely needs to be demonstrated. The earliest overt reference to the fear of God (Genesis 20: 11) shows that Abraham was well aware that the ethical standards which should regulate marital relationships would not be in evidence where the fear of God was absent. 'Surely the fear of God is not in this place; and they will slay me for my wife's sake.' There was more integrity in Abimelech than Abraham apparently expected. But Abraham's recognition that the absence of the fear of God produced an ethic other than that of integrity is in accord with the total witness of Scripture. 'Thou shalt not curse the deaf, nor put a stumblingblock before the blind; but thou shalt fear thy God: I am the Lord' (Leviticus 19: 14; cf. 25: 17, 36). 'The fear of the Lord is to hate evil: pride, and arrogancy, and the evil way, and the perverse mouth do I hate' (Proverbs 8: 13; cf. 16: 6). And surely the psalmist and apostle put this beyond question when they find the explanation of the catalogue of the transgressions

of the wicked in the fact that 'there is no fear of God before
their eyes' (Romans 3: 18; *cf.* Psalm 36: 1).

The relation of the fear of God to the keeping of the commandments of God is indicated by the 'Preacher' when he says, 'Let us
hear the conclusion of the whole matter: fear God and keep his
commandments; for this is the whole duty of man' (Ecclesiastes
12: 13). The most practical of mundane duties derive their
inspiration and impetus from the fear of God (*cf.* II Samuel 23: 3;
Colossians 3: 22). The highest reaches of sanctification are
realized only in the fear of God (*cf.* II Corinthians 7: 1).

This emphasis which Scripture places upon the fear of God
evinces the bond that exists between religion and ethics. The
fear of God is essentially a religious concept; it refers to the
conception we entertain of God and the attitude of heart and
mind that is ours by reason of that conception. Since the biblical
ethic is grounded in and is the fruit of the fear of the Lord, we are
apprised again that ethics has its source in religion and as our
religion is so will be our ethic. This is to say also that what or
whom we worship determines our behaviour. What then is the
fear of God?

There are at least two obviously distinct senses in which the
word 'fear' is used in Scripture.[1] Frequently it refers to the

---

[1] In Hebrew the notion of 'fear' is expressed usually by the two roots ירא
and פחד. The former is used of the fear of God most frequently and does service
for both senses in which we may fear God: (1) the fear of being afraid of God
and his punitive judgments; (2) the fear of reverential awe and adoration.
To express the latter the root ירא may be said to be the standard term. The
instances of this meaning are so numerous that it is unnecessary to cite them.
Of the former sense *cf.* Genesis 3: 10; Exodus 3: 6; Deuteronomy 5: 5; 17: 13;
19: 20; II Samuel 6: 9; Psalm 119: 120; Jonah 1: 16. We are not to think that
these two meanings are antithetical or incompatible. The 'terribleness' of God,
expressed by the Niphal Participle of ירא (*cf.* Exodus 15: 11; Deuteronomy
7: 21; 10: 17; 28: 58; I Chronicles 16: 25; Nehemiah 1: 5; Psalm 47: 2; 111: 9;
Daniel 9: 4; Malachi 1: 14), is that which demands awe, and it excites terror
in all who are subject to the judgments of his holy indignation. Deliverance
from this terror is the fruit of God's propitiatory grace. Exodus 20: 20 is an
interesting example of exhortation to put away the fear of terror and to
entertain the fear of reverence and obedience.

The root פחד bears more frequently the meaning of being afraid, of terror
(*continued on p. 232*)

terror and dread which we entertain when we are afraid of some person or thing or complex of circumstances. When we read, 'This day will I begin to put the dread of thee and the fear of thee upon the nations that are under the whole heaven, who shall hear report of thee, and shall tremble, and be in anguish because of thee' (Deuteronomy 2: 25), it is clear that the fear spoken of is that of being afraid, of terror and dread. Or again, 'Egypt was glad when they departed: for the fear of them fell upon them' (Psalm 105: 38); here the same meaning is apparent. But when we read, 'Ye shall fear every man his mother and his father' (Leviticus 19: 3) it is equally obvious that the meaning is not that of terror but of veneration and honour (cf. Joshua 4: 14).

It is this distinction that must be taken into account in dealing with the diverse injunctions of Scripture. When the Lord says to Joshua, 'Fear not, neither be thou dismayed' (Joshua 8: 1), what is in view is the fear of the enemies of Israel and has the same force as had been expressed earlier in different language, 'Be strong and of good courage; be not afraid, neither be thou dismayed: for the Lord thy God is with thee whithersoever thou goest' (Joshua 1: 9). It is the same cardinal thought, the avoidance of unbelieving anxious dread, that is pressed upon Israel: 'Fear thou not; for I am with thee: be not dismayed; for I am thy God' (Isaiah 41: 10; cf. verses 13, 14; 43: 1, 5; 44: 2; 51: 7; 54: 4, 14). The same is urged upon the disciples by our Lord, 'Fear not,

---

(cf. Exodus 15: 16; Job 3: 25; Isaiah 33: 14; 51: 13; Micah 7: 17). But that פחד can be used for reverential awe is apparent from the following instances: Genesis 31: 42, 53; Psalm 36: 1; 119: 120, 161; Jeremiah 2: 19; Hosea 3: 5. It is difficult to determine the precise shade of meaning in Proverbs 28: 14, but it is probable that the fear of coming short of God's commandments and of falling into sin is in the foreground. In any case the fear in view is commended. Isaiah 60: 5 is an interesting example of the use of פחד in the sense of joyful emotion. Apparently the thought is that the heart throbs with pleasure.

In the New Testament the terms generally used to express 'fear' are φόβος and φοβέω. They are used very frequently to express the idea of being afraid. In the sense of the fear that we owe to God these terms occur (cf. Matthew 10: 28; Luke 1: 50; 23: 40; Acts 9: 31; Romans 3: 18; 11: 20; II Corinthians 7: 1; Colossians 3: 22; Revelation 14: 7; 15: 4). They are also used with reference to the fear and trembling which are enjoined upon us in the path of obedience and perseverance (cf. I Corinthians 2: 3; Ephesians 6: 5; Philippians 2: 12; Hebrews 4: 1).

little flock; for it is your Father's good pleasure to give you the kingdom' (Luke 12: 32) and again, 'Fear not them which kill the body' (Matthew 10: 28; *cf.* Matthew 10: 31; Luke 12: 7, 32).

It would be unnecessary to adduce the evidence establishing so obvious a distinction were it not the case that these two meanings of 'fear' enter into the concept of the fear of God. There is the dread or terror of the Lord and there is the fear of reverential awe. There is the fear that consists in being afraid; it elicits anguish and terror. There is the fear of reverence; it elicits confidence and love. Scripture introduces us to the former when we read of Adam after his fall: 'And he said, I heard thy voice in the garden, and I was afraid because I was naked, and I hid myself' (Genesis 3: 10). Our moral and spiritual sensitivities are seared if we do not sense the religious catastrophe which this reply of Adam demonstrates. Made for communion with God, he now flees from his presence because he is afraid. And this dread of the presence of God is the reaction of his consciousness to the rupture which his sin had effected. Adam was afraid of God.

There is much loose thinking on this aspect of the question. Is it proper to be afraid of God? The only proper answer is that it is the essence of impiety not to be afraid of God when there is *reason* to be afraid. Adam's sin and his sin alone was the reason for the emotion of terror with which his soul had become stricken. But once he sinned the absence of this dread would have shown complete insensitivity to the revolution in which his sin consisted and which it also caused. For Adam to have behaved as if the rupture had not taken place would have been an unspeakable aggravation of his offence.

The Scripture throughout prescribes the necessity of this fear of God under all the circumstances in which our sinful situation makes us liable to God's righteous judgment. The person who did presumptuously in Israel and did not hearken to the priest who ministered in God's name was to be put to death, and we read, 'And all the people shall hear, and fear, and do no more presumptuously' (Deuteronomy 17: 13). The stubborn and rebellious son, a glutton and a drunkard, was to be stoned to death, and in this connection we read, 'And all Israel shall hear and fear' (Deuteronomy 21: 21). We must believe that in these contexts the fear mentioned is, principally at least, the fear evoked by the extreme punishment meted out to the transgressors involved, and the implication is that others would take warning from these examples and be inhibited from the commission of like offences by fear of the penalty. Again, lest we should think that this reflects a low plane of morality and motivation, worthy of the Old Testament but not of the gospel, we find this same kind of appeal in the New Testament itself. Nothing is more pertinent than our Lord's word, 'Be not afraid of them who kill the body, but are not able to kill the soul: but rather be afraid of him who is able to destroy both soul and body in hell' (Matthew 10: 28; cf. Luke 12: 4, 5). Jesus is pleading the necessity of that kind of fear which arises from the consideration of the judgment which God executes in the place of woe. It is futile to attempt to eliminate from the fear enjoined the terror which the thought of the final judgment of God is calculated to arouse. The writer of the Epistle to the Hebrews urges the fear of coming short as the incentive to diligence and perseverance. 'Let us fear therefore, lest by any means, a promise being left of entering into his rest, any one of you should seem to come short of it' (Hebrews 4: 1). And the same writer is not loath to bring the fearful expectation of judgment and the fierceness of the fire of God's vengeance, as the issues of apostasy, to bear upon the necessity of undeviating faith (Hebrews 10: 27). He brings the warning to a conclusion by reminding us that 'it is a fearful thing to fall into the hands of the living God' (verse 31).

The God of Scripture is holy and because he is holy his wrath rests upon sin. The strongest terms are enlisted to express the intensity of his indignation (cf. Exodus 15: 7; Numbers 25: 4; Isaiah 42: 25; 51: 17, 20, 22; 63: 6; Jeremiah 4: 8; 6: 11; 42: 18; Jonah 3: 9; Nahum 1: 6; Romans 2: 9; II Thessalonians 1: 8, 9; Revelation 20: 10, 14, 15). That those who are subject to this wrath should not dread it would be totally unnatural. It would be a violation of the infirmity inherent in our finitude not to be filled with horror and anguish at the thought of being subject to the fury of God's displeasure. Only the ignorant and hardhearted could be destitute of this terror. And to aver that the fear of God's wrath and of the judgments which execute his wrath is an improper motive to action is to go counter to all that sound reason would dictate. Once we are convinced of the reality of God's judgment our hearts must react with terror and to be content to contain that terror violates human psychology. Why do we resist the thought of God's wrath? Why do we try to suppress the conviction of its reality? Is it not because we do not wish to entertain the terror which the conviction involves and we do not wish to be placed under the necessity of fashioning thought and life in terms of this reality? And if we cannot resist or suppress the conviction, are we not compelled in the nature of the case to think and act in terms of the reality of which we are convinced? But whatever may be true in the realm of human psychology, it is quite obvious that the Scripture represents the dread or terror of God's wrath as belonging to the total concept of the fear of God. Even where there is no sin, and therefore no existent wrath, we cannot eliminate the fear of incurring God's displeasure as one motive deterrent to the commission of sin. We may not forget that the penal consequence of transgression was set forth to Adam before he fell: 'In the day thou eatest thereof thou shalt surely die' (Genesis 2: 17). And the same is adduced as a reason why he should not transgress. This is just to say that the fear of the consequence should have acted as a motive to deter him from sin. And shall we not say that the fear of incurring the displeasure of the Almighty is a motive in the ministry of the angels who have never sinned and have kept their first estate?

These foregoing considerations may help us to understand how this kind of fear is a necessity in the heart and life of the people of God. We should not be surprised when the psalmist proclaims: 'My flesh trembleth for fear of thee; and I am afraid of thy judgments' (Psalm 119: 120). It is the same piety of which Psalm 119 is redolent that could protest: 'The Lord is my light and my salvation; whom shall I fear? The Lord is the strength of my life; of whom shall I be afraid?' (Psalm 27: 1); 'I will not be afraid of ten thousands of the people that have set themselves against me round about' (Psalm 3: 6). Yet there is trembling and fear in the presence of God and of his judgments. The saint of God is not free from sin. He knows that sin is displeasing to God and he is keenly sensitive to the demands and judgments of his holiness. It is within this frame of thought and of feeling that we shall have to interpret those New Testament injunctions which never cease to have relevance to the believer during his sojourn here: 'Work out your own salvation with fear and trembling; for it is God who worketh in you both to will and to do for his good pleasure' (Philippians 2: 12, 13); 'And if ye call on the Father who without respect of persons judgeth according to each man's work, pass the time of your sojourning in fear' (I Peter 1: 17); 'Be not high-minded, but fear: for if God spared not the natural branches, neither will he spare thee' (Romans 11: 20, 21). Humility, contrition, lowliness of mind are of the essence of godliness. And the dispositional complex which is characterized by these fruits of the Spirit is one that must embrace the fear and trembling which reflect our consciousness of sin and frailty.[2] The piety of the New Testament is totally alien to the presumption of the person who is a stranger to the contrite heart and it is alien to the confidence of the person who never takes account of the holy and just judgments of God. The piety of the Bible is that of the contrite and humble spirit that trembles at God's Word. 'Blessed are the poor in spirit: for theirs is the kingdom of heaven. Blessed are they that mourn: for they shall be comforted. Blessed are the meek: for they shall inherit the earth' (Matthew 5: 3-5).

The fear of God which is the soul of godliness does not consist, however, in the dread which is produced by the apprehension of God's wrath. When the reason for such dread exists, then to be destitute of it is the sign of hardened ungodliness. But the fear of God which is the basis of godliness, and in which godliness may be said to consist, is much more inclusive and determinative than the fear of God's judgment. And we must remember that the dread of judgment will never of itself generate within us the love of God or hatred of the sin that makes us liable to his wrath. Even the infliction of wrath will not create the hatred of sin; it will incite to greater love of sin and enmity against God. Punishment has of itself no regenerating or converting power. The fear of God in which godliness consists is the fear which constrains adoration and love. It is the fear which consists in awe, reverence, honour, and worship, and all of these on the highest level of exercise. It is the reflex in our consciousness of the transcendent

[2] If Peter had feared and trembled by reason of his own frailty, he would not have indulged in the protestation that though all would be offended yet would not he (cf. Matthew 26: 31-35; Mark 14: 27-31).

majesty and holiness of God. It belongs to all created rational beings and does not take its origin from sin. The essence of sin may be said to be negation of God's fear. Perhaps the most eloquent example of this fear of God is the adoration of the angelic host in Isaiah's vision. 'In the year that king Uzziah died I saw the Lord sitting upon a throne, high and lifted up; and his train filled the temple. Above him stood the seraphim: each one had six wings; with twain he covered his face, and with twain he covered his feet, and with twain he did fly. And one cried unto another and said, Holy, holy, holy, is the Lord of hosts: the whole earth is full of his glory' (Isaiah 6: 1-3). The reaction of the prophet is likewise significant. The angelic host is overwhelmed with awe and reverence before the manifestation of God's transcendent holiness. But there is no abashment because of their sin. It is otherwise with Isaiah. 'Woe is me! for I am undone; because I am a man of unclean lips, and dwell in the midst of a people of unclean lips: for mine eyes have seen the King, the Lord of hosts' (verse 5). We have therefore the awe and adoration which the majesty of God must elicit from all rational creatures and we have also the complexion which the fact of our sinfulness must impart to that reverence and adoration.

It is this fear of God that Scripture has in view when it reiterates throughout, 'Thou shalt fear the Lord thy God'. The controlling sense of the majesty and holiness of God and the profound reverence which this apprehension elicits constitute the essence of the fear of God. When we attempt to analyse this fear there are various elements or, at least, corollaries. There is the all-pervasive sense of the presence of God. 'Whither shall I go from thy Spirit? Or whither shall I flee from thy presence? If I ascend up into heaven, thou art there: if I make my bed in Sheol, behold, thou art there. If I take the wings of the morning, and dwell in the uttermost part of the sea, even there shall thy hand lead me, and thy right hand shall hold me' (Psalm 139: 7-10). And there is the all-pervasive sense of our dependence upon him and responsibility to him (*cf.* Psalm 139: 1-6, 13-16, 23, 24; Acts 17: 26-28; Romans 11: 36; I Corinthians 8: 6; Hebrews 2: 10; Revelation 4: 11). The fear of God implies our constant consciousness of relation to God, that, while we are also related to angels, demons, men, and things, our primary relationship is to God and all other relationships are determined by, and to be interpreted in terms of, our relation to him. The fool says in his heart 'There is no God' and God is not in all the thoughts of the wicked (cf. Psalm 14: 1; 10: 4). The first thought of the godly man in every circumstance is God's relation to him and it, and his and its relation to God. That is God-consciousness and that is what the fear of God entails.

The Scripture graphically portrays the life of godliness in these terms. 'And Enoch walked with God after he begat Methuselah three hundred years, and begat sons and daughters . . . and Enoch walked with God: and he was not, for God took him' (Genesis 5: 22, 24; cf. 6: 9). 'And when Abram was ninety years old and nine, the Lord appeared to Abram and said unto him, I am God Almighty; walk before me, and be thou perfect' (Genesis 17: 1). The variation in the terms is likely intended to express the distinct facets of what is involved. Enoch walked with God and this, anthropomorphically, indicates his awareness of the presence of God and communion with him. Abraham is charged to walk before God and his life is represented as one lived in the constant consciousness of the inspection and direction of God. The anthropomorphism in the latter case points to the awe and circumspection which the knowledge of God's presence evokes, in the former case to the tenderness and intimacy of communion with God. These elements are correlative. That Abraham also walked with God and that he was distinguished by that trait, just as Enoch and Noah were, is apparent. He bears the distinction of being called the friend of God (II Chronicles 20: 7; Isaiah 41: 8; James 2: 23; cf. Genesis 18: 17-19).

The relation of the fear of God to ethics appears in the case of Abraham most conspicuously. We marvel at the magnitude of Abraham's character. His magnanimity: 'And Abram said unto Lot, Let there be no strife, I pray thee, between me and thee, and between my herdsmen and thy herdsmen; for we are brethren. Is not the whole land before thee? separate thyself, I pray thee, from me: if thou wilt take the left hand, then I will go to the right; or if thou wilt take the right hand, then I will go to the left' (Genesis 13: 8, 9). And though higher considerations than those of magnanimity prompted his reply to the king of

Sodom, yet these higher sanctions could not have found a place unless magnanimity had controlled his heart: 'I have lifted up my hand unto the Lord, God Most High, possessor of heaven and earth, that I will not take a thread nor a shoe-latchet nor aught that is thine,'lest thou shouldest say, I have made Abram rich' (Genesis 14: 22, 23). Yet there is an amazing example of the sense of justice in this same incident. 'Aner, Eshcol, and Mamre; let them have their portion' (verse 24). Magnanimity may constrain us to resign our own rights but never may it operate to deprive others of theirs—'let them have their portion'. We think also of Abraham's filial loyalty: 'And when Abram heard that his brother was taken, he led forth his trained men, born in his house, three hundred and eighteen, and pursued as far as Dan' (Genesis 14: 14); 'Cast out this handmaid and her son . . . And the thing was very grievous in Abraham's sight because of his son' (Genesis 21: 10, 11). And what is the secret of Abraham's nobility? The story informs us.

Obedience is the principle and secret of integrity. Next to his faith in God's promise, instant obedience to the commandment of God is the outstanding feature of Abraham's witness (cf. James 2: 21, 22). 'Take now thy son, thine only son Isaac, whom thou lovest; and get thee into the land of Moriah; and offer him there for a burnt offering' (Genesis 22: 2). The will of God was plain. Abraham did not hesitate. He rose early in the morning and set off to fulfil the command. The time for prayer was past, except the prayer for sustained strength of resolution. How different from Balaam who loved the wages of unrighteousness! And what is the Lord's word to Abraham? 'And the angel of the Lord . . . said, Lay not thy hand upon the lad, neither do thou anything unto him; for now I know that thou fearest God, seeing thou hast not withheld thy son, thine only son, from me' (Genesis 22: 11, 12). The inferences are obvious. God was proving Abraham and proving him in respect of his fear of God. Abraham's obedience demonstrated his fear of God. It was *because* Abraham feared the Lord that he obeyed God's voice.

The same relationship can be traced in the other virtues that adorned Abraham's character. Why could he have been so magnanimous to Lot? It was because he feared the Lord and trusted his promise and his providence. He had no need to be mean; he feared and trusted the Lord. Why could he have been magnanimous to the king of Sodom? It was because he feared the Lord, God Most High, possessor of heaven and earth, and might not allow the enrichment offered to prejudice the independence of his faith; he needed not to be graspingly acquisitive. He could offer up his son to whom the covenant promises were attached because he feared the Lord. It all amounts to this that nothing had value or meaning for Abraham except in terms of his relationship to God and God's to him, a relationship focused in covenant promise and faithfulness. *That* is all-pervasive God-consciousness, and it is God-consciousness conditioned by covenant-consciousness. This is the fear of God or its indispensable corollary.

The character of Isaac has been underestimated and sometimes he has been maligned. Inspiration, however, has accorded Isaac a unique tribute. It has inscribed on its record the most unusual title as applied to God, one which is derived from the fear of God which Jacob had witnessed in his father Isaac. That Jacob recognized his father as sharing the faith of his grandfather Abraham is apparent. 'O God of my father Abraham, and God of my father Isaac, O Lord, who saidst unto me, Return to thy country, and to thy kindred, and I will do thee good: I am not worthy of all the lovingkindnesses, and of all the truth, which thou hast showed unto thy servant; for with my staff I passed over this Jordan, and now I have become two bands' (Genesis 32: 9, 10). The humility, gratitude, and faith of Jacob are nowhere illustrated more clearly than in this prayer, and the place of Isaac in the legacy of faith which provided the background of Jacob's own faith is hereby certified. But the distinctive tribute to the godliness of Isaac resides in that title by which on two previous occasions the God of Abraham and Isaac had been identified. 'Except the God of my father, the God of Abraham, and the Fear of Isaac, had been with me, surely now hadst thou sent me away empty' (Genesis 31: 42). 'The God of Abraham, and the God of Nahor, the God of their father, judge betwixt us. And Jacob sware by the Fear of his father Isaac' (verse 53).

'The Fear of Isaac', as a name of God, witnesses to the profound and lasting impression produced upon Jacob by the fear of God which Isaac exhibited; it witnesses to the reality, depth, and per-

vasiveness of Isaac's godly fear; it shows that Jacob's conception
of the living God had been fashioned in terms of that which
Isaac's fear implied; it constitutes on the part of Scripture a
unique tribute to the place which the fear of God occupies in
the thought and life of Isaac. The only explanation of Jacob's
use of such a title is that Isaac's demeanour and behaviour bespoke
the profound sense of the majesty of God with which he was
imbued.

It is symptomatic of the extent to which the concept of the
fear of God and the attitude of heart and mind which it represents have suffered eclipse that we have become reluctant to
distinguish the earnest and consistent believer as 'God-fearing'.
Perhaps our reluctance arises from the fact that believers manifest
so little of the fear of God that we scarcely dare to characterize
them as God-fearing; we may even be hesitant to call them godly.
But whatever the reason, the eclipse of the fear of God, whether
viewed as doctrine or as attitude, evidences the deterioration of
faith in the living God. Biblical faith means the fear of God,
because the only God is 'glorious in holiness, fearful in praises,
doing wonders' (Exodus 15: 11) and his name is glorious and
fearful (cf. Deuteronomy 28: 58). If we know God we must know
him in the matchless glory of his transcendent majesty, and the
only appropriate posture for us is prostration before him in awe
and reverence. To think otherwise is to deny the transcendent
greatness of God, and that is infidelity. The pervasive emphasis
of Scripture upon the fear of God as the determinative attitude
of heart in both religion and ethics and as the characteristic mark
of God's people is exactly what must have been if the Bible is
consistent with itself. The doctrine of God could know nothing
else. To discount this emphasis and have any other is proof that
the faith of the Bible is not ours. Our consciousness is not biblical
unless it is conditioned by the fear of God.

The fear of God is the beginning of wisdom, and the perfection
of glory in the world to come will only intensify its exercise.
'Perfect love casts out fear' (I John 4: 18) but it is the fear of
torment, not that of reverence and adoration. 'Great and mar-
vellous are thy works, Lord God Almighty; just and true are
thy ways, O King of the nations: who shall not fear, O Lord, and

glorify thy name? for thou only art holy; for all the nations shall come and worship before thee, for thy righteous acts have been made manifest' (Revelation 15: 3, 4). God's dread majesty can never be dissolved and neither can the sense of it in those who serve him. The deeper the apprehension of God's glory the more enhanced will be our wonderment. It will not be the wonderment of perplexity or horror but of reverential and exultant adoration.

The fear of God could be nothing less than the soul of rectitude. It is the apprehension of God's glory that constrains the fear of his name. It is that same glory that commands our totality commitment to him, totality trust and obedience. The fear of God is but the reflex in our consciousness of the transcendent perfection which alone could warrant and demand the totality of our commitment in love and devotion. 'Thou shalt love the Lord thy God with all thy heart, and with all thy soul, and with all thy mind, and with all thy strength' (Mark 12: 30). It is the transcendent perfection of God, the fact that he is God and there is none else, that validates this totality demand. The fear of God in us is that frame of heart and mind which reflects our apprehension of who and what God is, and who and what God is will tolerate nothing less than totality commitment to him. The commandments of God are the concrete expressions to us of God's glory and will. If we are committed to him in devotion and love, we shall love his commandments, too. The fear of God and the love of God are but different aspects of our response to him in the glory of his majesty and holiness (cf. Deuteronomy 6: 2, 4, 14). 'The fear of the Lord is clean, enduring for ever: the judgments of the Lord are true and righteous altogether. More to be desired are they than gold, yea, than much fine gold: sweeter also than honey and the honeycomb. Moreover by them is thy servant warned: and in keeping of them there is great reward' (Psalm 19: 9-11).

APPENDIX A

WHATEVER view we adopt regarding the 'sons of God' mentioned in this passage, the wrong involved in the marriages contracted and the evils resulting therefrom bear directly upon the sanctity of marriage as the institution for the procreation of life. The interpretation of the passage obviously turns on the view we are to adopt respecting the 'sons of God'. Are they pre-ternatural angelic beings or are they members of the human race who are distinguished from the rest of humanity by this title?

The former view has been adopted by many interpreters and the identity of the 'spirits in prison' of I Peter 3: 19 has been, either wholly or partially, fixed in terms of that interpretation. The *Book of Enoch* has naturally exercised great influence in this direction because it definitely regards the episodes of Genesis 6: 1-3 as the sexual conjunction of angels with the daughters of men. 'And it came to pass when the children of men had multi-plied that in those days were born unto them beautiful and comely daughters. And the angels, the children of the heaven, saw and lusted after them, and said to one another: "Come let us choose us wives from among the children of men and beget us children." . . . Then sware they all together and bound them-selves by mutual imprecations upon it. And they were in all two hundred; who descended in the days of Jared on the summit of Mount Hermon . . . And these are the names of their leaders . . . And all the others together with them took unto themselves wives, and each chose for himself one, and they began to go in unto them and to defile themselves with them . . . And they became pregnant, and they bare great giants, whose height was three thousand ells: who consumed all the acquisitions of men' (VI, 1, 2, 5, 6, 7; VII, 1, 2, 3; *cf.* X. 1-15; XV, 1-12; LXIV, 1, 2; as translated by R. H. Charles: *The Book of Enoch*, Oxford, 1912). Most recently Bo Reicke: *The Disobedient Spirits and Christian Baptism* (Copenhagen. 1946) and E. G. Selwyn: *The First Epistle of Peter* (London, 1946), pp. 196ff., 314–362 have ably

presented the case for this interpretation of I Peter 3: 19 and, by
implication, of Genesis 6: 1-3. Without question, if I Peter 3: 19
refers to angelic beings, whether exclusively or partially so as to
include also the disembodied souls of men, this interpretation
would necessarily turn the scales in favour of the view that the
sons of God in Genesis 6: 1-3 were angelic beings.

Genesis 6: 1-3 does appear to lend support to the view that
'the sons of God' are non-human. We should naturally suppose
that 'the daughters of men' represent mankind and that those
designated 'sons of God' must not only be contrasted with the
women of mankind but also with mankind. We might expect
that if the contrast were simply between 'daughters' and 'sons',
that is between the women and the men, the distinction would
be drawn in terms of 'the daughters of men' and 'the sons of
men'. Also, it must be granted that angelic beings could be called
'sons of God' (cf. Job 1: 6; 2: 1; 38: 7).

If we are to be guided by considerations of a biblico-theological
character there are overwhelming objections to this interpretation.
However helpful extra-canonical literature may be in arriving
at the sense of Scripture, extra-canonical considerations may
never be pitted against the evidence which the Scripture itself
determinatively provides. The arguments in support of the view
that 'the sons of God' in Genesis 6: 2 refer to members of the
human race have been ably presented by C. F. Keil and F.
Delitzsch in their *Biblical Commentary on the Old Testament*
(Eng. Trans., Grand Rapids, 1949), Vol. I, pp. 127-139, and
by William Henry Green in an article, 'The Sons of God and
the Daughters of Men' (*The Presbyterian and Reformed Review*,
Vol. V (1894), pp. 654-660). With some abbreviation and
modification I shall present the argument as developed by them.

(1) There is no reason why הָאָדָם in Genesis 6: 1 should not be
used in a generic sense and בְּנוֹת הָאָדָם in Genesis 6: 2 in a specific
sense to designate a division within mankind. The evidence from
Hebrew usage adduced by Keil and Delitzsch (*op. cit.*, pp. 130f.)
and by Green (*op. cit.*, pp. 658f.) demonstrates the feasibility
of this construction. Besides, it may not be necessary to take הָאָדָם
in verse 1 in the generic sense; it may be used in the specific
sense in which it is used in verse 2 and thus in both verses con-

trasted with 'the sons of God' in the sense to be explained presently. But, in any case, usage indicates that there is no necessity to suppose that, because 'the sons of God' are distinguished from 'the daughters of men', 'the sons of God' cannot belong to the genus humanity. They may also be men; only they are called 'sons of God' to distinguish them from other men who do not belong to the classification by which the former are distinguished.

(2) In the preceding context the family of Seth is distinguished by the significant observation that within that lineage 'men began to call upon the name of the Lord' (Genesis 4: 26). There is an eloquent contrast between this mark of piety within the Sethite family and that delineation which we find in the immediately preceding context of the family of Cain. Notable distinction is shown to exist within the human family. This notification of distinction in terms of the fear and service of God is certified in the genealogy of Genesis 5 which follows. 'And Enoch walked with God after he begat Methuselah three hundred years . . . and Enoch walked with God: and he was not; for God took him' (5: 22, 24). 'And Lamech lived . . . and begat a son: and he called his name Noah, saying, This same shall comfort us in our work and in the toil of our hands, because of the ground which the Lord hath cursed' (5: 28, 29). We are thus definitely prepared for distinctions, drawn within the human family, in respect of the very relationship which the title 'sons of God' might be expected to connote or specify. It is neglect of this factor which appears so conspicuously in the two genealogies immediately preceding Genesis 6: 1-3 that gives plausibility to the argument that 'the sons of God' must refer to preternatural beings. When the contrasts of the preceding narrative are taken into account this plausibility dissipates. Quite naturally the title 'sons of God' can be taken as another specification of the discrimination already established.

(3) The passage implies that some grievous wrong had been perpetrated in the marriages concerned. Verse 3 refers to the judgment of God upon it. It is significant that the judgment has respect to man alone. If the sons of God were angels we should expect some intimation of the judgment executed upon them. The sons of God were the initiators of this travesty—'they saw

. . . they took'. If they were angels the severest penalty would have been inflicted upon them. But the narrative has in view only the judgment upon men. 'And the Lord said, My Spirit shall not rule in man for ever in their erring; he is flesh, and his days shall be a hundred and twenty years.' To say the least, we are led to suspect that only mankind was involved in the wrong.

Furthermore, if holy angels were the perpetrators of this wrong, they must have fallen from their holy estate, and if they fell thereby the heinousness of the sin would have been greatly aggravated. Since it occurred on the scene of this world we should all the more expect that the judgment upon them would have been intimated (cf. Genesis 3: 14, 15).

(4) There is no suggestion anywhere in Scripture that angels or demons are capable of sexual functions. As W. H. Green says, 'Sexual relations are nowhere in Scripture attributed to superior beings. There is no suggestion that angels are married or are given in marriage; the contrary is expressly declared (Matt. xxii. 30) . . . The whole conception of sexual life as connected with God or angels is absolutely foreign to Hebrew thought, and for that reason cannot be supposed to be countenanced here' (op. cit., p. 655).

(5) The phrase לָקַח אִשָּׁה used in verse 2—'and they took to them wives'—is the common Old Testament expression for marriage. It is not the expression that would conveniently denote the utterly abnormal and monstrous relationship constituted by the sexual conjunction of angels and the women of mankind. As we shall see later, there is no indication in this passage that the marriages as such were of an abnormal or monstrous character. The wrong is of a different type.

(6) Men are called 'sons of God' in the usage of the Old Testament and, more particularly, in the Pentateuch (cf. Exodus 4: 22, 23; Deuteronomy 14: 1; 32: 5, 6; Psalm 73: 15; 82: 6; Hosea 1: 10; Malachi 1: 6). There is no reason why some division of the human race, or certain persons by reason of religious privilege or political authority, should not be given this designation in order to distinguish them from others.

(7) The supposition that the *nephilim* mentioned in verse 4 are the offspring of these abnormal sexual conjunctions and that they were superhuman monsters because they were the issue of angelic

beings has absolutely no warrant in the text. The supposition is an importation which the syntax does not support and against which the terms definitely militate. All that is stated is that the *nephilim* were in the earth in the days in which the sons of God took wives from the daughters of men. And the natural construction is that they were already in the earth when these marriages took place, that after the offspring of these marriages were born the *nephilim* exercised the rôle of warriors, and that they long antedated these marriages and the situation arising from them. There is no suggestion of genetic connection between the *nephilim* and the marriages concerned. To insist that there is violates the canons of sober exegesis.

We must conclude therefore that there is no biblical support for the view that 'the sons of God' were angelic or preternatural beings. The biblical evidence militates against this interpretation and decisively supports the view that the marriages concerned were those between one classification of mankind that could be designated 'sons of God' and another classification that could not be thus designated. The narrative itself points to this discrimination as that between the Sethites and the Cainites, between those who feared the Lord and those who were worldly.

The lesson derived from this passage is directly pertinent to the sanctity of marriage. In the judgment pronounced upon this episode of human history we have the condemnation of unholy marital alliance. The point is not that these marriages were *per se* illicit, or that the sexual relations were of a monstrous character, but that they were contracted in disregard of the principles that should guide the people of God in the selection of marital partners. We have portrayed for us the evil that is entailed in, and results from, the failure to remember that in marriage we are not to please worldly and fleshly impulse but to seek wedlock that conserves and promotes the interests of godliness. In wedlock we must preserve the line of demarcation between the people of God and the ungodly world and have respect to the unity in faith and the bond of peace which will insure godly nurture. How early in the biblical history we have advertised and sealed the principle that marriage is not only for the increase of mankind with a legitimate issue but of the church with a holy seed. We have here what becomes more explicit in the onward progress of covenant revelation, that the godly should marry only in the Lord.

If the *nephilim* of verse 4 do not have genetic connection with the marriages of verse 2, what, we may ask, is the purpose of the reference to them in this sequence? We do not need a great deal of ingenuity to find the answer. The first three verses deal with the vice of mixed marriages and the judgment resulting from it. The succeeding part of the chapter (verses 5ff.) deals with the corruption which abounded in the earth and with the violence that became rampant—'all flesh had corrupted their way upon the earth' (verse 12) and 'the earth was filled with violence' (verse 11). What more significant datum could be mentioned as a transition than the reference to the *nephilim*? If the *nephilim* were in the earth and they exercised the rôle of warriors, the implication is that their prestige and activities had a decisive influence, either for good or for evil, in the abounding iniquity of that period.

If we were to suppose that the influence of the *nephilim* was for good, then we should have to regard them as the guardians of justice and order and as offering resistance to the rampant vice. On this hypothesis the resistance they offered would only accentuate the potency and prevalence of vice, for, notwithstanding their power and renown, violence still abounded. It is more reasonable to believe, however, that the *nephilim* were themselves agents in promoting violence. We are told that the whole earth was corrupt before God and it is not likely that the *nephilim* were notable exceptions. It is more natural to think that the *nephilim* were the main perpetrators of violence and because of their might and renown played the rôle of dictators or tyrants and thus gave impetus to the violence that filled the earth. The relevance of allusion to these *nephilim* in the narrative of events is apparent.

There is one further observation that may be made regarding the *nephilim* and the context in which allusion to them occurs. It is to the effect that the passage as a whole shows the close interaction of the various kinds of vice. While the connection between the *nephilim* and the marriages is not genetic, there is, nevertheless, a moral connection. The degeneration presupposed in, and again resulting from, these unholy alliances provided fruitful soil for the violence in connection with which the *nephilim* played a decisive rôle. The breakdown of moral and religious restraints evidenced by these marital alignments gave rein to the vice of violence and oppression. The indulgence of sex vice in any form kindles the flames of passion which break out in other directions, particularly in the direction of violence. Marriage is the institution for the procreation of life. Holy marriage is an indispensable means of conserving and promoting godly families and the nurture of faith; it is the institution for the propagation of godly life. When the proprieties which govern such marriages are desecrated, then the gates are flung open to the most violent of vices. This is the lesson written plainly on Genesis 6: 1-13.

APPENDIX B

THE first of these verses reads: 'Thou shalt not uncover the nakedness of thy brother's wife: it is thy brother's nakedness'. Since the Levirate law of Deuteronomy 25: 5-10 required the marriage of a man and his deceased brother's widow when the brother died childless, it might appear that the prohibition here has reference to the brother's wife only as long as the brother lived and could not apply to the deceased brother's widow. This does not follow, however. The Levirate law could well be an exception to meet a certain exigency and is quite compatible with the general provision that a man may not marry his deceased brother's widow. The latter could be the rule, the Levirate law the exception in the extreme exigency contemplated (*cf.* Neufeld: *op. cit.*, pp. 43, 44, 203). There are good reasons for this view.

1. Leviticus 20: 21 deals with the same subject as Leviticus 18: 16 and specifically with the penalty for such impurity. The penalty is that they shall die childless, apparently meaning that any offspring there might be would not be included in the public registers, 'so that in a civil sense they would be childless' (Michaelis: *op. cit.*, p. 114). But if the prohibition had in view sexual intercourse while the brother was still living, then the impurity involved would be an aggravated form of adultery for which the penalty would have been death in accordance with other Mosaic provisions. The relative mildness of the penalty, in contrast with the other cases mentioned in Leviticus 20: 14, 17 and probably 20: 18, can only be explained on the ground that marriage with a deceased brother's widow was not regarded as heinous as the offence in some other cases. This could not be by any means the case if the woman were the surviving brother's wife.

(2) Since Leviticus 20: 21 has marriage in view, the prohibition of Leviticus 18: 16 would have in mind a totally abnormal situation, in terms of Hebrew practice, if the brother is conceived of as living. For then we should have polyandry. Polygamy we have in the Old Testament but not polyandry. And to

think of such a monstrosity as visited with no greater penalty than that of Leviticus 20: 21 is contrary to all Old Testament analogy.

(3) The reason why marriage with a deceased brother's widow is not regarded with the gravity of some other prohibited degrees is apparent from Deuteronomy 25: 5-10. Since it is required in that exigency it is apparent that it cannot be intrinsically as grave an offence as that of Leviticus 20: 14, for example. But there could be no such explanation if the offence were marriage with a brother's wife while the brother lives.

That a widow can be called the wife (אִשָּׁה and γυνή) of her deceased husband is easily demonstrated (cf. Genesis 38: 8; Deuteronomy 25: 5, 7; Ruth 4: 5; II Samuel 12: 10; Matthew 22: 25; Acts 5: 7; see George Bush: *Notes, Critical and Practical, on the Book of Leviticus*, New York, 1843, pp. 177ff.). Hebrew has a word for widow (אַלְמָנָה), but it is not Old Testament usage to identify a widow as the widow of such an one. As the above instances show, it is the usage to call her the 'wife' (אִשָּׁה) of such an one. Hence the presence of the word 'wife' here rather than widow is what we should expect, even though the person concerned is, in our terminology, actually the widow.

Leviticus 18: 18 has given occasion for much dispute. Most frequently the expression אִשָּׁה אֶל־אֲחֹתָהּ is interpreted as meaning 'a wife to her sister' and the prohibition is regarded as dealing with the relation of a man to his wife's sister. In terms of this interpretation the verse would read as follows: 'And thou shalt not take a wife to her sister, to vex her, to uncover her nakedness, besides the other in her lifetime'. The precise force of certain expressions (לִצְרֹר and עָלֶיהָ) is doubtful. But the main thought is that a man may not take his wife's sister to uncover her nakedness during the lifetime of the other. Many expositors are emphatic to the effect that what is expressly forbidden is simply and solely that a man may not be married to two women who are sisters at the same time and that the concluding term 'in her lifetime' (בְּחַיֶּיהָ) makes it unmistakeably clear that the prohibition has nothing whatsoever to do with the question of marriage to a *deceased* wife's sister, that only neglect of the express limitation contained in the verse could ever allow for such an interpretation.

Michaelis (*op. cit.*, p. 113) says: 'As to his doing so in the life-time
of the first, I cannot comprehend how it should ever have been
imagined that Moses also prohibited marriage with a deceased
wife's sister . . . What Moses prohibited, was merely *simultaneous
polygamy* with two sisters; that sort of marriage in which Jacob
lived, when he married Rachel, as well as her sister Leah.' *Cf.*
S. H. Kellogg: *The Book of Leviticus* (*The Expositor's Bible*), New
York, 1891, p. 382, who says: 'No words could well be more
explicit than those which we have here, in limiting the application
of the prohibition to the life-time of the wife'. *Cf.* also C. F.
Keil and F. Delitzsch: *Biblical Commentary on the Old Testament*
(Edinburgh, 1882) *ad* Leviticus 18: 18.

It must be admitted that, if the prohibition in question has
reference to a man's wife's sister, that is to say, if אָחוֹת is to be
understood in the sense of sister properly understood, then the
limiting expression בְּחַיֶּיהָ is to be interpreted as limiting the
prohibition to the lifetime of the wife mentioned in the text, and
this verse could not be reasonably pleaded as in itself forbidding
marriage with a deceased wife's sister. The expression לִצְרֹר?,
whatever may be its precise force, would strengthen this conclusion. It could not be supposed that the sister would be a rival or
the cause of vexation to the wife after the latter was deceased.

There is also much to be said in favour of the view that אָחוֹת
in this verse is a sister, literally understood. In the passage אָחוֹת
is used in this sense in verses 9, 11, 12 and 13, and we should
reasonably expect that it would be used in the same sense in verse
18. Only strong considerations to the contrary would carry
weight in support of another conclusion.

However, an entirely different view of the import of Leviticus
18: 18 must be accorded serious consideration. It is the view that
the expression אִשָּׁה אֶל־אֲחֹתָהּ is not to be rendered 'a wife to her
sister' but rather 'one wife to another' and that what is prohibited
here is digamy or polygamy. The verse would then be rendered
as follows: 'Thou shalt not take a wife to another, to vex her, to
uncover her nakedness, besides her in her lifetime.' *Cf.* Matthew
Pool: *Annotations upon the Holy Bible, ad* Leviticus 18: 18; Charles
Hodge: *The Biblical Repertory and Princeton Review*, 1842, Vol.
XIV, pp. 518f.

This view of the verse would have to be abruptly dismissed, as is done by many, were it not for the fact that in Hebrew usage of the Old Testament the expression which occurs in Leviticus 18: 18, to wit, אִשָּׁה אֶל־אֲחֹתָהּ is used elsewhere in the sense of 'one to another' without implying that the persons concerned are sisters in the proper sense. In fact it is an idiom of the Hebrew Old Testament in the sense of 'one to another' even when persons are not in view at all (cf. Exodus 26: 3, 5, 6, 17; Ezek. 1: 9, 23; 3: 13). In this respect it is like the expression אִישׁ אֶל־אָחִיו (literally 'a man to his brother') which occurs more frequently and does not imply more than 'one to the other' or 'one to another' (Genesis 42: 21, 28; Exodus 10: 23; 16: 15; 25: 20; 37: 9; Numbers 14: 4; Isaiah 9: 18; Jeremiah 13: 14; 23: 35; 25: 26; Ezekiel 24: 23). Of course, on occasion the persons involved may be literally brothers but this is not necessary. The expression אִישׁ אֶל־אָחִיו is similar to other expressions (cf. Genesis 13: 11; Exodus 32: 27; Leviticus 7: 10; 25: 14; Deuteronomy 1: 16; Jeremiah 31: 33; Ezekiel 4: 17; 18: 8; 38: 21; Joel 2: 8; Zechariah 7: 9, 10; Malachi 2: 10).

Hence the expression with which we are concerned, as far as Old Testament usage is concerned, can perfectly well mean 'a wife to another', 'one woman to another' and need not reflect upon two women who are sisters in the proper sense of the term. The only reason why this has been abruptly dismissed is that sufficient attention has not been paid to the force of this expression and its analogues elsewhere.

If this interpretation is adopted, then the verse has no bearing whatsoever upon the question so keenly debated, namely, that of marriage with a deceased wife's sister. Indeed, it would bear upon the question of a man's relation to his wife's sister in terms of the prohibition of digamy in general. But it would have no relevance, of itself, to the question of the deceased wife's sister. And, furthermore, this verse would be express condemnation of digamy and polygamy and would hark back to the original ordinance of monogamy (Genesis 2: 23, 24).

There are difficulties encountering this interpretation. If it is such an express prohibition of digamy or polygamy, why were digamy and polygamy practised subsequent to the time of Moses without overt condemnation in terms of this statute? If digamy is here expressly forbidden we should expect a penalty in terms of the Pentateuch itself. And why should there be at Leviticus 18: 18 such a sudden transition from prohibitions concerned with marriages within certain degrees of kinship to a provision of an entirely different character?

This last objection is not as cogent as it might at first appear to be. The paragraph divisions of our English Bibles do not have any necessary validity. It may be that the transition from questions pertaining to kinship occurs at the end of verse 17 rather than at the end of verse 18. It is obvious that verse 19 introduces prohibition of a different category. Why should not transition take place at verse 18? Verse 20 deals with adultery. Why should not verse 18 deal with a closely related sin, that of digamy or polygamy? In Leviticus 20: 10-21 the penalties instituted are concerned to a large extent with violations of the proprieties that should govern near of kin, but there is sudden transition from this category of wrong to different categories (cf. verses 15, 16, 18 and Deuteronomy 27: 15-26). The objection therefore as it pertains to transition has little, if any, weight.

The objection that we should expect to find appeal to this prohibition of digamy and penal legislation for violation is much more cogent. Yet it is not of sufficient weight to rule out the possibility that Leviticus 18: 18 should be interpreted in the way proposed. It may not be pointless in this connection to note that, in the list of penalties imposed in Leviticus 20: 10-21 and in the curses pronounced in Deuteronomy 27: 15-26, there is no reference to marriage with a wife's sister. We might expect some reference to this wrong if it is so expressly forbidden in Leviticus 18: 18. On the assumption that it refers to marriage with a wife's sister while the former is alive, this violation would surely carry with it no less a penalty than that upon marriage with a brother's widow (Leviticus 20: 21).

The case is such therefore that we may not assume and dogmatically insist that Leviticus 18: 18 deals with the question of a wife's sister whether the wife is contemplated as living or dead. The verse may concern something very different. If this is so, then there is nothing express and overt in the Mosaic law pertaining to the matter of the deceased wife's sister. Is there anything implicit? This is the whole question of the implications of these relevant passages in the Pentateuch. Are marriages within similar or equal degrees of kinship prohibited as well as those expressly mentioned by Moses? For example, the prohibitions in Leviticus 18: 7-18 are viewed from the standpoint of the man; they are stated in terms of the kinship he sustains to the woman in question in each case. But must we not suppose that if we take the standpoint of the woman and think in terms of the kinship she sustains to the man the prohibitions apply to the same types of kinship? To be specific, Leviticus 18: 12 reads: 'Thou shalt not uncover the nakedness of thy father's sister'—a man may not marry his father's sister. But does it not follow by inference, because of the identical nature of the kinship, that a woman may not marry her father's brother or, for that matter, her mother's brother? This is the question on which much division of opinion has existed. In reference to our precise question, that of the deceased wife's sister, the matter turns on the implications of Leviticus 16: 16. There a man is forbidden to marry his deceased brother's widow. Stating this from the standpoint of the woman it means that *a woman may not marry her deceased husband's brother*. Does it not follow by inference that *a man may not marry his deceased wife's sister*? In the judgment of the present writer it is here that the matter of the deceased wife's sister enters and not in connection with Leviticus 18: 18. On either interpretation of the latter text, it is not the deceased wife's sister that is in view. But we are confronted with this question inescapably in connection with the possible implications of Leviticus 18: 16; 20: 21. It would take us beyond reasonable limits to enter into this discussion. But it seems to me necessary to understand that Moses has not specified all the prohibitions which are involved in the degrees of consanguinity and affinity enunciated. Leviticus 18: 6-17 provides us with the *principles* in terms of which the prohibited degrees of consanguinity and affinity are to be determined. Of course Moses does not do this in the *form* of principles. That would not be consonant with Old Testament method. Moses declares the law in terms of the concrete. But these concrete instances are not to be isolated from the kind of relationship which they exemplify. And that is what is meant when we say that Leviticus 18: 6-17 provides us with principles, that is, with the principles of relationship in terms of which we are to interpret the degrees of consanguinity and affinity within which marriage is illicit. This is surely in accord with the analogy of Scripture. The ten commandments are concrete but they exemplify far-reaching principles. None has shown this more clearly than our Lord himself. In the matter of divorce the New Testament *expressly* gives the right of divorce only to the man. But we infer, and surely rightly, that the same right belongs to the woman in the event of adultery on the part of her husband. By similar reasoning may we not draw certain inferences from Leviticus 18: 6-17?

This position implies that Moses was selective and gave a representative list but not a complete catalogue. That he could be selective appears from Leviticus 20: 10-21 and Deuteronomy 27: 15-26. In the former the penalties are specified, in the latter curses are pronounced. But he does not specify all the cases mentioned in Leviticus 18: 6-17, particularly not in the curses pronounced. Yet we cannot suppose that those omitted carry no penalty or curse. In Leviticus 20: 10-21 there is no explicit mention of the penalty for uncovering the nakedness of a uterine mother, the first of the prohibitions in Leviticus 18. We could not believe that the penalty would be less than that for intercourse with a father's wife (Leviticus 20:11), namely, death. Apparently the reason for the omission is that the penalty would be understood without any overt prescription.

What the principle of selection adopted in these various passages was it would be difficult to say. Perhaps Mace's suggestion (*op. cit.*, p. 152) is as good as any that the incestuous unions expressly prohibited were those of 'fairly frequent occurrence at the time'. But that we do not have a complete list and that we may apply the same principles of kinship to near of kin not expressly specified is the conclusion to which the relevant data would point (*cf.* Mace: *op. cit.*, pp. 152-164).

Hence the conclusion to which the present writer is driven is that the prohibition of marriage with a deceased wife's sister is implicit in the prohibition of marriage with a deceased husband's brother (Leviticus 18: 16; 20: 21).

APPENDIX C

ADDITIONAL NOTE ON I CORINTHIANS 5: 1

In addition to the fact that Paul so severely condemns this violation of the law governing affinity there are other considerations which show the universality of the ethic involved.

There is, first of all, the consideration that the heathen nations had been condemned for the violation of these precepts of Leviticus 18: 6-17. 'Defile not ye yourselves in any of these things: for in all these the nations are defiled which I cast out before you: and the land is defiled: therefore I do visit the iniquity thereof upon it, and the land itself vomiteth out her inhabitants. . . . For all these abominations have the men of the land done, which were before you, and the land is defiled' (Leviticus 18: 24, 25, 27; cf. 20: 22, 23). If these violations of marital propriety are among the abominations and iniquities which the Lord abhorred, it was because they were iniquities for the nations concerned and therefore departures from the law of God by which they were bound. The precepts had application, therefore, to all men and not simply to Israel.

Secondly, Paul says that the kind of fornication in view, that a man should have his father's wife, was not even among the Gentiles (καὶ τοιαύτη πορνεία ἥτις οὐδὲ ἐν τοῖς ἔθνεσιν). It is, of course, difficult to understand this statement in view of the practices of peoples proximate to the Graeco-Roman world. It is likely that Paul has in mind Roman law and custom (cf. John Fulton: *The Laws of Marriage*, New York, 1883, pp. 31ff.; Edward Westermarck: *The History of Human Marriage*, New York, 1922, Vol. II, p. 149; especially August Rossbach: *Untersuchungen über die römische Ehe* (Stuttgart, 1853), pp. 420-443, particularly on affinity pp. 435-439). The following excerpts from the Latin sources quoted by Rossbach are of particular interest. 'Inter eas enim personas, quae parentum liberorumve locum inter se optinent, nuptiae contrahi non possunt nec inter eos connubium est, velut inter patrem et filiam, vel matrem et filium, vel avum et neptem, et si tales personae inter se coierint,

257

nefarias atque incestas nuptias contraxisse dicuntur' (*op. cit.*, p. 424). '(Ducere non licet) item eam quae nobis quondam socrus aut nurus, aut privigna aut noverca fuit.' 'Eam denique, quae noverca vel privigna vel nurus vel socrus nostra fuit, uxorem ducere non possumus.' 'Nec socrum nec nurum, privignam nec novercam aliquando citra poenam incesti ducere licet' (*ibid.*, p. 435).

Paul's statement need not be understood as a universal negative. It may refer simply to the fact that there was the recognition even among the Gentiles of the impropriety of sexual relationship within this degree of affinity. Paul's appeal to this fact is for the purpose of indicating that outside the pale of covenant revelation there was abhorrence of this kind of marital relationship. This implies that the prohibition in question had relevance to mankind in general.

Thirdly, Paul is not here *establishing* a law in the exercise of apostolic inspiration. He is simply applying the law which he recognizes as established and expresses his consternation that a law of universal obligation should be violated within the Christian community and the violation regarded so lightly by the church there. Paul's exasperation underlines the grossness of the wrong involved.

APPENDIX D

AN interesting chapter in the history of the debate is provided by the General Assembly of the Presbyterian Church in the U.S.A. In 1818 a report of a committee directed to prepare such a report was adopted unanimously by the Assembly. This report declared: 'We consider the voluntary enslaving of one part of the human race by another, as a gross violation of the most precious and sacred rights of human nature; as utterly inconsistent with the law of God, which requires us to love our neighbour as ourselves, and as totally irreconcilable with the spirit and principles of the gospel of Christ . . . it is manifestly the duty of all Christians who enjoy the light of the present day, when the inconsistency of slavery, both with the dictates of humanity and religion, has been demonstrated, and is generally seen and acknowledged, to use their honest, earnest, and unwearied endeavours, to correct the errors of former times, and as speedily as possible to efface this blot on our holy religion, and to obtain the complete abolition of slavery throughout Christendom, and if possible throughout the world' (*Minutes of the General Assembly*, 1818, p. 692). This report did not advocate precipitate measures for the emancipation of the 'unhappy Africans'. That would be to 'add a second injury to the first, by emancipating them in such manner as that they will be likely to destroy themselves or others' (*ibid*., p. 693). But the report does insist that it is a 'duty indispensably incumbent on all Christians to labour for its complete extinction' (*idem*), that is, of slavery.

It is difficult, if not impossible, to harmonize the position taken in this report, unanimously adopted by the Assembly, with the action of the Old School General Assembly of 1845 which resolved by a vote of 168 to 13 that 'the existence of domestic slavery, under the circumstances in which it is found in the southern portion of the country is no bar to Christian communion' and that 'the petitions that ask the Assembly to make the holding of slaves in itself a matter of discipline, do virtually require this judicatory to dissolve itself' (*Minutes*, 1845, p. 18). These resolutions carried with them the endorsement of 'principles and facts' which were stated in the earlier part of the committee's report where we read: 'The question, therefore, which this Assembly is called upon to decide, is this: Do the Scriptures teach that the holding of slaves, without regard to circumstances, is a sin, the renunciation of which should be made a condition of membership in the church of Christ? It is impossible to answer this question in the affirmative without contradicting some of the plainest declarations of the Word of God. That slavery existed in the days of Christ and his Apostles is an admitted fact. That they did not denounce the relation as sinful, as inconsistent with Christianity; that slaveholders were admitted to membership in the churches organized by the Apostles; that whilst they were required to treat their slaves with kindness, and as rational, accountable, and immortal beings, and if Christians, as brethren in the Lord, they were not commanded to emancipate them; that slaves were required to be "obedient to their masters according to the flesh, with fear and trembling, with singleness of heart as unto Christ," are facts which meet the eye of every reader of the New Testament. This Assembly cannot, therefore, denounce the holding of slaves as necessarily a heinous and scandalous sin, calculated to bring upon the Church the curse of God, without charging the Apostles of Christ with conniving at such sin, introducing into the Church such sinners, and thus bringing upon them the curse of the Almighty. In so saying, however, the Assembly are not to be understood as denying that there is evil connected with slavery. Much less do they approve those defective and oppressive laws by which, in some of the States, it is regulated . . . Nor is this Assembly to be understood as countenancing the idea that masters may regard their servants as *mere property*, and not as human beings, rational, accountable, immortal . . . The Assembly intend simply to say, that since Christ and his inspired Apostles did not make the holding of slaves a bar to communion, we, as a court of Christ, have no authority to do so' (*ibid.*, pp. 16f.).

In the following year, 1846, the General Assembly (Old School), in answer to memorials and petitions on the subject of slavery, adopted the following minute by a vote of 119 to 33:

'Our church has, from time to time, during a period of nearly sixty years, expressed its views on the subject of Slavery. During all this period, it has held and uttered *substantially* the same sentiments. Believing that this uniform testimony is true, and capable of vindication from the word of God, the Assembly is, at the same time, clearly of the opinion that it has already deliberately and solemnly spoken on this subject with sufficient fulness and clearness. Therefore, *resolved*, that no further action upon this subject is, at present, needed' (*Minutes*, 1846, p. 206). On the same day a resolution offered by R. M. White was adopted. It reads as follows: '*Resolved*, that in the judgment of this house, the action of the General Assembly of 1845 was not intended to deny or rescind the testimony often uttered by the General Assemblies previous to that date' (*ibid.*, p. 207).

In 1863 the General Assembly (Old School) adopted the following report: 'This Assembly has, from the first, uttered its sentiments on the subject of slavery in substantially the same language. The action of 1818 was taken with more care, made more clear, full, and explicit, and was adopted unanimously. It has since remained the true and scriptural deliverance on this subject, by which our church is determined to abide. It has never been repealed, amended, or modified, but has frequently been referred to, and reiterated in subsequent Assemblies. And when some persons fancied that the action of 1845 in some way interfered with it, the Assembly of 1846 declared, with much unanimity, that the action of 1845 was not intended to deny or rescind the testimony on the subject, previously uttered by General Assemblies; and by these deliverances we still abide' (*Minutes*, 1863, p. 55). If there is a way of resolving the discrepancies between positions taken in 1818 and those of 1845, the present writer is not able to find it. That the climate had changed between 1818 and 1845 is apparent. In 1831 the 'abolitionist' furore had become intense. That was the year in which William Lloyd Garrison launched *The Liberator*. The excesses of the 'abolitionist' movement aroused the opposition even of those who believed slave-holding to be intrinsically wrong as well as of those who did not hold that position but believed in ultimate emancipation. To say the least, the situation in 1845 required that those who did not believe in the wrong of slavery *per se* should say so explicitly.

Other factors could be adduced to explain the change of temper in the General Assembly. *Cf.* on the discrepancy between 1818 and 1845 Lewis G. Vander Velde: *The Presbyterian Churches and the Federal Union* 1861-1869 (Cambridge and London, 1932), pp. 26f., and on the history of the period John R. Bodo: *The Protestant Clergy and Public Issues* 1812-1848 (Princeton, 1954), pp. 112-149; Alice Felt Tyler: *Freedom's Ferment: Phases of American Social History to* 1860 (Minneapolis, 1944), pp. 463-547.

The General Assembly of 1864 adopted with almost entire unanimity a pronouncement on the question of slavery which endorsed the declaration of 1818, quoting from it at length, approved the emancipation proclamations of 'the highest executive authorities', and recommended to all in its communion 'to labour honestly, earnestly, and unweariedly in their respective spheres for this glorious consummation (the extirpation of slavery), to which human justice, Christian love, national peace and prosperity, every earthly and every religious interest, combine to pledge them' (*Minutes*, 1864, pp. 296-299). For discussion of the actions of the General Assembly in 1863 and 1864 *cf.* Lewis G. Vander Velde: *op. cit.*, pp. 123-128.

Samuel J. Baird's digest of 1856 called *A Collection of the Acts, Deliverances and Testimonies of the Supreme Judicatory of the Presbyterian Church* (Philadelphia, 1856) gives a satisfactory account of the actions of the General Assembly until 1856 (see the same, pp. 808-814). William E. Moore's *Digest* of 1873 (pp. 481-483), of 1886 (pp. 593-595), the *Digest* dated 1923 (Vol. I, p. 467), the *Digest* dated 1938 (Vol. I, p. 668) are distinctly misleading—they refer expressly to the deliverance of 1818 but not to that of 1845.

For actions of the New School Assembly *cf. Minutes*, 1862, p. 24; *Minutes*, 1863, p. 244. These actions are more in accord with the deliverance of the undivided Assembly of 1818.

APPENDIX E

IN view of Emil Brunner's dialectic it is admittedly difficult to find coherence and consistency of statement. In his book *Das Gebot und die Ordnungen* (Tübingen, 1932, translated by Olive Wyon under the title *The Divine Imperative*, New York, 1937) he insists that the believer has to obey the law from obedience to God (p. 126; E.T., p. 146) and that the law has for the believer its *usus didacticus* (p. 133; E.T., p. 149). Although it is the Holy Spirit who guides us, yet the Spirit does this through the law which he expounds to us (p. 132). And Brunner says much that is relevant and cogent against legalism. But when we read: 'Was man aus Liebe tut, das tut man eben nicht aus Pflicht, sondern—mit Schiller ironisch zu reden—"leider aus Neigung"' (p. 47) or 'Sollen und Wahres Gutsein schliessen sich gegenseitig aus' (p. 61; E.T., p. 74) or 'Für den Glauben, im Glauben ist das Gesetz abgetan' (p. 67; E.T., p. 80) and numerous other statements of like effect, we cannot but discover a radical deviation from the perfect complementation and co-ordination which we find in the Scripture of love and duty, of goodness and oughtness, of faith and obedience to law. This complementation is not to be equated with legalism. It is the complementation which existed in man's original state and it is restored in the operations of saving grace. Brunner warns against the error of fanatical antinomianism and regards it as being as dangerous as what he calls orthodox legalism (p. 107; E.T., p. 122). But there is implicit in this dialectic a type of antinomianism that is perhaps the most virulent of all. When we read: 'Man of himself knows God's Law, it is true, but not His Command, and because he does not know the Law as His Command, he does not rightly know the meaning of the Law, which is love' (p. 100; E.T., p. 115), and again, 'I cannot know beforehand the content of the Command as I can know that of the Law; I can only receive it afresh each time through the voice of the Spirit' (p. 97; E.T., p. 111), we have the same existentialist dialectic applied to ethics that appears elsewhere in connection with revelation: Scripture is not itself the revelatory Word; the law of God is not in itself the divine Command. The former destroys the normative character of Scripture as a whole; the latter destroys the normative character of the law of God as revealed in Scripture. It is this kind of antinomianism that Brunner represents.

In modern dispensationalism a sharp antithesis in respect of governing principle is set up between the dispensation of law (Sinai to Calvary) and the dispensation of grace (Calvary to Christ's second coming), as also, perhaps to a lesser extent, between the kingdom dispensation (millennial reign of Christ) and the dispensation of grace. A great many of the statements of dispensationalists are perfectly correct insofar as they express the antithesis that does exist, and on which Scripture lays the greatest emphasis, between obedience to law as the way of justification and acceptance with God and the way of grace. Every evangelical must recognize and appreciate this absolute antithesis. The error of dispensationalism in this connection is twofold. First of all, it applies this sharp antithesis to the successive dispensations and interprets the Mosaic as exemplifying law in contrast with grace, and the gospel dispensation as exemplifying grace in contrast with law. Secondly, this antithesis which is applied to the successive dispensations in respect of governing principle leads dispensationalism into a false view of the place of law within the sphere of grace.

This bias of dispensationalism appears, for example, in the Scofield Reference Bible in its comments on the sermon on the mount (pp. 999f., 1002). In the literature of dispensationalism perhaps no one sets forth the position more insistently than Lewis Sperry Chafer (cf. Systematic Theology, Dallas, 1948, Vol. IV, pages 180-251). One or two examples will illustrate. 'The very nature of grace precepts precludes them from being reduced to a decalogue. They are free in character in the sense that they are not required for acceptance with God' (p. 184). Of course the precepts of the gospel, those which regulate the life of the believer, are not the way of acceptance with God. But what has this to do with the question as to whether or not the ten commandments are comprised in the precepts of the gospel? Again, 'Must Christians turn to the Decalogue for a basis of divine government in their daily lives? Scripture answers this question with a positive assertion: "Ye are not under the law, but under grace"' (p. 209). Although Chafer proceeds to argue that the 'great moral values of the Decalogue' are retained yet he insists that they 'do not reappear under grace in the character and coloring of the Law, but, rather, in the character and coloring of pure grace' (*idem*). These quotations illustrate the kind of antithesis that is conceived of between the decalogue and the precepts of the gospel. The construction of the relations of the law of God, as expressed in the decalogue, to the provisions of grace, which these quotations evince, is the construction which is being controverted in chapter VIII.

INDEX TO SCRIPTURE TEXTS DISCUSSED

INDEX OF SUBJECTS

INDEX OF AUTHORS